The Great Society and Its Legacy

THE GREAT SOCIETY

AND ITS LEGACY

Twenty Years of U.S. Social Policy

Edited by Marshall Kaplan and Peggy L. Cuciti

Duke University Press   Durham, 1986

© 1986 Duke University Press
All rights reserved
Printed in the United States of America
on acid free paper ∞
Library of Congress Cataloging in Publication Data
appear on the last printed page of this book.

Contents

Acknowledgments

This book reflects the thoughtful work of many contributors. They graciously permitted us freedom to make mistakes in interpreting their respective analyses. To them belongs the essential wisdom, if any, in this text. They are a unique group of scholars and practitioners bound together by a shared commitment to an America premised on decency and choice.

Former president of the University of Colorado, Arnold Weber,* deserves a special thanks for co-hosting the Great Society conference with the University of Colorado's Graduate School of Public Affairs. The conference permitted friends and critics of the Great Society and America's domestic policies in the seventies to share thoughts and develop the papers for this book.

Appreciation is also extended to Princeton University's Urban and Regional Research Center, to the Massachusetts Institute of Technology's School of City Planning, to the University of California's School of Public Policy, and the *Denver Post*. They provided either direct financial help to the conference or supported the involvement of one or more of their key scholars.

Books like this consume much time and require the efforts of many people. We would be remiss if we didn't thank our colleagues in the University of Colorado's Graduate School of Public Affairs and its centers—the Center for the Improvement of Public Management and the Center for Public-Private Sector Cooperation—for their patience while we were diverted, at times, during the course of editing and writing parts of this book; and our secretary, Michelle Sprague, for her tireless efforts in typing numerous versions of the manuscript. Finally, we need to extend more than the usual symbolic thanks to our respective families for listening to us endlessly debate the virtues of America's efforts to ame-

* Weber became president of Northwestern University in early 1985.

liorate poverty and expand opportunity. We hope their willingness to tolerate us while we were completing this book will not be for naught if the book helps to foster a needed dialogue concerning America's domestic future.

Marshall Kaplan
Peggy Cuciti

Introduction

The early sixties were a time of affluence, idealism, optimism, and belief in the problem-solving abilities of government. While President Kennedy embraced all of these themes in his New Frontier, it was President Johnson who in challenging the nation to create a Great Society left a rich legislative legacy. The eighty-ninth Congress, which responded to the Johnson initiatives, was described as one of "accomplished hopes . . . realized dreams," having "brought to a harvest a generation's backlog of ideas and social legislation."[1] Some of the initiatives, such as Medicare, were first conceived during Roosevelt's New Deal; others, such as the War on Poverty, were truly Great Society creations.

Almost twenty years later another activist (albeit conservative) president was elected who led Congress to another burst of legislative activity. The changes enacted during the first administration of Ronald Reagan are perceived by many to be as fundamental as those of the Great Society. Unlike President Johnson who was concerned about "private affluence and public squalor," President Reagan worries about public confiscation of resources from the private sector.[2] While Johnson saw government as the preeminent problem solver, Reagan sees government as a large part of the problem. Interestingly, however, both presidents wrought their changes after a period characterized by deadlock and malaise.

With the perspective of hindsight, it now appears that the interim administrations of Nixon, Ford, and Carter offered continuity. While not characterized by the moral fervor of the Great Society period, they essentially accepted the premises set forth during the Kennedy-Johnson years. The federal government continued to grow; new programs were enacted and resources were committed in the hope of finding solutions to the domestic problems of the day. Certainly there were quibbles with the design of some Great Society programs and the priorities they represented. Some programs were amended; others were scrapped. Even so, the basic initiatives of the Great Society remained more or less intact.

Changes generated by the "Reagan Revolution" force us to adopt a new perspective and recognize how much policy continuity was maintained from the mid-sixties through the late seventies. In light of the challenge posed by this administration to the recent past, it seems desirable to reassess the performance of federal domestic programs over the last twenty years. To this end a conference was convened by the University of Colorado's president and its Graduate School of Public Affairs. It brought together individuals from the policy analysis and academic communities. Many had had a role in shaping federal policy. All were committed by the norms of their profession to an objective evaluation of what had been accomplished. They were asked to assess the development of federal programs since 1960 in light of the goals and aspirations of the architects of the Great Society and to assess their impact on the structure of American political and social life.

The vision of the Great Society entailed "an end to poverty and racial injustice."[3] Its goal was to provide an opportunity for *full* participation in American political and economic life so that all might have a share of its abundance. Poverty in the midst of plenty was deplored and the federal government assumed primary responsibility for achieving change. Residents of the "other America" were to be pulled out of the "cycle of poverty" so that they might become an integral part of the national community.

The problems of the poor, the disabled, and minorities were viewed as national in scope. According to the Great Society warriors, state and local governments could not or would not take the steps necessary to expand opportunity and extend choices of low-income households and black and brown individuals. Lower-level governments were viewed as lacking the imagination, talent, institutional capacity, fiscal resources, and political will to tackle the problem. If progress was to be made, the federal government would have to take the lead. Its leadership was seen as legitimate, for we were one nation, a single community, indivisible, committed to justice for all.

While the federal government was to be the primary Great Society player, it could not act alone. Few of the Great Society programs called upon the federal government to administer services directly. Instead a variety of partnerships were formed that changed the functioning of governments nationwide. Cities, once the orphans of the federal system, became the favored partners of many federal agencies and the implementors of numerous Great Society efforts. Direct federal support generated other relatively new participants in the system including neighborhood groups, nonprofit agencies, and regional entities. Only state governments, it often seemed, remained outside looking in.

The Great Society sought to achieve its goals in part by providing services to individuals and in part by reshaping the environment.

Service programs were intended to provide the resources and skills that would allow many poor and near poor individuals to compete for jobs effectively. Much of the emphasis was on youth and on education and training programs. Some of the key legislative changes included the Manpower Development and Training Act, Job Corps, Elementary and Secondary Education Act, Head Start, and the Work Incentive Program.

The effort at reshaping the environment extended to the social and economic fabric of the community as well as its physical contours. Various types of discrimination were outlawed. Efforts were made to strengthen organizational life in impoverished communities and to develop a new leadership cadre among disenfranchised minorities and poor people. Key legislative actions included the Community Action Program enacted as part of the Economic Opportunity Act of 1964, The Public Works and Economic Development Act of 1965, The Civil Rights Act of 1964, the Voting Rights Act of 1965, and the Model Cities Program of 1966.

While the emphasis on the creation of opportunity was relatively unique, other parts of the Great Society program are best thought of as extending the New Deal. Federal responsibility for managing the economy was reaffirmed, professional economists assumed a greater role in government, and greater use was made of the tools of fiscal policy. There was a tremendous expansion of social welfare programs that constitute the social safety net and modestly equalize the distribution of income. Medicare and Medicaid were initiated in 1964. The food stamps program was set up on a demonstration basis in 1961 and subsequently was enacted nationwide in 1964.

Ironically, while Kennedy, Johnson, and their domestic policy architects were interested primarily in the creation of opportunities for the poor to participate in the economic mainstream, the primary legacy of the period was the expansion of income security programs. The Great Society emphasis was on education, training, and jobs. At the same time, however, it created (or took advantage of) the conditions that allowed the expansion of welfare-type programs. For example, it promoted organizations at the local level, such as Legal Aid, that encouraged the poor to seek welfare assistance, it fostered a shift in attitudes regarding the poor, and it recruited microeconomists, who believe in cash transfer programs, into the bureaucracy in policy positions.

The Great Society was characterized by an interest in experimentation and *new* initiatives. There was little interest in pursuing incremental change within preexisting programs. Indeed, this infatuation with innovation may have prevented the Great Society from achieving more lasting and important changes, such as basic reform of the tax code or social insurance programs.

Another characteristic of the Great Society was its confidence in the contribution that could be made by social science research and systematic policy analysis. President Johnson sought to integrate social scientists into the policy formulation process either by inviting them to sit on task forces or by bringing them formally into government. In addition, he mandated that all agencies adopt Planning, Programming, and Budgeting Systems (PPBS.) While that initiative has been faulted by some, the integration of sophisticated analytic tools into the political and administrative process is a lasting accomplishment.

THEMES AND PREMISES

The initial essay by Robert Wood examines the prevailing wisdom concerning the Great Society. Critics, whose views have dominated debate, conclude that the Great Society was both an aberration and a failure. They hold that it was unrealistic in its goals of "equality in life and quality of life" and that it constituted an unwise departure from the more traditional practice of pragmatic and incremental program change. Wood faults many analyses for placing too much emphasis on Lyndon Johnson's personality and on tumultuous, unpredictable events such as urban riots and the war in Vietnam. He would prefer to see an evaluation based on the quality of the ideas and on the capacity of the system to implement programs. Wood agrees with the critics that many of the Great Society's ideas were indeed based on untested theories but he argues that subsequent research has supported many of the initial contentions. The issues of institutional capability and the adequacy of program evaluation are then addressed, but Wood concludes that the jury is still out. Wood notes that Johnson himself was a very strong advocate of critical program evaluation and in a second administration would have reviewed and revised many of the Great Society initiatives.

William Schambra explains the transition from the Great Society to the New Federalism in terms of long-standing competing American political traditions. The Great Society was premised on a vision of a national community and public spirit. In Schambra's view the idea of national community is very fragile and can only be maintained in times of emergency or disaster. When the community-mindedness of the nation begins to recede, federal programs undertaken on its behalf lose their moral underpinning; all that remains is the sense of an intrusive, bureaucratic, centralized government. Schambra concludes that the problem with the Great Society was that it could not sell its idea of national community. The ideal of the "small republic" is too deeply rooted in American society. Americans yearn for the kind of community found in small participatory groups such as the family, church, voluntary associations, or local government. This ideal is so pervasive that attacks on the Great Society came from the left as well as the right, from Democrats as well as Republicans as early as the late sixties. Schambra concludes that "the idea of constructing a great national community will continue to recede and the idea of rebuilding 'small republics' will continue to grow."

THE MACROECONOMIC CONTEXT

The performance of the economy and the macroeconomic policies established to manage that performance set the context for many of the programmatic and policy decisions of the sixties and seventies. Indeed, the unprecedented prosperity of the period is viewed by many as critical to the forging of a consensus to aid the disadvantaged. Absent a rapidly expanding economic pie, support for such programs tends to wane. The decline in economic performance from the sixties to the eighties constitutes an alternative explanation for the shift from the Great Society to New Federalism in American politics.

Barry Bosworth begins his chronicle of the evolution of economic policy by noting the magnitude of the change that occurred over the ·last two decades. The sixties were a period of tremendous optimism characterized by both strong economic performance and confidence in the ability of fiscal and monetary policy to achieve sustained economic expansion free of recession. By the end of the seventies, optimism regarding the economy and government's ability to manage its performance had faded. Bosworth argues that changes in the broader economic environment as well as in the policy-making process led to the deterioration of economic performance. He concludes that many of these changes are irreversible and that we should expect continued wide cyclical swings. A major focus of the paper is the mix between fiscal and monetary tools for achieving economic goals, and the burden now placed on monetary policy. Both tools were available in the past but structural deficits now effectively preclude the use of fiscal policy as a stabilization tool. Bosworth fears this may result in too great a burden being placed on monetary policy.

Joseph Pechman argues that Kennedy and Johnson had relatively little interest in tax reform per se. The only tax legislation passed during their administrations is best viewed as a successful exercise in fiscal policy formulation. Pechman then reviews the relationship between tax policy and income distribution in the United States. He concludes that the combined federal-state-local tax system is substantially less progressive now than it was in 1966, and that the distribution of income after taxes is less equal now than it was twenty years ago. He attributes this in part to the change in the tax system and partly to increasingly unequal market outcomes.

PROBLEMS, POLICIES, PROGRAMS AND EVALUATION

The Great Society was premised on the idea of a national community where all are appropriately concerned about the status and achievement (or lack thereof) of each of its members. While poverty was hardly a new problem for the United States, it was rediscovered as a public policy issue. The Great Society warriors designed a range of programs to enhance "equality in life and quality of life." While there is disagreement regarding the programs' effectiveness in altering the opportunities of the poor, there is little doubt that the Great Society altered the scope and structure of governance in the United States.

Poverty: the central focus of the Great Society. Paul Ylvisaker's chapter examines the extent of the nation's success in its war on poverty. The initial declaration of war arose out of strong commitment but relatively little knowledge regarding the dimensions or character of the problem. Since that time our knowledge base has greatly expanded but our commitment to the eradication of poverty may have waned. An unrepentent Great Society warrior, Ylvisaker argues that the programs launched in the sixties and seventies were successful. The nation saw a reduction in poverty between 1966 and 1978; indeed, among the elderly there was a tremendous improvement in economic status. Ylvisaker laments the reversal of the trend since 1978; a weak economy and cutbacks in social programs have resulted in a substantial increase in the number of poor Americans. Minorities, female-headed households, and children are especially at risk.

Bernard Gifford takes a less positive view of the Great Society's efforts to reduce poverty. He traces alternative views of the causes and cures for poverty and concludes that the War on Poverty was a failure because it was built on the wrong view of the problem. The Great Society program took a "therapeutic" or "rehabilitative" approach designed to alter the "culture of poverty," when what was required for real progress were structural changes in the economy. Besides failing to eradicate poverty at its root cause, Gifford argues, the War on Poverty programs had an unintended and undesirable side effect. The programs led to increased dependency among the poor by expanding claims to welfare-type programs that in the absence of jobs were the best way to meet basic needs.

In Gifford's view, the only innovative part of the War on Poverty was its effort to involve citizens in key decisions regarding program design. Interestingly, it was this feature that led to the demise of many of the programs, since it threatened social services professionals as well as the local politicians who were an important source of support for the Democratic party. Gifford concludes that the problem of poverty is best understood in economic terms, using a class-based analysis. The solution to the problem, in his view, lies in the creation of jobs that pay adequate wages and in the elimination of discrimination.

The program legacy: expanding individual opportunity. Sar Levitan and Clifford Johnson describe the wide range of social programs initiated during and after the Great Society and argue that most were effective in meeting and solving the real needs of the poor. "The nation's welfare system," they argue, "has improved lives . . . by expanding opportunity and reducing deprivation throughout the life cycle." Using the life cycle concept as the organizing principle, the authors remind the reader of the many large and small social programs affecting health, nutrition, education, skill development, access to jobs, income security, etc., that were enacted. The results of numerous evaluation studies are also reported. While they are positive regarding the Great Society legacy, the authors argue the needs of the poor would be better met if greater emphasis were placed on education and training as opposed to income support. The Great Society, they believe, was correct in its initial emphasis on "opportunity expansion."

Employment training and job creation efforts are addressed by Peter Edelman. While welfare programs must be maintained, Edelman argues, employment is the key to reducing poverty. He reviews the history of efforts to deal with the problems of the unemployed and concludes that "our public policy has gone from the mistake of providing jobs without training and back again." A multidimensional policy "offered in combination that will differ depending on the age, skill gaps, and other characteristics of the client group involved" is needed if we are to make progress. Edelman then proposes numerous program options to increase the total number of jobs available in the United States, to improve access to these jobs by both the "old" and the "new" poor, and to improve income for those in low-wage jobs.

Henry Aaron focuses his attention on income maintenance programs. Neither Kennedy nor Johnson was interested in welfare reform; their war on poverty consisted of programs designed to expand opportunity. The focus on welfare as an important instrument for combatting poverty came later under presidents Nixon and Carter. Aaron goes on to discuss factors that frame public perceptions of need for assistance and the relationship between welfare, willingness to work, and family stability. The current welfare system is categorically based, requiring specific family status or disability to qualify for aid. Reform has generally been cast in terms of noncategorical cash assistance based solely on economic need. Advocates of reform have argued that such a system, properly designed, would have no effect on work effort and would enhance family stability. Aaron suggests that recent research (initiated by the reformers to prove their case) had the effect of casting both of these propositions in doubt, hence, he says, "the intellectual case for that kind of reform has collapsed." Under President Reagan the entire approach to welfare has shifted; categorical distinctions have been strengthened, benefit reduction rates increased, and "workfare" programs promoted.

Wilbur Cohen assesses reforms achieved in the health policy arena during the Great Society. With the passage of Medicare and Medicaid in 1964, the elderly and some of the poor achieved greater access to physicians' services and hospital care. Using the criteria of equity, efficiency, adequacy, administrative acceptability, ideology, and provider response to evaluate these programs, Cohen assigns Medicare a high score and Medicaid a passing grade.

Another focus of Cohen's essay is on the political realities of social reform. He postulates a cyclical theory of social reform and the necessity for compromise to achieve acceptance of programs when there is a window of opportunity. Programs that result will be imperfect but modifications are possible in the interim periods when major reforms are politically impossible. Cohen argues strongly that every major piece of legislation should provide for evaluation to enhance the prospects for mid-course corrections and enhancements. He offers numerous other insights regarding the political process, including the need for mythology and the importance of radicals to the achievement of more modest social reforms.

Restructuring the urban environment. The Great Society placed the problems of cities and their poor high on the national policy agenda. Even so, Marshall Kaplan argues that a comprehensive urban policy was never developed—either by the Great Society or during subsequent administrations. Policy development was hampered by a lack of an adequate theory of urban development and of sufficient political clout by urban residents. Kaplan highlights the tension between "people-oriented" and "place-oriented" policies, suggesting that a mix is probably necessary for both political and substantive reasons. He describes the evolution of policy in terms of a series of contrasts. Twenty years ago, policy was ambitious and comprehensive; today efforts are more limited in scope. We have moved from an emphasis on citizen participation to a reliance on established institutions and decision processes. A complex federal structure dependent on narrow categorical programs and numerous direct relationships between the federal government and local agencies is giving way to the more traditional dual federalism model. States are assuming a more important role. Discrete urban initiatives are less likely than broad policies changing the ground rules governing the social and economic behavior of Americans. Kaplan notes a shift in focus from the public sectors' role in problem-solving to an interest in public-private partnerships.

Bernard Frieden and Lynne Sagalyn provide an in-depth analysis of several public-private partnerships that have resulted in several large downtown retail redevelopment projects. These projects were dependent in part on an improvement in underlying factors such as the revitalization of the downtown office market. But, more important, these projects owe their existence to innovative entrepreneurial urban policy. This essay shows how current city policies evolved from the experience gained from redevelopment efforts launched under federal auspices, including Great Society programs. At the same time the cities' activities represent a clear departure from past economic practice. A totally new kind of relationship has emerged between the public and private sectors, characterized by joint decision-making and shared risk-taking.

USE AND MISUSE OF INFORMATION

Role of the media. Two very different views of the role of the media are presented: Ian Menzies of the *Boston Globe* suggests that the press can be an independent force influential in shaping public policy, while Charles Green of the *Denver Post* argues that the power of the media has been overstated.

In looking back on the Great Society, Menzies observes that the media were an uncritical supporter of the Great Society. The media made the effort to understand the perspective of the poverty community, but they failed to make the same effort to develop "street-level" knowledge of the concerns of working and middle-class people. Had the media done so, they might have supported policy modifications that would have facilitated development of a broader constituency for the liberal reform efforts of the sixties and seventies. Menzies suggests that the press can influence policy in two ways—through its editorial content and through its detailed portrayals of life as it happens at the local level. Administrations must work more closely with the media, preferably the editors and staff at the local offices, explaining their view of problems and proposed solutions so that the media can undertake coverage that will facilitate public understanding and enhance critical debate.

Chuck Green takes a broad view of the role of the media in shaping public policy. He suggests that the press has been credited with more power than it really has: "The prevalent myth is of the Imperial Media, an awesome force which somehow bestride the Republic like a colossus, working their will and whim upon a passive populace." The myth is wrong in Green's view. The media are admittedly important because they focus attention on events and issues; ultimately, however, their role is passive, in that the media cannot control events or the public and private decisions shaping those events. The media report public opinion more than they shape it.

Role of social science. An important conclusion regarding the Great Society involved the new role it established for the social sciences during the Great Society—both as the generator of ideas and program options and as the evaluator of policy. Evaluations in turn enter the policy debate and affect future options. Richard Nathan sets forth a typology of research in which he distinguishes between analytical studies, evaluation studies, and demonstration studies. Each type may be quantitative or qualitative in approach. Analytical studies are intended to produce systematic, objective statements about social and economic trends and conditions. These studies burgeoned in the mid-sixties. Nathan argues social scientific resources, while important, are better directed toward evaluation research and demonstration studies. Evaluation research could be improved if more attention were directed to the hard-to-quantify institutional and political variables. Nathan argues for interdisciplinary efforts that combine qualitative and quantitative approaches to the understanding of program causes and effects. Demonstration studies are a special form of evaluation. An activity is initiated and assessed in order to define its impact and learn about costs and benefits. Nathan concludes optimistically that social research need not be a conservative force, and that if topics are selected and applied correctly such research can be an important determinant of policy.

THE IMPACT ON GOVERNANCE

The Great Society set in motion changes in the relationships among the federal, state, and local levels of government and in how each level relates to its citizenry. Essays by Robert Reischauer, David Walker, and David Rosenbloom address these changes in the character of institutional relationships and governance.

Reischauer argues that the Great Society marked the beginning of an era of fiscal federalism that lasted for approximately fifteen years. In 1964 no resource constraints existed at the federal level and there were relatively few federal programs directed at social problems. State and local governments were characterized by fiscal starvation, limited administrative capacity, and little interest in reform. The Great Society put in place a strategy of categorical grants designed to provide resources to state and local governments but also to dictate the services to be provided, the decision process, the delivery mechanism, and the beneficiaries (for example, the poor and underprivileged). Often the federal government chose to bypass the states and deal with local governments or community organizations. Reischauer details the critique of the system that emerged during the seventies but notes the presence of political forces that made it difficult to secure major change. President Reagan has managed to change key contours of the grants landscape, reducing the total number of programs and the flow of dollars, increasing recipient discretion, and enhancing the role of the states. Reischauer concludes that the Great Society achieved many of its goals. It succeeded in broadening the scope of government so that federal, state, and local governments administered programs directed at solving social problems. It played an important role in opening state and local decision processes and broadening their constituencies. Finally, it helped professionalize administration at the state and local level.

While David Walker's conclusions are consistent with Reischauer's regarding the changing shape of American federalism, his essay reads quite differently. Walker starts by examining the four political traditions that gave rise to the Johnson program—two of which he sees as liberal and two as conservative. On the liberal side of the ledger, he identifies new nationalism and liberal federalist traditions. The first emphasizes the "national community," a theme also addressed by Wood and Schambra. Johnson tempered his belief in the national community with a distrust of strong central administration; consistent with the liberal federalist tradition, his initiatives relied on a partnership with state and local governments. Countering these liberal expansionist traditions were two more conservative influences. In Walker's view, Johnson was a pragmatist and a fiscal and administrative conservative. Had these latter traditions been honored by Johnson's predecessors, Walker suggests, the counterreaction to the Great Society might never have occurred.

Walker characterizes the change in intergovernmental relations in terms of the increase in grant programs and dollar flows, a shift in favor of urban and metropolitan interests, a broad expansion in the definition of the national interest, a tendency to bypass state governments, increased involvement of states and localities in federal regulatory efforts, and efforts to manage intergovernmental programs better. Despite widespread criticism of many of these developments, Walker contends that the seventies produced much of the same. President Reagan's fiscal, programmatic, and revolutionary attacks on the system are described; Walker concludes that "despite some successes" there has been no "wholesale eradication of major programs nor even overall funding reductions." Due to Reagan economics, the federal government is unlikely to propose new social programs, but in Walker's view the Johnsonian programmatic legacy remains largely intact.

David Rosenbloom describes the growth of juridical federalism. The Great Society is credited with fostering this development in two ways. First, it legitimated the premise that individuals' rights were being violated by the states and that the federal government had an obligation to provide some protection. Second, President Johnson appointed numerous judges who shared his philosophy of activism. The courts assigned themselves a new role by reinterpreting section 1983 of the Civil Rights Act of 1871 and by allowing public law litigation. As a result of the first action, governmental entities and individual officeholders can be held liable if their policies result in violations of individual rights. Public law litigation, usually involving class action suits against governmental agencies, permits the court to fashion comprehensive solutions to social problems such as school desegregation. Rosenbloom concludes with a critique of juridical federalism, arguing that it represents an encroachment on state sovereignty and a breach of the principles of representative government. He suggests that judicial decisions have put pressure on state budgets and have circumvented normal procedures for allocating resources.

LEGACY OF THE GREAT SOCIETY: A VIEW TO THE FUTURE

To conclude the volume, the editors have written an essay summarizing what is known about the effectiveness of federal domestic policies in reducing poverty. Was the reduction in poverty achieved in the sixties and seventies a function simply of economic growth or did the programs designed to enhance opportunity and income play a role?

We conclude that economic growth alone was not responsible for the lowering of the poverty rate. While some federal initiatives failed and while consistency among policies was not always apparent, federal efforts played an important role in expanding opportunity and in reducing poverty. While some indices suggest that little progress was made in ameliorating social problems, others suggest a more positive picture.

A concern for the poor and their problems is currently not fashionable. Many of the budget cuts implemented during the first Reagan administration were in the programs benefiting the less fortunate. As a result, the incidence of poverty has increased.

Our proposed agenda is based on the social commitments of the Great Society. It also reflects, however, resource constraints and changing federal, state, and local government relationships. While further federal budget cuts may be warranted, they should not be made in the means-tested programs. Furthermore, while policies to secure strong economic growth are essential, they must be joined by policies that facilitate participation by the poor and minorities in the economic and social life of the nation. A commitment by the public and private sectors to eradicate discrimination and expand education and job opportunities is a logical component of an effective, efficient, and equitable overall strategy.

The Great Society has shaped the national political agenda for twenty years. An activist role for the federal government, in designing solutions for domestic problems, working in concert with state and local governments, has been accepted until recently. A claim by the poor and minorities for assistance and protection has generally been acknowledged as legitimate by most Americans.

The presidency of Ronald Reagan has clearly changed the agenda. The tax reductions enacted during his first year and the subsequent budget deficits virtually ensure that no additional resources will be available for new initiatives to solve social problems. The federal role in shaping "quality of life and equality in life" will almost certainly diminish, even if federal spending remains constant. This is the logical consequence of the administration's commitment to increase defense spending, its unwillingness to consider tax increases, and its desire to preserve middle-class entitlements.

It is to be hoped that America will retain the basic commitment made during the Great Society to expand minority choices, eliminate racism, and reduce poverty. The essence of the Great Society was not the specifics of its programs; indeed, some of the solutions of the sixties and seventies are inappropriate in the eighties. What is important to remember as we try to devise a path for the future is the Great Society's commitment to a national community, its recognition of responsibility for improving the position of the least advantaged and for shaping the quality of the physical and social environment, its willingness to experiment and to be evaluated, and finally its trust in government as the lever for achieving desired change.

||||| ★ |||||

B O O K   O N E

Background

1

Themes and Premises

———

The Great Society in 1984:
Relic or Reality?
ROBERT WOOD

Ventures in retrospection can be perilous, especially when you are looking back on events in which you were directly involved. Twenty years is a long enough time to provide reasonable detachment in perspective. It is, however, also long enough for memories to become unreliable, for facts to be embellished, for contributions to be magnified, and for errors to be ignored. It is important, then, to forswear remembrance in any romantic sense and to make sure reflection has as solid an empirical base as one can muster. Nevertheless, the utility of the participant-observer in the evolving field of public analysis, where properly constrained, is generally acknowledged. When combined with observations derived from more sophisticated techniques of external research, the effects can be reinforcing and one hand washes another.

The conventional judgment about the programs launched twenty years ago, advanced by academic commentators and popular columnists alike throughout the seventies down to today, runs something like this. A suddenly powerful, politically seasoned president, megalomanical in his ambitions, driven by personal insecurities, ineffective with the media, and haunted by the Kennedy legacy, deviously first co-opted and then manipulated experts and scholars. These guileful, irresponsible individuals, drawn like moths to the candle flame of power, reached into their bags of half-formulated unverified hypotheses and theories and seized the opportunity to translate preposterous notions into law. A series of unpropitious events and a recalcitrant bureaucracy at all levels of the federal system doomed their ill-considered, unproven schemes to failure.

And it was just as well—for authoritative evaluations show that their models of man, their conceptions of reality, and their suggestion that equality *in* life and quality *of* life were simultaneously achievable for America was hopelessly utopian.

To be sure, there have been occasional dissenters—Sar Levitan and Robert Taggart during the seventies,[1] and John Schwarz in the eighties.[2] But the overwhelming weight of conventional wisdom is that the Great Society is best regarded as an aberration, a blip on the computer screen, and an affront to the American tradition of pragmatism, of incrementalism, of reliance on capitalism, and of distrust of government. Is that characterization valid? Does it hold up? Let's take observations from five distinct and different vantage points.

First, the role of President Johnson. Do we explain the Great Society as the creature of his drives, visions, insecurities, compulsions, an exercise in power, a desperation to overachieve, to outdo the New Frontier?

Second, the impact of unpredictable tumultuous events. Vietnam, of course. The assassination of the Kennedys and King. The riots, the counterculture culminating on the streets of Chicago at the Democratic Convention of 1968. What domestic program could survive, be tested, and be proven or disproven in such a hostile environment?

Third, the quality and character of the ideas that shaped the programs. Were they the product of New Class, High Tech and Low Mandarin, degree-bearing animals whose native language is CCD—Carefree and Critical Discourse? Were they fashioned from reputable thinking and reliable knowledge? Did their inferences and recommendations exceed their data bases?

Fourth, did the institutions responsible for program execution possess the capability to carry out the tasks? Did the Great Society represent the expansion of the federal government into unsurveyed territory, the appropriation of powers legitimately belonging to states and cities, the "overloading" of the federal system?

Fifth, were the evaluations of program performance professionally reliable, authoritatively objective? Did the avalanche of neoconservative commentary and study represent an easily found consensus by impartial, uninvolved observers, or was it a rush to judgment, heavily ideological in its first premises, tinged with envy by those either not invited to participate or personally committed to political adversaries?

As I sift and sort the evidence, looking back with the dispassion that time allows, I am disposed to minimize two factors, hold a third in abeyance for further examination, and concentrate on two: the validity of the concepts, and the reliability of the evaluations.

First, I am disposed to set aside the role of the President, for all the fascination he holds for psychohistorians and political scientists. Whatever the interpretations of Kearns,[3] Caro,[4] Burns,[5] and the others—whatever the interplay between extraordinary intelligence, experience, and competence on the one hand, and extraordinary inferiority, defensiveness, vulgarity, and deception on the other—I still hold Merle Miller's oral biography in high regard, and Tom Johnson's quote therein as the most apt.

> All of the people who came in contact with Lyndon Johnson—his family, his friends, his political associates, the members of the White House Staff—each of them has his or her slice of Lyndon Johnson. . . .
> But nobody has ever put all of the slices together. The things that have been written about him, all of them are very limited, taking in a very small slice. What has to be done is to put all the slices of the pie together. If it can be done.[6]

I am content to say that Johnson provided an extraordinary political opportunity to put into law a set of domestic initiatives, aimed at realizing our nation's promise of justice and a reasonable quality of life for all. The new initiatives derived for the most part from the capital stock of the social sciences as understood and practiced a generation ago.

As for the president's view on the use of experts, let me recall a passage from one little-remembered address (somewhat understandably since it was on the academic occasion celebrating the Brookings Institution's fiftieth anniversary on September 29, 1966). The phrase-making was Harry MacPherson's, but the sentiments, I am persuaded, were Lyndon Johnson's, searching for "something better than a visceral, emotional response" to "the enormous complexity of modern living." The president said:

> We have seen, in our time, two aspects of intellectual power brought to bear on our nation's problems: the power to create, to discover and propose new remedies for what ails us; and the power to administer complex programs in a rational way.

Then, and somewhat curiously but important for our purposes here, he went on to say,

> But there is a third aspect of intellectual power that our country urgently needs tonight . . . less glamorous . . . less visible . . .

[It is] the power to evaluate . . . to say about public policies and private choices: this works, but this does not . . . this costs more than it is worth. This is worth more than it costs. Of all these powers, that of the critical facility, I think, is most deeply associated with the intellectual. . . .

I took then, I take now, the president at his word. If a second term had occurred, there would have been evaluations of major dimension and with major personal and professional consequences.

Second, I discount more heavily now than then the significance of exogenous events. One can make a plausible argument that the Great Society was not aberrant so much as it was aborted. The second- and third-order consequences of the drive for civil rights, transformed from nonviolent revolution in the political process to violent protest in the streets, provoked a backlash of majority opinion. It pushed the administration from experimental, innovative activities to full-scale production, as represented by the Housing and Urban Development Act of 1968, that went far beyond the original assumptions and specifications.

The assassinations, Vietnam, the calamity of the Chicago Democratic Convention, the defeat of Hubert Humphrey, all cut short the progress of the Great Society. The expectation had been a continuity of administration and program development at least until 1972. How well are programs expected to fare when they are placed in hostile hands? It may be reasonably argued that they would not fare well. But I discount that argument if our purpose is to judge the objectives and policies and their appropriateness today. Some programs, such as Model Cities, endured for a spectacularly long time. Some concepts, such as block grants, creative federalism, and environmental legislation, were appropriated by successive administrations, folded in, repackaged.

One simply must expect the unexpected in the American political process. Good luck and bad luck, unwelcomed occurrences, and happy surprises have come to every administration. Those who believe that constitutional reform, congressional reform, executive reform, or party reform will somehow produce a stable, rational, political decision-making process, unaffected by outside events, either misread our history or are having a love affair with a political ghost that never was.

What of the institutional factor, the problems of interdepartmental and interjurisdictional bureaucratic warfare, that has spawned an entire new field of study called "implementation?" Frieden and Kaplan have made much of the problems of coordination, regulation-making, and local counterpart capability in their evenhanded and responsible study of model cities. Wildavsky, Pressman, Bardach, Edwards, Sundquist, Nakamura, Smallwood, and others have traced the torturous trail of program execution or nonexecution from Oakland eastward.[7] The inference I draw from their works is that models of optimization and Weberian order are being replaced by models of "coping," negotiation, and mediation.

But the field is too volatile and the prescriptions are too contradictory for me to draw a reasonable conclusion that another administrative framework would have meant Great Society "success." I do believe that the most erroneous assumption most of us proceeded on was an adequacy of resources, an expectation that a rising economic tide combined with extensive federal assistance would float all boats, that interagency coordination, amply funded, would make a real contribution toward helping the poor and revitalizing their communities. But until we understand the skill requirements of implementation in a federal system better, I suspend judgment.

We are left then with two components, from two vantage points. How good were the ideas and how good were the evaluations?

Let me treat the ideas both in the context of what was known then and what has been learned since. On balance, I suggest we had reasonable empirical grounds and more than plausible hypotheses for a good number of the programs. Headstart's emphasis on the importance of early childhood learning has been increasingly strongly confirmed over the years. So has the efficacy of special attention to the education of poor children. So (although this is more complex depending on which survey of James Coleman you read at which time) has been the beneficial educational impact of desegregation. Levitan and Taggart have documented concrete achievements in health care, housing, education, manpower employment. John Schwarz has established the benefits of the economic growth-oriented policies, as well as the advances of Medicaid and Medicare and the decline in infant mortality. For the new ventures that lay at the heart of the Great Society—programs that undertook to modify human behavior and the human condition—the ideas by and large stand up.

I make two exceptions. My own political science discipline was muddle-headed in its formulation and application of the concepts of citizen participation. We advocated Rousseau and Madison simultaneously; we failed to perceive the intimate relation with the concurrent civil rights movement; we confused deliberation as to ends and means in neighborhood development. That is to say, the Community Action Program proceeded on a theory of direct democracy in its purest form, to empower poor people in neighborhoods with authority not only to choose among values but also among techniques of implementation. The Model Cities program was more constrained: advocating the sharing of power between neighborhoods and city hall, enlarging past patterns of participation but maintaining final authority in formal institutions of government. Both found difficulty in distinguishing neighborhood delegations of authority with the new thrust of black power. Over the years the practice of citizen participation produced a new generation of savvy ward politicians and imparted valuable political skills to future councilpersons, mayors, and legislators; it also produced financial scandals, poor program management, and sordid personnel practices. Whatever the effects of whichever version, we uncorked the bottle impetuously and the genie of participation is now forever with us.

Second, our colleagues in demography led us astray by projecting the doubling time in population, housing, and community facilities to be thirty-five years. The president said that "by the year 2000 America would have to build an inventory of homes, roads, hospitals, museums, centers equal to all we had built before in the past two hundred years of our history." I know he said it because I wrote that sentence. I believed our colleagues who calculated population growth and change. I was wrong.

Finally, *how do we evaluate the evaluators?* Like purple elephants, very carefully. If we set aside the appraisals by the print and electronic media as devastating in impact but fatally flawed by the compulsions of that enterprise, what of the more scholarly studies? Here I rely on a true authority: Peter Rossi, in his already classic essay, "Issues in the Evaluation of Human Services Delivery," published in 1978. Rossi conditionally propounds the "Iron Law of Social Program Evaluation"; to wit, that the expected value for any measured effect of a social program is zero. "In short, most programs when properly evaluated, turn out to be ineffective or at best marginally to accomplish their set aims." Accordingly as the programs seem to continue, Rossi concludes, "nothing succeeds like failure."[8]

Rossi holds that in the extraordinarily difficult task of affecting human behavior—addressing "pockets of deficiencies" in the conditions of individual and household life—the effectiveness of the treatment prescribed, the design of the delivery system, and its applicability on an appropriate scale are all interrelated and each capable alone of preventing a desired result. As he carefully takes us through the methodological complexities of analyzing each stage and establishing a strategy for more professional evaluation, one is struck by how primitive and biased most of the evaluations of the Great Society, based on conventional wisdom, have been. Take these popular conclusions, for example:

—Public housing is a failure—look at Pruitt Igo or Columbia Point, and ignore the 1,200 other projects that work.

—The Early and Periodic Screening, Diagnosis, and Treatment Program of Medicaid lacked the "solid backing" of the scientific community and therefore failed—without reference to child health statistics.

—Another example, based on my favorite quotation from President Reagan: federal expenditures for education went up in the seventies but test scores went down. This correlation is so spurious that even if the vast changes in the national student body had been acknowledged, it still would have been meaningless.

Taken in aggregate, what do we make of the Great Society evaluations? Judging from Rossi's work, it is at least a toss-up whether it is better to reconsider the programs or reconsider the evaluations. And since there are few incentives for evaluators and academia or government to discover success and many incentives to find failure, it seems right to be skeptical of the pronouncements today. It is indeed ironical that of President Johnson's three stated roles for the experts, the one he emphasized the most—the use of the critical facility "to be critical—to be precise, to be sharp, and to be piercing"—is the one that has received the least attention, and may be the one where we have failed him most.

Until we are much more critical and examine the evaluation process more thoroughly, I suggest we hang on to the goals and the policies of the Great Society. Certainly the quests for equality for minorities and for women are as yet unrealized—and relevant today. Certainly the needs of the helpless, the young, the poor, the old, and the sick are unfilled—and relevant today. Certainly our cities need to be safer, cleaner, more attractive, and our neighborhoods more vibrant and healthy. These are relevant concerns. Certainly air, water, and land should be nonpoisonous as much in the eighties as in the sixties. Certainly access to public power is still a value to be cherished.

Compared to goals most often articulated today—to stand tall in the world, to promote space wars, to body-count and double body-count the homeless, to evade environmental responsibilities, to deprecate the poor, to relieve the burden of taxes on the rich—the aspirations of the Great Society do not seem aberrations from the American experience. They seem in the mainstream of the American tradition, the best of our people's values.

The quotation that President Johnson and Vice President Humphrey were always so fond of using, sometimes to the point of boring their captive audiences, bears one more recital. It is, of course, from Thomas Wolfe:

> To every man his choice—to every man regardless of his birth, his shining gold opportunity—to every man the right to live, to work, to be himself and to become whatever thing his manhood and his vision can combine to make him—This . . . is the promise of America.

Rid Wolfe of his chauvinism, embrace men and women as true equals, understand that citizenship is universal; even in the eighties, I can relate to that.

Is New Federalism the Wave of the Future?

WILLIAM A. SCHAMBRA

Some analysts[1]—perhaps friendly to the Great Society—have said, "President Reagan's New Federalism proposals . . . have challenged the . . . premises [that have formed the basis of] America's domestic policies since 1964," the year President Johnson first enunciated those premises in his "Great Society" speech at the University of Michigan. There is more than a slight suggestion here that the Great Society was healthy and robust, that it was the widely accepted basis of American domestic policy, until conservative Republican Ronald Reagan perversely but nonetheless successfully challenged it in 1980. One even detects here a note of hope, that the American people will soon realize the gravity of the error they made in 1980 and will return to the orthodoxy of the Great Society.

The history of the sixties and seventies, of course, tells us something quite different about the popularity of the Great Society—namely, that it had come under severe and mounting criticism throughout this period; that the most effective criticism came *not* from conservative Republicans but from the left, and from within the Democratic party; and therefore that the Great Society Ronald Reagan challenged in 1980 was *not* healthy and robust but ailing and decrepit. (Indeed, when Ronald

Reagan *had* challenged a young and healthy Great Society—as a prominent supporter of Barry Goldwater in 1964—the election results differed considerably from those of 1980.) It is important to understand the nature of the concerns raised about the Great Society during this period, because Reagan's New Federalism is, in a sense, simply a reflection and refinement of those concerns.

The noisiest challenge to the Great Society in the course of the sixties came, of course, from the New Left. The New Left maintained that the federal government—so central to the Great Society's scheme—was in fact a distant, alienating, bureaucratic monster and that its social welfare programs were intended not to vanquish poverty but to reconcile the poor to the domination of America by corporations and other megastructures.[2] The alternative to the Great Society, according to the New Left, was "participatory democracy." A society organized according to that principle would presumably devolve all political and economic decision-making to small local groups, within which people would—as the Students for a Democratic Society's Port Huron statement put it— "share in those social decisions determining the quality and direction of their lives." Local participatory politics would overcome the alienation characteristic of the Great Society's megastructures and would, the statement said, "bring people out of isolation and into community."[3]

The Black Power movement of the sixties and seventies was another strand of resistance to the Great Society. That movement rejected the integrationist premise of President Johnson's civil rights measures, because integration was based, Stokely Carmichael and William Hamilton asserted, "on the assumption that there is nothing of value in the black community and that little of value could be created among black people." Blacks, they said, should instead "redefine themselves, and only *they* can do that," by creating "their own sense of community and togetherness." The authors of *Black Power* continue: "only when black people fully develop this sense of community, of themselves, can they begin to deal effectively with the problem of racism." Like the New Left, then, Black Power reflected a profound skepticism about the intentions of federal programs and a desire to reorganize society along ethnic, communitarian lines.[4]

A final element of opposition to the Great Society—and the one that packed by far the greatest electoral punch—was the white ethnic movement within the Democratic party. George Wallace appealed to the sinister side of this movement with his surly references to "pointy-headed bureaucrats" and "pseudo-intellectual elitists," but others— Michael Novak foremost among them—argued that the basic outlook of the "unmeltable" white ethnics was not at all unlike that of the New Left and Black Power movements: namely a dissatisfaction with programs that ignored or disrupted local communities and neighborhoods in order to satisfy objectives established in faraway Washington. Novak urged the Democratic party to move away from the Great Society's reliance on a powerful central government toward a politics based on "the organic networks of communal life: family, ethnic group, and voluntary association in primary groups."[5]

Beneath these different and seemingly antagonistic movements, I think we can see a common theme: a dissatisfaction with intrusive, bureaucratic, centralized government and a desire to build (or preserve) small local communities, within which people could once again begin to shape their own lives. The Great Society—because it ignored or undermined "participatory democracy," neighborhoods, voluntary associations, and ethnic groups—stood accused of being anticommunity. This dissatisfaction with the Great Society convulsed the Democratic party from 1968 to 1980, permitting the minority Republican party to win the presidency three out of four times during this period.

As it turns out, the charge that the Great Society was anticommunity is not altogether fair. Indeed, the Great Society may be understood as the (perhaps last) great flowering of a grand and noble vision of community—the vision of *national* community—that had informed progressive liberalism from the beginning of the twentieth century. That vision summoned Americans to substitute for their traditional laissez-faire individualism the compassion, concern, and willingness to share benefits and burdens that are usually to be found only within families or tightly knit communities. The sense of national society would manifest itself in federal programs designed to "integrate" marginal groups into the broader national society and to ameliorate material inequalities and other differences that tended to disrupt national oneness. As Samuel Beer put it, the function of the liberal state was to "make the community more of a community."[6]

Given this vision, it is not surprising that the Kennedy-Johnson War on Poverty was sparked by a book that described the poor as "the other America," an America cut off from the national community.[7] Nor is it surprising that the rhetoric of the Great Society turned on the idea of pulling the poor out of a "cycle of poverty" and folding them into the national community, through programs that would change cultural attitudes as much as incomes. President Johnson insisted that he was trying to give the poor not "more relief" but "opportunity," the opportunity "to be part of a great nation."[8] Finally, we should not be surprised at

President Johnson's choice of "the Great Society" as the image for his administration—it conjures up perfectly the vision of national oneness or community that would inspire Americans to make the appropriate sacrifices on behalf of the disadvantaged. It was designed to lift Americans above material self-interest into a new realm of community-consciousness. "The Great Society," according to President Johnson, "is a place where the city of man serves not only the needs of the body and the demands of commerce, but the desire for beauty and the hunger for community."[9]

It is by no means accurate to describe the Great Society as anticommunity, then—it was solidly a part of the progressive liberal tradition that had tried from the beginning of the twentieth century to establish a true national community in America. There is a problem with this noble vision of national community, however; while there *are* moments when we must and can become "one nation"—namely, in times of grave national crises, such as severe depressions or wars—such moments of national oneness are extraordinarily difficult to sustain, because wars and depressions are, happily, not the steady diet of the republic. Liberalism thus comes to rely on dynamic, articulate presidents, who try rhetorically to re-create in ordinary circumstances the extraordinary atmosphere of crisis-period community. A favorite device for doing so is the use of the phrase, "moral equivalent of war"—a kind of war that will galvanize the national community without spilling blood. President Johnson turned to the image of a *"war* on poverty" for precisely this reason: the "military image" would "rally the nation," and "sound a call to arms which will stir people . . . to lend their talents to a massive effort to eliminate the evil."[10]

The extraordinary community-mindedness of war—with the strenuously self-forgetting public-spiritedness it seems to demand—cannot be sustained long, however, even by the most finely crafted moral equivalent of war. When the community-mindedness of the nation begins to recede, the federal programs undertaken on its behalf lose their moral underpinnings. They begin to seem intrusive, bureaucratic, alienating, expensive—and expendable—rather than proper expressions of the public interest. Such seemed to be the fate of the Great Society and its programs as the sixties ended. The process was speeded along by those critics of President Johnson who constructed fanciful parallels between the moral war on poverty at home and the shooting war against Communism abroad.

One message of the three currents of dissent in the sixties and seventies, then, was the fragility of the idea of national community. Another and equally important message was the enduring appeal of a much older idea of community—the kind of community to be found in small participatory groups, in the family, neighborhood, church, ethnic and voluntary association, and local government, stretching back to the Anti-Federalist opposition to the proposed new Constitution at the time of the nation's founding. The Anti-Federalists distrusted the nationalizing features of the Constitution because they believed that true republican communities—communities that could inspire citizenship, sacrifice, and public-spiritedness and that would permit citizens genuinely and democratically to shape their own lives—were possible only within the small spheres of local communities and the states.[11] Progressive liberalism rested on the assumption that such communities had been doomed by twentieth-century industrialization and urbanization; liberalism's chief purpose was to restore a similar degree of community at the level of the nation. The movements of the sixties and seventies indicated both that the "small republic" spirit had by no means perished in modern industrialized America, and that the national community idea simply was not an adequate substitute.[12]

The resurgence of "small republican" sentiment was sufficiently strong in the late sixties and seventies that presidents throughout the period—Republicans and Democrats alike—were compelled to accommodate it with appropriate rhetoric and programs. The Nixon and Ford administrations, for instance, emphasized the shift of authority from Washington to state and local governments through revenue sharing and block grants.[13] As President Ford said of the Community Development Block Grant, such measures were designed "to return power from the banks of the Potomac to the people in their own communities." And Ford was ushered from office by a man who charged that the Republicans had, rhetoric notwithstanding, permitted the federal government to become bloated and inefficient. Jimmy Carter promised, by contrast, a new emphasis on local community. He insisted during the 1976 campaign that "our neighborhoods and families can succeed in solving problems where government will always fail," and that "the only way we will ever put the government back in its place is to restore the family and neighborhood to their proper places."[14]

This is not to deny that federal programs grew tremendously during this period, in spite of rhetoric and initiatives to the contrary. The point, however, is that such growth came increasingly often to be described as illegitimate—the product of entrenched interest groups, "iron triangles," "new class" bureaucrats, a fragmented congressional structure—even by the presidents under whom such growth occurred. Watergate vividly dramatized the notion of a central government spinning out of control. Federal programs no longer seemed to express or reinforce the profound moral and political project of building a national community. After 1968 presidents seldom affirmed in Lyndon Johnson's confident tones the centrality of the federal government in American life. No president spoke of building a "Great Society" in America.

This context—the decline of the idea of national community and the resurgence of the idea of the "small republic" throughout the sixties and seventies—is essential for understanding the character of President Reagan's New Federalism. It is not, to be sure, the context in which we usually discuss it. We now tend to assume that New Federalism is, at best, a well-intentioned effort to straighten out the administrative details of service delivery in America, or, at worst, an ill-intentioned effort to slash federal assistance to the poor and throw the burden of social programs back on the states. Without denying that there are those in the administration who subscribe to one or the other of these programs, I think we have to understand New Federalism differently: namely, as the latest and by no means last manifestation of the "small republican" renaissance in America.

President Reagan himself certainly understands it this way. He made federalism the centerpiece of his 1976 campaign for the presidential nomination, not because he saw it as a way to cut federal spending— this was well before current budget problems—but because he saw it as the best way to restore to prominence local "participatory democracies" such as neighborhoods, voluntary associations, ethnic groups, and local governments. A renewed federalism, he insisted, was the best way to bring about "an end to giantism, [and] a return to the human scale, a scale that human beings can understand and cope with, the scale of the local fraternal lodge, the church organization, the block club, the farm bureau." Such a return was necessary, Reagan maintained, because "activity on a small, human scale creates the fabric of community."[15] This "small republic" spirit infused the 1981 block grant proposals, the private sector initiatives task force, and, of course, the 1982–83 initiatives for a "New Federalism" in America.

Reagan's New Federalism was launched under perhaps the least propitious of circumstances, during the deepest recession since the 1930s. We may not see again such a sweeping federalism initiative from this administration. Given Reagan's long-standing interest in federalism, however, we may expect more modest initiatives during his second term. And the failure of the 1982–83 initiative should not obscure what are in fact quite considerable achievements in the area of federalism: the block grants of 1981 and a reinvigoration of state and local government activity so pronounced that a recent Advisory Commission on Intergovernmental Relations (ACIR) publication could describe it as a "de facto New Federalism."[16] Such achievements are all the more remarkable given the severe recession—a circumstance that in the past would have produced almost automatically a vast expansion of federal power.

Nor should the results of 1982–83 divert our attention from a more fundamental point: small republican sentiment seems to be growing throughout the nation. As a result, we will probably see increasing numbers of initiatives designed to reach the goals implicit in the New Federalism, and fewer and fewer initiatives resembling those of the Great Society. The idea of constructing a great national community will continue to recede, and the idea of rebuilding local "small republics" will continue to grow.

Nowhere is this trend more pronounced than within the Democratic party today, as it struggles to define its future. The struggle was clearly apparent during the competition for the presidential nomination in 1984. Walter Mondale—the eventual nominee—is a loyal adherent to the New Deal–Great Society tradition. At the center of his speeches is precisely the vision of national community that underlay progressive liberalism for much of the twentieth century. Ronald Reagan, he charges, has disrupted national oneness, splitting America into prospering rich and languishing poor. Mondale's America, by contrast, he describes as "a civilization, a community, a family where we care for each other."[17] He noted before the California Democratic Conference in January 1983, ". . . we need . . . a community. There's nothing more basic to the principles of America than that we are in this country and this society together. We belong to one another."[18] True to the liberal tradition, Mondale's vision of national community is reflected in a pledge to restore federal programs to their former splendor.

While Mondale was nominated by the Democrats in 1984, I think the future of the party does not belong to him. Instead, it seems to belong to those who, like Senator Gary Hart, are skeptical of massive federal programs and of the vision behind them. In a speech to the Yale Divinity School in 1982, Senator Hart spelled out his alternative vision for America, centering on the restoration of local community. "Local control in politics, in social issues, and in the business world" must now be a central element of public policy, he maintained, because "room for human growth can be provided best within small units." "To have richness instead of isolation in our personal lives," he continued, "we must allow communities to grow."[19]

The future of the Democratic party may also lie with the likes of Jesse Jackson, and it is important to remember that Jackson came to leadership within the black community precisely by criticizing its reliance on massive federal programs and by calling on black neighborhoods and local groups to assume the initiative in solving their own problems. He argued in 1976 that "the first and immediate task for American blacks is to rise up from the decadence in which we too often find ourselves in the cities, and to do so by the force of our will, our intellect, our energy, and our faith in ourselves."[20] Jackson's vision of America, then, also seems to be built on the vitality of local communities, neighborhoods, and ethnic groups, not on a return to the liberal national community.

Such trends in thinking within the Democratic party suggest that if Reagan's New Federalism is *not* the wave of the future, then a "federalism with a human face" or some other Democratic equivalent is. Both parties seem to be trying to address speech and action to the growing "small republic" sentiment, and they will probably continue to do so for some time to come. What is least likely is a return—by either party—to the grand vision of the Great Society, with its ringing affirmation of the centrality of the federal government in American life.

It is a mistake to look at the sixties and seventies as a period of solid consensus behind the assumptions of the Great Society, suddenly and inexplicably interrupted in 1980 by the New Federalism. In fact, the Great Society's vision of national community had all but disappeared by the late sixties, and new (or rather very old) ideas about cultivating community through neighborhoods, voluntary associations, ethnic groups, and local government were on the rise. These ideas appeared first and most forcefully within the Great Society's own party. President Reagan's New Federalism is but the latest manifestation of the "small republic" renaissance, and if trends within both parties are any indication, it will not be the last. The New Federalism as such may not be the wave of the future. But it is trying to ride a wave that began to rise in the sixties, and that is giving no sign of subsiding, or even cresting, as it rolls through the eighties.

2

The Macroeconomic Context

The Evolution of Economic Policy

BARRY P. BOSWORTH

The public perspective on the economic history of the last two decades might be entitled "The Rise and Fall of Macroeconomic Policy." The 1960s are often viewed as a period of growing optimism about the ability of fiscal and monetary policies to achieve sustained economic expansion free of business-cycle recessions. Economic growth was something we came to take for granted and attention in the early 1970s shifted to a greater concern for the distributional implications of that growth.

That optimism was destroyed by the events of the 1970s. The rate of inflation accelerated to double-digit levels by the end of the decade. At the peak of the expansion of 1979, the unemployment rate was 6 percent compared to 3.5 a decade earlier; and today we speak of an unemployment rate of 6.5 to 7 percent as the minimum rate consistent with nonaccelerating inflation. Average real hourly earnings (adjusted for inflation) of production workers rose by 17 percent in the 1960s. Today real earnings are slightly below the levels of 1970. Most recently, fiscal policy itself has become caught up in an ideological debate over the size of government that seems to have eliminated government as an effective tool of stabilization policy for the foreseeable future.

It is reasonable to ask, "What went wrong?" Was the optimism and faith in the ability of government to control the course of the economy misplaced? While stabilization policy failed to live up to the expectations it engendered during the 1960s, was the deteriorating economic performance the fault of poor policy decisions, or was it a case of making the best of a bad situation? In the effort to draw some lessons for future policy, it is useful to examine what went wrong.

In this essay I argue that changes in both the economic environment in which policy was made and the policy-making process led to the deterioration of the outcomes, that many of these changes are irreversible, and that fond reminiscenses of the 1960s are unlikely to provide useful guidance for the future. I concentrate my comments in three areas: (1) the change in the environment in which economic policy is made, (2) the evolution of the policy-making process, and (3) implications for the future.

CHANGES IN THE ECONOMIC ENVIRONMENT

The 1960s represent the longest episode of sustained economic expansion in this century, but in citing the contribution of stabilization policy to that experience, we frequently overlook the favorable environment in which the policy operated. A critic could argue that the policy-makers of the 1960s inherited an economy of absolute price stability— a goal achieved at the cost of two severe economic recessions in the prior decade, and that in less than five years of recklessly stimulative policies, they threw away those hard-earned gains for a temporary reduction in unemployment. Such criticism goes too far, but we often forget the highly favorable initial conditions of price stability and the very benign external environment, free of any major international economic disruptions, that economic policy-makers faced in the 1960s.

Since that time the situation has changed in three major respects: inflation emerged as a far more complex and difficult problem than anticipated by economists of the 1960s; the United States became a more open economy subject to international developments beyond its own control; and productivity growth emerged as a major new economic problem.

Inflation. The failure to comprehend fully the difficulties of controlling inflation and the simplicity of the analytical models used to explain the inflation process constituted, I believe, the major failure of economic policy in the 1960s. Initially the problem was seen to be political in origin, as the president and the Congress were unwilling to raise taxes to finance the Vietnam War. Taxes were ultimately increased, however, and while a combination of fiscal and monetary policy restraint did slow the rate of demand growth in 1969–70, it failed to slow inflation. Instead the reduction in demand largely translated into reduced output and a rise of unemployment from 3.5 to 6 percent of the labor force. Economists at first viewed the problem as one of the lags in the response of prices and wages; they recommended patience and a continuation of restrictive policies. By the beginning of 1971, however, wage-rate increases had actually accelerated slightly (despite the high unemployment), and once excess inventories had been disposed of, the rate of price increase also picked up. Demand restraint was abandoned in 1971; the government now shifted to a policy of fiscal-monetary stimulus with wage and price controls.

Thus the key to the breakup of the demand-management policies of the 1960s was the failure to control inflation, together with the unexpectedly high unemployment cost of fighting inflation by means of demand restraint. These problems were exacerbated by the political difficulties of obtaining an adjustment of fiscal policy to offset the stimulus created by the Vietnam War expenditures.

At the same time, major discussions occurred within the economics profession. Milton Friedman and others insisted that the benefits of a demand-stimulus policy that reduced unemployment to low levels would only be temporary. They held that at low levels of unemployment, inflation would steadily accelerate, particularly as participants in the economy came to incorporate past rates of inflation into their expectations of the future. The result, they said, would be a tendency toward escalating inflation at low levels of unemployment. This debate over inflation continued within the economics profession throughout the 1970s. Given the growing difficulties of the policy-makers, the public became more aware of this dissension and more sensitive to the wide range of professional opinion that existed.

Economic research since 1970 has not provided a new solution to the control of inflation; but there is a better understanding of the basic process, and we are more realistic about the difficulties of achieving an acceptable balance between inflation and unemployment goals by stabilization policies alone. In addition, shifts in the composition of the labor force substantially raised the level of unemployment associated with any given degree of inflation pressures. The rapid entry of young adults and women into the labor force left the United States with a very inexperienced labor force and created some transitional problems of absorbing such a large influx of new workers. Estimates of unemployment that correct for the demographic factors imply that they added about 1.5 percentage points to unemployment—that is, an equivalent to 4 percent in 1960 had increased to 5.5 percent by 1979.

Open economy. Stabilization policy has been enormously complicated by the growing openness of the U.S. economy. The increased role of international economic development is evident not only in the rise in imports from 6 percent of the gross national product in 1970 to 10 percent today but also in the increased interrelationships of international financial markets and in the critical dependence of the U.S. economy on a few major international markets, such as petroleum and agriculture. Developments in international oil and grain markets were the dominant factors behind the surge of inflation in 1974 and 1979. The appreciation of the dollar exchange rate, with the consequent reduction in imported goods prices, was a major contributor to the slowing of inflation in the early 1980s.

Increased involvement with other countries yields substantial benefits in the form of a more efficient resource utilization, expanded consumption opportunities, and a higher standard of living. However, it becomes more difficult to formulate fiscal-monetary policies and the outcomes of these policies are more uncertain. For example, under flexible exchange rates, policies that alter interest rates have strong effects on the net trade balance with the rest of the world. Higher interest rates in the United States attract foreign capital, increase the demand for dollars, and lead to an upward revaluation of the dollar. The result is an increase in imports and a fall in exports. If stimulus to the domestic economy is achieved through monetary policy, interest rates will fall and the effect on the trade balance reinforces the domestic policy change. Stimulus provided by fiscal policy, however, raises interest rates and the change in the trade balance offsets the domestic policy actions. Furthermore, any policy action—fiscal or monetary—that raises domestic incomes tends to raise imports and, if pursued too far, will lead to higher rates of domestic inflation and a consequent fall in the exchange rate. The net outcome becomes highly complex and variable.

Productivity growth. In the period between the end of World War II and the late 1960s, labor productivity (output per man-hour) expanded at a relatively steady rate of about 3 percent annually. In the early 1970s that growth rate fell off to about 2 percent. Many observers attributed this to the poor performance of the economy as a whole; they expected a strong recovery after the 1975 recession. However, the growth rate has continued to slow, averaging less than 1 percent annually since 1973.

The issue of stagnant or declining real incomes is only now becoming a significant public issue. While the decline in productivity growth was already evident in the previously mentioned failure of real wages to grow during the 1970s, it was not reflected in real family incomes; these continued to rise at the same rate as they had in the preceding decade.

This was made possible largely by a rapid shift to two-income-earner families, together with a sharp expansion of non-wage-transfer income financed principally by reducing the defense share of government budget and by higher deficit financing. The tax burden on individuals actually rose less rapidly in the 1970s than in the 1960s.

It is impossible for these trends to be sustained in the 1980s. Neither job opportunity nor demographic projections promises continued increases in the portion of the population employed; also, strong pressures now exist to increase defense spending as a share in total budget outlays. Without a growth in total income, the past growth transfers can be sustained only by offsetting tax rate increases. Thus in the 1980s the implications of slow productivity growth on standards of living must become more evident.

A pattern of little or no growth in general living standards is likely to have major implications for a heterogeneous population like that of the United States. In the past, a portion of each year's productivity dividend was generally used to improve the Social Security programs, expand private health and retirement benefits, and raise the relative income of most disadvantaged; yet there remained a residual amount sufficient to allow for a significant general increase in real incomes. Mediation among conflicting groups was accomplished by promising more to some without actually reducing the incomes of others; thus slow productivity growth seems to be an almost certain prescription for increased social conflict.

If labor productivity had continued to expand after 1973 at the same rate as in prior decades, the current real income of the average American family would be 25 percent greater. Income increases of that magnitude would have gone a long way toward financing the increases in social, defense, and private sector needs that are today the source of so much contention. In fact, the current debate over government budget policy might be viewed as but a symptom of the shrinking growth rate of the economy as a whole.

Unfortunately, the causes of the decline in productivity growth remain in large part a mystery. Existing studies have evaluated a large number of potential explanations. Among these factors are the growth in the proportion of the labor force that is young and inexperienced, increased government regulation, the rise in energy prices, a reduction in research and development, a reduced rate of growth of capital per worker, and two major economic recessions. Yet much remains unexplained. Many of the factors affecting productivity growth are outside the control of government. It can, however, influence the pace of investment by minimizing its claims on private saving, maintaining a sustained expansion of the overall economy, reducing the taxation of income from capital, and ensuring the availability of credit at reasonable cost.

The point of highlighting these changes in the economy since the 1960s is not just to provide an excuse for policy but to emphasize the extent to which the concerns that policy must address have changed. At least in the early 1960s the basic economic problem was one of generating increases in demand sufficient to maintain a high utilization of the economy's resources. External price shocks and the collapse of productivity growth presented policy-makers with a whole different set of problems in the 1970s.

Nor should we forget that in at least one dimension the U.S. economy performed amazingly well: 21 million new jobs were created between 1970 and 1980. That compares with employment gains of 13 million in the 1960s, and it contrasts with the decline in jobs in Western European economies during the 1970s. The need to create a large number of new jobs for the emerging baby boom generation placed major strains on the economic system in the 1970s. This is one area where the economic challenges of the 1980s will be much less severe, as the inexperienced work force of the 1970s becomes the mature work force of the 1980s.

THE RISE OF MONETARY POLICY

The economic policies advocated by the Kennedy-Johnson administration did represent a break with the past, but the primary change was in the emphasis on a more activist fiscal policy. Before then, a consensus had gradually developed around the use of fiscal and monetary policies as countercyclical tools to offset extreme fluctuations in economic activity that were believed to originate in the private sector. At the level of fiscal policy, this was evident in the emphasis on automatic stabilizers and the popularity of the concept developed by the CED (Committee for Economic Development) of maintaining a constant high employment-budget balance—rather than attempting to balance the budget at all stages of the business cycle. Similarly, there was a gradual freeing up of monetary policy to allow it to act in a countercyclical fashion—something that was often described as "leaning against the wind."

The 1960s marked the introduction of fiscal policy as a more aggressive tool aimed at altering the secular growth of the economy—not simply to smooth out the business cycle. The role of monetary policy in that framework was secondary; to a large extent, its obligation was seen as accommodating the basic thrust of fiscal policy. In part that definition of its role reflected the notion that monetary policy was more effective as a tool of restraint rather than of expansion—analogous to pushing versus pulling on a string.

Several factors account for the emergence of a more dominant role for monetary policy since the mid-1960s. In 1966 the active pursuit of monetary restraint was the result of a failure to obtain a more restrictive fiscal policy—that is, it was perceived as the second best policy. But by 1969 the perspective on monetary policy had changed to the point that a significant shift toward restraint was viewed as a necessary counterpart to the fiscal actions to raise taxes. Throughout the 1970s there was a continued evolution of thought as monetary policy proved to have a stronger effect on the economy than had been anticipated in earlier decades. While the economics profession has not yet reached agreement on how to operate monetary policy, today no one seriously argues that it does not matter.

The growing role of monetary policy has also been a reflection of the breakdown of the national consensus on the appropriate goals for stabilization policy, and of the growing conflict between unemployment and inflation. In the early 1960s the emphasis was on expansion to reduce unemployment. In the 1970s the emphasis was on restraint to hold down inflation. Monetary policy would naturally play a greater role in such changed circumstances. But in the national debate of unemployment versus inflation goals, the Federal Reserve, like its constituents, tended to focus on the cost of inflation, in contrast to the more expansionist-minded Congress.

The experience of the 1930s left most industrial western economies with a heightened concern for unemployment and a commitment to using national policies to reduce it. The 1970s was a decade of transition. Everyone became more aware of the inflation cost of such efforts. In addition, the generation that experienced the 1930s has been gradually replaced by individuals born in the postwar period and who have had no personal experience with prolonged periods of economic depression. Unemployment remains an ominous personal prospect, but public concern with the issue is high only during periods of rising unemployment—associated with the fear that when others are losing their jobs, we could be next. When unemployment is not rising, even though it is high, the problem is perceived as affecting only a minority and it becomes more popular to argue that unemployment is the result of structural problems or a reflection of weak incentives to work.

Today public opinion in the United States seems to have shifted toward tolerating permanently higher levels of unemployment as an acceptable cost of reduced inflation—that is, on top of the changes in the composition of the workforce that imply a higher unemployment rate for any given degree of inflation pressures. Much of the current policy discussion implies a minimum future goal for unemployment of 6 to 6.5 percent, instead of the 4 percent or less previously considered acceptable.

Finally, the growing importance of monetary policy may have had a perverse effect of weakening the discipline of the fiscal policy process. It was not unusual during the 1970s to hear some congressional leaders justifying the continuation of budget deficits during expansionary periods on the grounds that fiscal policy had no effect on inflation—it was, the monetarists argued, a purely monetary phenomenon. This kind of argument reached extreme levels in 1981 when the new administration argued that monetary restraint provided a painless solution to inflation and that it could be combined with a stimulative fiscal policy to expand the economy and reduce unemployment.

Today we have reached a point where discretionary fiscal policy is no longer an available stabilization tool. On the one side, there is the administration view that as long as monetary authorities pursue a restrictive anti-inflation policy and taxes are kept low to promote private saving and investment, the deficit itself is of little consequence. On the other side, there is a concern for the long-run structural implications of large deficits, but the magnitude of the required expenditure reductions or tax increases seems beyond reach. No presidential candidate, for example, is willing to articulate a program that would bring the budget anywhere close to balance any time in this decade. Yet with deficits of this magnitude, there would be equally strong political objections to any further increase in the deficit in the event of a future recession.

One result of this shift in the relative roles of fiscal and monetary policy has been a weakening of accountability for policy decisions. Presidents are still held responsible for overall economic conditions, but in a very general way that focuses on outcomes rather than on any evaluation of how well the challenges have been addressed. Thus presidents not only are vulnerable to external events over which they have no control, but are also dependent upon the decisions of an independent monetary authority as to how to respond to the problems or opportunities that may develop.

While the Federal Reserve is an independent agency, it is not apolitical. At the extreme, it must be responsive to political concerns if it is to maintain its independence. Within these broad limits, however, the monetary authorities are free to pursue their own preferences as to policy goals, and this freedom of action is considerably greater than that of either the president or the Congress. Political concerns were one factor behind the greater emphasis placed in recent years on targets for monetary aggregates (money supply and reserves) in public statements on monetary policy. In the past, policy was articulated in terms of interest rates. Such an emphasis led, during periods of monetary restraint, to sharp attacks on the Federal Reserve as the basic cause of high interest rates. In recent years policy has been stated in terms of targets for monetary supply and reserves growth. This has allowed the Federal Reserve to deny any responsibility for interest rates and to cite variations in the demand for credit—particularly borrowing by the government—as the basic cause of interest rate fluctuations. The Federal Reserve avoided becoming the focus of public dissatisfaction over high interest rates in 1980–81 and was able to pursue a policy of restraint for a longer period than in earlier recessions.

The rise of monetary policy as a major tool of economic policy has also heightened concern about the coordination of policy actions. At present, no mechanism exists to force a reconciliation between the monetary policy decisions of the Federal Reserve System and the budgetary actions of the Congress. In recent years the collision between a restrictive monetary policy and an expansionary fiscal policy has been costly in terms of high interest rates and the sharp rise in foreign exchange rates. Those costs are likely to continue to grow in future years.

The design of an appropriate fiscal-monetary policy must differentiate between two fundmental issues: the appropriate target for overall economic activity, and the mix of policies to achieve that target. The first issue revolves around the balancing of the cost of inflation against the benefits of lower unemployment. It involves difficult economic and value judgments. However, it makes little sense to conduct fiscal or monetary policy on the basis of independent and often contradictory determinations of the goals one or both are trying to achieve. The United States has a history of using monetary restraint at the peak of business cycles as a means of reducing inflation, and then adopting expansionary fiscal measures as a response to the subsequent recession and rise in unemployment. The result has been an economy that goes up and down like a roller coaster, a secular rise in both inflation and unemployment, and a continuing drift in the mix of policy toward larger deficits and increased monetary restraint.

The second issue, the appropriate mix of fiscal and monetary policy to achieve a given target of output is more relevant to the division of re-source use between current consumption and investment for the future. A consideration of the responses of saving, investment, and the foreign exchange rate to interest rates and tax incentives suggests that economic growth would be favored by a mix of policy tilted in the direction of fiscal restraint to provide for an increase in national savings, and a monetary policy that encourages, with lower interest rates, the pass-through of the savings into investment: that is, a policy mix exactly the reverse of that which emerged from the decisions of recent years.

FUTURE IMPLICATIONS

The economic policies of the 1970s suffer by comparison with those of the 1960s if the focus is on outcomes. A consideration of the nature of the challenges faced by policy-makers, however, weakens the argument that policy has performed less well. The 1960s provided a very benign environment within which a domestically oriented economic policy could operate. By comparison, the 1970s were fraught with problems that would have led to a deterioration of economic performance regardless of the policies adopted.

At this point the question of whether the decade of the eighties will resemble the 1960s or the 1970s, in terms of the challenges and opportunities it poses for policy, is largely problematic. The prospects for sharp increases in energy or food prices throughout the eighties seem less than in the 1970s. The problems raised by a rapidly expanding labor force are largely behind us. Much as in the late 1950s, inflation has been beaten down at the cost of a severe recession. On the other hand, we are no closer to defining a successful program to reverse the prior slow-down in productivity growth. On the inflation front, it appears that we have simply exchanged one problem—inflation—for another—unemployment. There is little evidence that we have achieved any structural changes to allow a more satisfactory balance between the two.

The greatest cause for concern lies with the loss of fiscal policy as an effective stabilization tool. This has drastically increased the burden being placed on monetary policy. Monetary policy can successfully offset the economic stimulus provided by the budget deficits in order to avoid another episode of accelerating inflation, but only at the price of very high interest rates. And, while the United States is currently enjoying the benefits of an economic expansion dominated by high levels of public and private consumption, the continuation of a policy of large deficits and high interest rates does raise serious concerns for the longer term. Budget deficits that consume two-thirds of private saving will in a high-employment economy severely restrict the resources available for capital formation. Large trade deficits and continued borrowing of resources abroad place a large burden on those sectors of the economy that are unable to compete in international markets. In addition, the rapid accumulation of public and foreign debt imposes significant costs on future generations. Finally, developing economies find that they must devote a much larger share of their export earnings simply to repay the escalating interest costs on their existing debt, leaving very little room for expansion of their own domestic economies. They find themselves in sharp competition with the richest country in the world for saving in the international financial markets. While the United States preaches that the poorer countries should reduce their domestic consumption and live within their means, it refuses to follow its own advice.

Tax Reform From 1964 to 1984— A Brief Retrospect

JOSEPH PECHMAN

Tax reform was not a major emphasis of either the New Frontier or Great Society. Given eight years of prosperity and the principles underlying the Democratic party philosophy, the Kennedy and Johnson administrations should have done much better in terms of reforming the tax system. Subsequent developments made matters worse, and we are now saddled with a tax system that is inequitable, inefficient, and exceptionally complicated. Tax reform is regaining its priority on the legislative agenda, but the forces arrayed against it remain powerful.

LEGISLATIVE HISTORY

The Revenue Act of 1964, the only major piece of tax legislation during the Great Society period, is best viewed as part of fiscal policy. Its major objective was to promote economic growth. Overall, the objective was achieved; for one fleeting moment, in 1965, we really did achieve our fiscal and monetary objectives. At the end of that year, the federal budget was in balance. The economy was growing at 5 percent a year.

Unemployment was down to about 3 or 3.5 percent. The balance of payments was in good shape, and so on.

Even if tax policy is viewed as an extension of fiscal policy, the Johnson administration did well only for a while. In looking over this whole period, the greatest disappointment to a fiscal economist was the failure of President Johnson to accept the suggestions of his Council of Economic Advisors and many other economists to increase taxes in 1967. The economic consultants were unanimous: taxes had to rise if military expenditures were to go up. As the nation became more deeply involved in the Vietnam War, military expenditures did rise but taxes did not.

At President Johnson's suggestion, I worked with a number of economists to develop some legislative momentum for a tax increase. We turned in a thousand signatures suggesting we ought to increase taxes to finance the Vietnam War. But political considerations overruled a tax increase. Failure on the tax front explains why we did not achieve many of the objectives of the Great Society. Had we conducted our fiscal affairs correctly during the Vietnam War, economic and tax history would have been very different.

From the point of view of tax reform, very little was accomplished during the Democratic administrations of the sixties. A part of the Revenue Act of 1964 that was intended to reform the system was virtually scuttled by Congress. Neither Kennedy nor Johnson worked toward it very hard. Nor was Kennedy or Johnson willing to embrace the concept of a negative income tax. Unfortunately, those of us who were outside of government were not able to persuade them that we ought to have a counterpart to the positive tax system.

While tax reform was not a priority of the New Frontier or the Great Society, the Treasury Department worked intensively during this period on the details of tax reform. Its staff prepared several volumes of analysis of tax problems, later published by the House Ways and Means Committee. These volumes set the stage for the tax reforms passed in 1969.

The high water mark of tax reform occurred after the Nixon administration came into office. The Tax Reform Act of 1969 included increases in the tax on capital gains, increases in exemptions, a minimum tax, and other reform provisions.

We never approached that degree of interest in tax reform in the seventies and certainly, until recently, not in the eighties. There was a small flourish of interest in 1976 after the recession of 1975–76. Percentage depletion was eliminated for the major oil companies and an earned income credit was introduced for low-income people. On the whole, however, tax reform lost ground during the seventies and of course fell apart completely in 1981, when the Reagan tax cut and many new loopholes were approved.

Now that large deficits are in the offing for years to come, there appears to be a resurgence of interest in improving the tax system. Newspaper articles are appearing about the complexity of the system and the need for simplification and reductions in tax shelters—changes that will reduce the difference in actual tax payments by people with the same income. These are not new issues; they are the same ones that were on the tax reform agenda twenty years ago.

A number of tax reform plans are now being seriously considered. There is the Bradley-Gephardt proposal for a comprehensive income tax with lower tax rates. Some Republicans have also recommended comprehensive tax reform plans that would both improve the equity of the tax system and simplify it a great deal.[1]

It is difficult to assess changes in the tax system by reviewing tax legislation. Research at the Brookings Institution offers several quantitative measures of changes in the tax system and consequences regarding the distribution of income in the United States. The research is based on large data files built by merging large samples of income tax returns with the family income survey of the Census Bureau.

Over the last twenty years there has been a substantial shift in the mix of taxes as well as changes in the structure of specific taxes. The result of these changes is a shift in the burden of taxes by income group, with an overall decline in progressivity. This in turn has had some negative consequences on the overall distribution of income in the United States.

Starting with the Kennedy administration, we have been deemphasizing the corporate income tax. Currently the contribution of this tax to federal revenues is about 10 percent, down from about 30 percent in the early years of the post–World War II period. Unlike many in the business community, I believe that the corporate income tax is borne by capital. Therefore, a shift away from this tax reduces the progressivity of the overall tax system. It has revenue consequences as well, since in addition to the individual income tax the corporate income tax was a major source of tax receipts.

While the federal corporate tax has been decreasing in importance, the payroll tax has become more prominent. Some of the increase could have been anticipated. The rest is the result of recent changes introduced to cover the cost of rising real Social Security benefits.

In the late 1960s many of us had hoped to introduce general revenues into the financing of the Social Security system to moderate the regressive impact of the payroll tax. But we were never able to persuade the American public. Use of general revenues still makes sense since benefits are not related exactly to the taxes paid by individuals through the payroll tax.

The importance of the individual income tax to the overall system has remained stable. Nominal rates have declined but due to a combination of economic growth and "bracket creep," collections have increased. The ratio of individual income taxes to total federal tax receipts has held at around 45 percent throughout this entire period.

State and local governments raised their income and sales taxes during the 1980s, while the effective rate of property taxation declined. On balance, state and local taxes rose from 9 percent of the gross national product in 1962 to 12 percent in 1977, and have remained just below 12 percent since then.

THE DISTRIBUTION OF THE TAX BURDEN

The estimates of changes in tax burdens presented below are based upon assumptions regarding tax incidence. Taxes on capital are assumed to remain stable; they are not shifted to consumers. Payroll taxes are borne by workers, whether the tax is paid by the employer or the employee. Taxes on consumption—excise taxes and sales taxes—are paid by consumers. Taxes on income are borne by those who pay them.

The combined federal, state, and local tax systems were mildly progressive in 1966. In the lowest decile of the income distribution, taxes were equal to about 17 percent of total income. In the top decile they amounted to about 30 percent. By 1985 the tax burden shifted dramatically. At the bottom the average tax rate has risen slightly—to about 22 percent of income. At the top it has declined to 25 percent. Almost all the progressivity that remains in the system is due to the individual income tax (see table 1).

THE DISTRIBUTION OF INCOME

What is the impact of these changes on income distribution? The distribution of income *before* taxes has remained remarkably stable over the last twenty years (see table 2). In 1966 the bottom quintile of the population had 2.9 percent of total income. In 1985 this same group had just over 4 percent. The second quintile had 10.0 percent in both 1966 and 1985. The top fifth had 47.7 percent in 1966 and about the same

Table 1 Effective rates of federal, state, and local taxes, variants 1c and 3b, by population decile, 1966 and 1985

Population decile	1966	1985
First*	16.8	21.9
Second	18.9	21.3
Third	21.7	21.4
Fourth	22.6	22.5
Fifth	22.8	23.1
Sixth	22.7	23.5
Seventh	22.7	23.7
Eighth	23.1	24.6
Ninth	23.3	25.1
Tenth	30.1	25.3
All deciles	25.2	24.5

* Includes only units in the sixth to tenth percentiles. The first five percentiles were eliminated because they included negative as well as positive incomes.

Source: Joseph Pechman, *Who Paid the Taxes 1966–1985?* (Washington, D.C.: Brookings Institution, 1985). For incidence assumptions, see table 3-1, variant 1c.

Table 2 Distribution of adjusted family income before and after federal, state, and local taxes, variants 1c and 3b, by population quintiles, 1966 and 1985

Population quintiles	1966	1985
Before tax		
First	3.9	4.2
Second	10.0	10.0
Third	16.3	15.8
Fourth	22.0	23.3
Fifth	47.7	47.7
After tax		
First	4.3	4.4
Second	10.3	10.2
Third	16.4	15.8
Fourth	23.3	22.4
Fifth	45.7	47.3

Sources: Brookings MERGE files. Same incidence assumptions as table 1.

share in 1985. These figures hide the fact that factor incomes—capital, land, labor—are becoming more unequal. The ratio of transfer payments to income has increased sharply during this period. Transfer payments, consisting of Social Security benefits, food stamps, and other income-maintenance programs, are concentrated at the lower end of the income distribution. If the distribution of total income including transfer payments remains constant, the distribution of income before transfer payments becomes more unequal. In other words, the incomes that go to individuals from the market system (returns to labor and capital) have become more unequal. The system of transfer payments has done nothing more than counterbalance that development.

Given our finding earlier that the tax system has grown less progressive, it is not surprising that the distribution of income *after* taxes is less equal now than it was twenty years earlier. The top fifth, for example, had 45.7 percent of income after tax in 1966, and had 47.3 percent in 1985 (see table 2). The difference is not great, but given the stability of the numbers overall, it is significant.

In brief, a fairly progressive tax system existed in the 1960s. As a result of the deemphasis of corporation income tax, increases in the payroll tax, and the absence of individual income tax reform, the distribution of tax burdens has become less progressive. The goals for tax reformers in the future should be to stimulate more interest on the part of the public, the Congress, and the administration to modify the tax system so that it will raise enough revenue, conform more nearly with ability to pay criteria, and reduce the costs of compliance and administration.

|||||| ★ ||||||

B O O K   T W O

Problems, Policies, Programs, and Evaluation

1

The Discovery of Poverty

Poverty in the United States
PAUL N. YLVISAKER

My purpose here is to trace the long journey this country has taken in its dealing with poverty, from 1964 when the War on Poverty became a high presidential priority to the present when it seems to have no significant place on the White House agenda. My mood is that of an unrepentant poverty warrior, still persuaded that what was launched in the sixties was essentially noble and successful and that a continuing commitment to develop this nation's wasting human resources is a pragmatic and moral imperative.

The journey has been a long one: from the euphoria of that early period when decimal points in budgetary proposals could be moved blithely to the right, to the melancholy of retrenchment with decimal points moving inexorably to the left; from the rather quaint conviction in the sixties that we were mopping up the last vestiges of poverty within an affluent nation, to the chastening awareness that we are today coping with a global flood.

Despite those shifts in environment and perception, I still view both past and future with optimism. The War on Poverty *was* essentially a success: it helped convert the powerful social forces breaking suddenly upon the United States during the sixties—surging energies of the young and the minorities—into constructive elements; it built bridges between ghettos and the establishment over which an extraordinary percentage of contemporary leaders have passed; it released the creative potential of indigenous populations through the novel vehicle of community action; and it left a remarkable residue of innovative techniques (early childhood education, advocacy and legal services, employment training, foster grandparents, etc.) that have survived tenaciously and have become respected parts of America's social repertoire.

The War on Poverty had its failings, but it was not a failure. Calling it so has become a partisan excuse for calling it off.

Having confessed to those beliefs, let me proceed in a more measured way with an accounting of poverty in America over the course of the past two decades.

CONTEXTUAL CHANGES, 1964–84

Nineteen sixty-four was in many respects a different time, a different world. It was an age when the nation was feeling its power, a time of military, industrial, and scientific hegemony, a mood that reflected the optimism of a flourishing suburbia and the exuberance of a swelling generation of youth.

Poverty was a potent political issue. Kennedy had given a promise to West Virginia; big-city mayors in the same 1960 campaign had exacted another presidential pledge to address their gray-area concerns; the urban poor were growing restive; the civil rights movement was in full cry; both the old aristocracy and the newly affluent were feeling a mixture of guilt and altruism; young turks in the church had seized upon poverty and civil rights as the twin handles of ecclesiastical reform; burgeoning philanthropies were breaking out of conventional patterns and daring to move at the street level; and then Lyndon Johnson suddenly became president, determined to match and even exceed the social dedication of his predecessor.

Concepts of poverty and what to do about it also bore the mark of the times. Without sophisticated analyses to go on, there was a tendency to think and deal in undifferentiated terms. There were easy references to "the poor," as though they were a homogeneous and near-permanent cohort of the population, along with exaggerated expectations of mass support, as though the poor were a solid constituency. With the administrative expansionism of the New Deal and World War II so close in history there was an almost automatic resort to "programs" and bureaucratized delivery of services as the way to proceed. Even the refreshing heresy of community action soon carried the conventional labels.

Nor was it measurable at the time how much of the force of the War on Poverty was linked to, and stemmed from, the civil rights and Black Power movements that were simultaneously stirring, as well as the fear generated by urban violence.

And since the sixties? American hope and hegemony have been seriously eroded. Sophistication has brought skepticism, even passivity. There is a perception of impotence—impotence of citizen action, of bureaucracies, of economic and social engineering. There has been a slackening and even a reversal of allied forces: religious fundamentalism replacing church reform; the civil rights movement placed on the defensive. Old institutional stalwarts have departed the scene: the Office of Economic Opportunity, Area Development, and even Housing and Urban Development, left with only its Cheshire smile.

Demographics have changed, with society dividing into aging majorities and youthful minorities. Distance is also growing between minorities of higher and lower socioeconomic status, with former leadership having difficulty crossing the gap. Signs of an underclass have begun to appear, and individual isolation has increased with the rapid disappearance of the two-parent family and with the multiplying numbers of latch-key children.

Changes in the economy—most fundamentally the shift from manufacturing with its familiar ladders of advancement to a service-information society—are powerfully influencing the patterns of poverty and the chances of moving into and out of it. A restratification appears to be taking place—the relatively few "good jobs" are becoming the prizes of select professionals, the more numerous "so-so" jobs are giving static prospects and insecure tenure to an ever-enlarging fraction of the work force, and increasing numbers of older workers and minority males are being consigned to no jobs at all.

Perhaps the most significant shift over the two decades has been in American attitudes: from a perception of continuing economic growth and affluence to one of diminishing prospects and economic instability. "The poor," it turns out, are not so much what we once thought: an identifiable group set apart as "they." There exists much more of a flow in and out of poverty, involving a quarter of the population over a ten-year period. In this rapidly changing world, "we" can at any time become "they." Consequently an ambivalence has arisen: a resentment at having to spend dwindling resources on a safety net for others, along with a chilling second thought that we may need one ourselves.

Changes in scale and incidence. Not the least of the legacies of the sixties is sophisticated research on poverty and its measurement, stimulated in those years and steadily maturing ever since. The early work of Molly Orshansky and the University of Michigan's Survey Research, the continuing studies by the University of Wisconsin's Institute for Research on Poverty, and the time series of the Census Bureau (to mention but a few) all have made it possible to speak about the nature and incidence of poverty in America in more precise terms. I have relied heavily on these sources in the sections that follow, and I have profited immensely from the recent aggregation of statistics on poverty published in October 1983 as "Background on Poverty" for the Subcommittees on Oversight and on Public Assistance and Unemployment Compensation of the Committee on Ways and Means of the U.S. House of Representatives.[1] (Data reported for 1983–84 are briefly analyzed in the concluding epilogue.) That document and the testimony of experts at hearings subsequently held by those subcommittees are a rich mine of information that leaves one not only grateful but wondering how differently we might have proceeded in the sixties had such carefully wrought analyses then been available.

Current data and analyses still leave room for differing numbers and interpretations. Scholarly and partisan debate still continue. What I have attempted to do in the generalizations that follow is to distill a reasonable consensus from what the various data and interpretations suggest.

POVERTY IN AMERICA, 1964–1982:
FIVE GENERALIZATIONS

(1) *The incidence of poverty declined over the period 1965–78 and since then has been on the increase.* As measured by the Bureau of the Census, the poverty rate dropped from 15.6 percent of the U.S. population in 1965 to 11.4 percent in 1978, then rose sharply to 15.0 percent in 1982. When adjusted for in-kind transfers, taxes, and underreporting, the corresponding percentages become: 1965—12.1 percent; 1979—6.1 percent; and 1982—8.8 percent.[2]

The principal factors entering into the recent increase in the incidence of poverty are the federal budgetary cutbacks of 1981 and the economic recession of 1981–82.

(2) *Minorities remain the most vulnerable.* In 1966 the poverty rate for blacks was 42 percent compared to 11.5 percent for whites; in 1978 it was 31 percent versus 9 percent and in 1982, 35.6 percent versus 12 percent. Blacks currently account for 11.9 percent of the population, but 28.2 percent of the nation's poor.

In 1978 Hispanics experienced a poverty rate of 21.8 percent, sharply rising to 29.9 percent in 1982. By then 6 percent of the population, they accounted for 12.5 percent of the nation's poor.[3]

Poverty rates for minorities are consistently higher whatever the sub-classification—age group, gender, etc.

(3) *Children are especially at risk.* The Bureau of the Census reports the following differentials:

Age group	Poverty rates		
	1966	1978	1982
0–17	17.7%	15.7%	21.3%
18–65	10.6	8.9	12.3
65+	28.5	14.0	14.6

Children (0–17) in 1982 constituted 27.2 percent of the American population, but 37.7 percent of the nation's poor. Between 1978 and 1982 the number of children under six in poverty increased by 40 percent. (Note the contrast in trends for the elderly, whose escape from poverty is rightly heralded as one of the success stories of recent decades, accountable in large part to income transfers. Still, elderly blacks experienced three times the poverty rate of elderly whites.) Again, black children are conspicuously at risk. Nearly one-half (47.3 percent) of all black children in 1982 were poor, compared to 17 percent of all white children.[4]

(4) *Poverty is concentrating dramatically in female-headed families.* Between 1978 and 1982, the number of persons in female-headed families increased by 15 percent, two-and-a-half times the rate of increase of the general population. By 1982 the poverty rate for those families had climbed to 48.2 percent. These trends were even more pronounced for black female-headed families: their number doubled between 1969 and 1982 and their poverty rate increased to 57.4 percent (versus 35.6 percent for all black persons). In 1982 black female-headed families constituted 71 percent of all poor black persons against 54 percent in 1969.

Children in female-headed families are especially disadvantaged. They now constitute 52 percent of all poor children; their poverty rate moved from 70 percent in 1966 to a low of 48.6 percent in 1978, then shot up to 56 percent in 1982—roughly five times the rate of children in two-parent families.[5]

(5) *More and more of the nation's poor are concentrating in the central cities.* The proportion of the nation's poor living in central cities grew from 33 percent in 1969 to 37 percent in 1982—an interval during which those cities lost 4 percent of their total populations. During the same period metropolitan areas increased their share of the nation's poor from 54 percent to 62 percent.[6]

SOME REFLECTIONS: GOOD NEWS, BAD NEWS

Reflecting on experience and inquiry over the past twenty years, one moves through light and shadow. Among the brighter spots:

First, research suggests that many Americans who become poor do not remain long in poverty. A longitudinal study by Bane and Ellwood (cited by David Stockman in his testimony before congressional subcommittees) indicates that 25 percent of Americans who fell into poverty during the decade 1969–78 usually escaped within two years. Only about 1 percent remained poor during the entire period. Another search (published in 1974), this one covering a seven-year period, found only 5 percent classified as poor in five of those years. Encouragingly, too, another longitudinal study (by Martha Hill and colleagues at the University of Michigan) revealed considerable upward mobility among children of the poor—poverty is not necessarily a transmitted condition.[7]

There's also hopeful evidence that income supplements in tandem with service programs have proved effective in reducing poverty. In testimony before the congressional committee, Sheldon Danziger reported that the amalgam of income transfers (cash and in-kind) had brought significant numbers of the "pre-transfer" poor out of poverty: 43.2 percent in 1965; 71.9 percent in 1976; declining to 63.3 percent in 1982. The results have been most dramatic in the case of the elderly, whose poverty rate in 1982 (14.6 percent, slightly below the national rate) would have been 43 percent had it not been for income transfers.[8] Recent budgetary cutbacks have begun to close this escape route.

A third source of reassurance is the tenacious way in which the issue of poverty, the determination to do something about it, and an ever-regenerating supply of institutions and ideas have perservered—despite the cold water of skepticism, self-centeredness, budget-cutting, and presidential indifference that has lately been doused upon them. Such apparently neutral processes as the gathering and publication of time series data have prevented the issue from being ignored. Philanthropy, even when spending at the margin, has helped keep consciences alive; so have the innumerable nonprofit agencies that somehow manage to survive and proliferate; so have the surprising numbers of community action agencies still alive despite the loss of federal parentage and patronage; so have the scholars and program designers and think centers who keep evaluating and inventing formulae for legislative and voluntary action; so has that hardy American penchant for fairness that keeps cropping up, particularly now with the specter of the homeless, the hungry, and the jobless looming larger on the streets of every town.

But the bad news is still writ in bolder type. The numbers of poor people have increased in America. Poverty is having the heaviest impact on those least capable of mounting an economic, social, or political defense: minorities, children, and generally those at the bottom of the ladder. The Congressional Research Service estimated in July 1984 that 557,000 persons, most of them children, have been made poor by the budget cuts of 1981 (not counting the additional persons impoverished by subsequent cuts). The General Accounting Office reported in April 1984 that in the five cities it studied, 493,000 families, many of them with incomes below the poverty line, had been cut from Aid to Families with Dependent Children (AFDC) rolls and had lost from $1,400 to $2,700 of their annual incomes; substantial numbers of these families were left with no health-care coverage and with budgetary shortfalls for food and utilities. AFDC benefits generally have been depressed, their purchasing power having dropped a third since 1973.[9]

The pattern is repeated in recent tax policy and income distribution. The Congressional Budget Office estimated in April 1984 that recent budget and tax policies would remove, between 1983 and 1985, $23 billion from families with incomes below $10,000, and would add $35 billion to the income of families over $80,000. At the individual family level, the calculations worked out as follows:

	Family income	
	Under $10,000	Over $80,000
1983		
Cash benefits	$ −170	$ −40
In-kind	−110	−30
Taxes	10	7,140
	$ −270	$ 7,070
1984		
Cash benefits	−250	−90
In-kind	−160	−40
Taxes	20	8,390
	$ −390	$ 8,270
1985		
Cash benefits	−280	−100
In-kind	−200	−40
Taxes	40	9,070
3-year total	$−1,100	$24,270

Source: Congressional Budget Office. Cited in "A Further Look at the Budget Debate," *Monitor* (Washington, D.C.: Center for Community Change, April 1984), p. 8.

Another indicator: corporate taxes are continuing to fall as a percentage of federal revenue. Their share dropped from 23 percent in 1960 to 16.9 percent in 1970, to 12.5 percent in 1980, and fell sharply to 6.3 percent in 1983.[10]

This nation resolved in the 1960s to share its affluence more equitably. Presidential leadership now seems intent on distributing the hardship of the times more inequitably. The general rule seems to be to take from those who have not and to give to those who have. There has been a direct correlation between the amount of benefits that have been cut and the voting power of those affected: the elderly, for example, have been handled with political respect while the children of the minorities and the poor have had their votes counted and come up wanting.

This is the saddest of all commentaries on current presidential leadership and on that fraction of the American nation which goes along. Contrast that indifference with a criterion set by the United Nations as the mark of a good society: that a child born into that society immediately and continuously feels wanted, needed, and nurtured.

The current administration's posture toward our poor and minority children is the more incomprehensible when a look at the demographics reveals how much our future depends upon these very children; they are indeed a generation too precious to waste. The number of adolescents and high school graduates in the United States will be falling sharply (by around 25 percent) over the next decade; the most rapidly growing proportion of that diminishing cohort will be minority and poor. The nation will become dependent upon them in every facet of our life: keeping the United States economically competitive; providing a skilled and reliable work force; replenishing our scientific, educational, artistic, athletic, humanitarian, and political sectors; maintaining our national defense; ensuring the viability of our Social Security and other mutual support systems. Why then the withdrawal of support, the failure to invest in this next generation? From a War on Poverty to a war on children?

One could cite other ominous signs: the reduction in nutritional programs and health care, the reluctance to provide adequate day care, the allowed deterioration of schools and housing in central cities where so many children of the minorities, the immigrants, and the poor are concentrated. All this occurs within the political framework of an aging majority population voting its more immediate self-interests, of parents of public school children outnumbered 4–1 by other voting adults, of a dwindling generation of youngsters with no access to the ballot.

The prospects appear bleak—and one can the more appreciate and applaud those who against the odds have taken up the cause of poor children: the network of child advocate groups across the nation, and most notably the Children's Defense Fund headed by Marian Wright Edelman.

Further backing will come with the rising political activism of the minorities, especially black and Hispanic, whose children and families are immediately at risk and whose swing vote will be more and more frequently cultivated and respected.

My guess is that we are not far from a national burst of interest in America's children as a precious but wasting resource. If so, it should not come primarily as a political and bureaucratic concern, but as a moral imperative. And while recognizing the pragmatic need for sophisticated mechanisms—"programs that work"—I would be looking first for presidential leadership to promote a national climate of respect for those whose potential goes far beyond their present status and voting power.

EPILOGUE: 1983–84

The last two years of the nation's improving economy brought the welcome news of a drop in the overall poverty rate from 15.2 percent in 1983 (versus the 15 percent reported above for 1982) to 14.4 percent in 1984. The overall rate for blacks fell from 35.7 percent to 33.8 percent; the rate for Hispanics rose from 28.1 percent to 28.4 percent; the rate for whites dropped from 12.2 percent to 11.5 percent.

Again, the elderly gained significantly. Their poverty rate dropped from 14.2 percent to 12.4 percent. Another notable improvement was in the poverty rate for families headed by women, whose rate declined from 36.1 percent to 34.5 percent, and whose numbers fell from 16.8 million to 16.4 million—the biggest such drop since 1966. Still, this group accounts for 16 percent of all families and 48 percent of the poor.

While there have been some improvements, the facts still present an ominous picture of poverty in America. Poverty rates for children and youth (0–18) still are dismal: 46.5 percent for blacks (unchanged from 1983); 39 percent for Hispanics (up 1.1 percent since 1983); 16.5 percent for whites (down only one percent since 1983). Most discouraging, no real dent—and worse, no presidentially led, stimulated, or even articulated effort—has been made in halting the disinvestment in our youngest children. Poverty rates for children under the age of six eased down by a mere 1 percent (24 percent in 1984 versus 25 percent in

1983). For blacks and Hispanics the rates remained inexcusably high: 51.1 percent for blacks (up from 49.4 percent in 1983); for Hispanics 40.6 percent (versus 41.8 percent in 1983).[11]

War on Poverty:
Assumptions, History, and Results,
a Flawed but Important Effort

BERNARD R. GIFFORD

In the last year we seem to have suddenly awakened, rubbing our eyes like Rip Van Winkle, to the fact that mass poverty persists and that it is one of our . . . gravest social problems.—Dwight MacDonald, 19 January 1963

Some Americans may have awakened abruptly to the realization that poverty still afflicted millions, but the inquiry and discussion that led to America's rediscovery of poverty in the early 1960s had been percolating beneath the surface of the public mind since the mid-1950s. John Kenneth Galbraith's work at that time provides one excellent example of elite liberal attitudes toward the American poor. The election of John Kennedy brought Galbraith and other proponents of the slightly condescending but intensely optimistic liberal social conscience closer to the source of policy-making. However, public policy did not come fully to reflect their views until after Lyndon Johnson succeeded to the presidency late in 1963.

Poverty never became a mass political issue in the 1960s. It did not mobilize the electorate as it had during the Depression, because the specter of poverty did not threaten the American mainstream. Those most concerned with poverty in the 1960s were liberal social engineers, who believed in the American ideal of universal prosperity and whose faith in Keynesian economics and in the ability to manipulate the political economy of capitalism led them to believe they could eliminate deprivation and want. While in the 1930s attention centered largely on the unemployed work force, rendered destitute by the Depression, in the early 1960s critical attention fell upon the disadvantaged, the neglected, and the hard-core poor—those who stayed poor in so-called "good times." This marked the first time since the Progressive era that American intellectuals and public policy-makers had focused specifically on the "disreputable poor."

Information documenting the unabated suffering and deprivation among America's poor population appeared during the Kennedy years in the work of journalists, economists, activists, and government researchers. Their findings did not reach a widespread audience until after the War on Poverty began.[1] But in the early 1960s, these thinkers did capture the attention of some American intellectuals, politicians, policy-makers, and other establishment figures who constitute the circle of "enlightened public opinion."

Much of the credit for bringing the persistence of poverty to the attention of this enlightened public belongs to Michael Harrington, whose book *The Other America: Poverty in the United States* was published in 1962. Harrington, arguing that we had drastically underestimated the number of poor people in America, placed the actual figure at 40 to 50 million—roughly a quarter of the population. He defined the poor as "those who are denied the minimal levels of health, housing, food and education that the present stage of scientific knowledge specifies as necessary for life as it is now lived in the United States."[2] Harrington thus cast his vote for a relative definition of poverty. Throughout the 1960s discussion of the problem rested on the assumption that absolute poverty was a thing of the past.

Despite the wide differences in political outlook between Harrington and Galbraith, the work of both men reads as if it had evolved from the same postwar school of enlightened liberal criticism of American capitalism. Harrington criticized Galbraith for underestimating the extent of poverty in America but praised him for being "one of the first to understand that there are enough poor people in the United States to constitute a subculture of misery."[3] He went on to codify the assumption behind Galbraith's analysis of why many Americans were still poor: "The poor," wrote Harrington, "live in a culture of poverty."[4] By defining poverty in cultural as well as economic terms, Harrington opened the door to a social services approach to the abolition of poverty and helped to recast, as a form of social pathology, what in the past had been considered principally an economic problem.[5] Thus even Harrington—politically well to the left of Galbraith and the elite liberals in the Kennedy White House—adopted the cultural critique of the poor that soon became a cornerstone of the War on Poverty.

Harrington's work led the parade of publications on poverty that appeared in the early 1960s. Discussion of much of this material ultimately found its way into a long review article by Dwight MacDonald, published in January 1963 in *The New Yorker* magazine. There, his pages sandwiched between advertisements for expensive vacations, restaurants, and luxury goods, MacDonald proceeded to sift through the findings of Galbraith, Harrington, Gabriel Kolko, and a host of government research panels. In a brilliantly conceived examination of contemporary data, MacDonald ripped apart the mythology that economic progress since the war had substantially benefited all Americans. Moreover, he wisely avoided the culture-of-poverty argument and focused instead on the problem of distribution in America's burgeoning corporate economy.[6]

MacDonald's article is said to have influenced President Kennedy, among others.[7] The author's sensible emphasis on poverty as an economic problem, however, appears not to have rubbed off on those who designed and finally implemented the War on Poverty—the federal government's ultimate response to the dilemma exposed by Harrington and the rest. John Kennedy's advisors articulated the ideological shape of the War on Poverty long before Lyndon Johnson had a chance to exert any influence on it. The social scientists among Kennedy's advisors, especially, subscribed to the culture-of-poverty theory, under which the attempt to eliminate poverty would be based on therapeutic intervention, rehabilitation, and retraining.[8] The emphasis on rehabilitation instead of redistribution (inherent in the culture-of-poverty approach) served to mollify the touchy sensibilities of the middle-class constituency whose support Kennedy sought for his domestic economic and social policies.[9]

It is almost impossible to understand the logic behind the War on Poverty without considering its companion piece of legislation, the tax cut. The War on Poverty formed part of a larger strategy—to achieve rapid new growth through stimulation of the economy. According to this plan, the tax cut would free up new resources for investment and job creation, while rehabilitative antipoverty programs would equip the poor to take advantage of the economic opportunities sure to arise in the near future. The notion that "a rising tide lifts all boats" was central to this two-part strategy. War on Poverty programs would render all boats seaworthy in anticipation of the rising economic tide.[10]

Walter Heller, one of the chief architects of the War on Poverty, was characteristically optimistic about the degree to which economic growth stemming from a tax cut would decrease unemployment and create new economic opportunities. In 1961, for example, he predicted that an 8 percent increase in the gross national product would reduce unemployment from 6.4 percent to 4 percent. In fact, although the gross national product actually increased an astonishing 15 percent, unemployment went down less than 1 percent, to 5.5 percent.[11]

In domestic as well as foreign policy, President Johnson inherited Kennedy's advisors and sought to demonstrate the continuity between his administration and his predecessor's.[12] When Johnson declared war on poverty in 1964, he spoke as an enthusiastic proponent of the best type of Kennedy-inspired liberalism:

> The war on poverty is not a struggle simply to support people, to make them dependent on the generosity of others.
>
> It is a struggle to give people a chance.
>
> It is an effort to allow them to develop and use their capacities, as we have been allowed to use ours, so that they can share, as others share, in the promise of this nation. . . .
>
> It strikes at the causes, not just the consequences of poverty.
>
> It can be a milestone in our one-hundred-eighty-year search for a better life for our people. . . .
>
> Through this program we offer new incentives and new opportunities for cooperation, so that all the energy of our nation, not merely the efforts of government can be brought to bear on our common enemy.[13]

In spite of Johnson's rhetoric the actual War on Poverty plan was predictably conventional. With the exception of individual communities being given the right to decide how federal antipoverty funds were spent, the rest of the plan—job training, work-study, a call for volunteers, and establishment of the Office of Economic Opportunity (OEO) as a bureaucratic umbrella—represented new versions of older poverty-fighting strategies. The most noteworthy aspect of the War on Poverty was not originality of design but rather the level of financial support it was able to command from the outset.

The critical thinking which underlay War on Poverty programs— much like the assumptions embraced by Progressive era antipoverty reformers as well as New Deal relief advocates—rested on a flawed and shallow assessment of the causes of poverty. In each of these three assaults on the poverty problem, the persistence of poverty was held to stem from some set of circumstances extrinsic to the regular function of the American system for distributing opportunity and resources, whether in good times or bad. Moreover, the remedies for poverty proposed by War on Poverty strategists—especially their reliance on thera-peutic intervention and social casework to help the poor out of poverty[14]—ignored the persistent tendency of the evolving American dis-tribution system to create slowly a dependent class of American poor. Contemporary liberal analysis in the 1960s offered no sensible assess-ment of the phenomenon of dependency, even though sound work had existed for years. In short, although the War on Poverty represented a more massive commitment to the eradication of poverty in the United States than had previously taken place, it failed to correct fundamen-tally the errors that had plagued past responses to the problem.

The War on Poverty began, auspiciously enough, as an attempt to zero in on the dependent poor by articulating the idea that its victims were somehow cut off from the rest of society. But instead of focusing on their estrangement from the day-to-day economic and political life of American society, policy-makers concentrated on the alleged defects of the culture of poor people, especially blacks. Instead of trying to fight dependency by opening economic opportunities to mobility, advance-ment, employment, and self-respect, money was poured into programs designed to alter the worldview of the poor. No realistic commitment was made to change the fundamental economic and social conditions under which poor Americans lived.

On the one hand, the federal poverty approach made aid easier to obtain. The attention the War on Poverty focused on the plight of the poor did remove some of the stigma from receiving relief payments from the government. The agencies dispensing relief funds, swelled by an in-flux of federal resources, ceased trying to discourage clients.[15] The pro-liferation of government aid ensured that an even greater number of those who could not find work or were physically or mentally unfit to work would fall under the jurisdiction of the welfare bureaucracy. These individuals surrendered control of and responsibility for their lives. They became even more dependent and unlikely ever to become self-sufficient again.

An explosion in the welfare population resulted during the 1960s from changes in state and federal government approaches to the poor. According to statistics cited by Piven and Cloward, the number of families receiving AFDC (Aid to Families with Dependent Children) rose an astonishing 225 percent (to 2,400,000 families) between 1960 and 1970, most of the increase coming after 1964. James Patterson cites similar sources, reporting that the number of Americans receiving aid under AFDC increased from 3.1 million in 1960 to 10.8 million in 1974.[16] Both friends and foes of the War on Poverty universally conclude that a revolution in social welfare occurred during the 1960s. While Piven and Cloward see this trend as making up for a previously existing short-fall in aid, which arose from eligibility restrictions, Patterson offers the view that the expansion of welfare aid during the 1960s represented a "striking improvement" in government efforts to provide for the needy.[17] Neither Piven and Cloward nor Patterson emphasizes the increase in dependency brought about by the massive expansion of the welfare rolls.

Evidence of the steady decline of wage income in the poorest American households since World War II suggests that the increased aid coming from higher transfer payments to the poor during the 1960s was cancelled by lower family income.[18] If this is true, then, despite the War on Poverty the poor merely held their own, relative to the rest of the nation. Their dependency on government assistance grew, and the country as a whole paid a higher social cost.

The welfare explosion in the 1960s represented the final step in the urbanization of poverty that had been under way since World War I. More specifically, it represented the long-awaited impact of the enormous demographic transition begun after the turn of the century and accelerated during the New Deal and World War II.

The agricultural policy of the Roosevelt administration forced many hundreds of thousands of agricultural workers off the land into cities. Soon thereafter, the demand for industrial workers during World War II opened the door of opportunity to many more rural migrants, but it also provided false hope for those destined to become the victims of continuing discrimination. America's urban poor in the 1960s inherited the legacy of this denial of opportunity, education, and training that affected a growing minority of rural migrants and their descendants, especially those who were black. In essence, their difficulties were neither cultural nor inherited but stemmed instead from the inequality of opportunity and the lack of distributive justice of the American political economy. To the degree that the War on Poverty did not address these issues head-on, it failed to offer constructive solutions to the problem of dependent poverty and thus had little impact on the long-term prospects of the growing number of dependent poor.

POVERTY WARRIORS—MISTAKEN ASSUMPTIONS

The liberal social scientists who conceived the War on Poverty voiced concern about the destruction of the black family, an issue that became the essential companion to the culture-of-poverty theory in the 1960s.

In his 1965 report "The Negro Family: The Case for National Action," Daniel Patrick Moynihan made his famous reference to the "tangle of pathology" affecting the lives of ghetto blacks and argued that destruction of the black family was the "fundamental source of weakness of the Negro community at the present time."[19] Moynihan further contended that "it was by destroying the Negro family under slavery that white America broke the will of the Negro people" and that three centuries of injustice had brought about deep-seated distortions in the life of the Negro American.[20] Publication of the Moynihan report set off shock waves of protest and action among critics of various persuasions who accused Moynihan of racism, middle-class bias, and bad scholarship, to name only a few instances.[21]

Unfortunately, the ensuing debate over the report did not help to clarify the issues involved; neither did it bring observers closer to understanding the plight of the ghetto family nor the larger impact of dependent poverty on the poor. Some critics of the Moynihan report argued that the author overemphasized the importance of family as a social institution and that this drew attention away from the real issues— poverty and racism. The works of Lee Rainwater and Christopher Lasch, however, demonstrate that these issues cannot be considered in isolation from their impact on the family, because of the family's essential role in mediating "between social conditions and individual experience."[22]

Another set of Moynihan's critics argued that the female-headed black household represented, in the words of Bayard Rustin, a "healthy adaptation" to ghetto realities.[23] This argument ignores the almost universal preference among poor blacks for two-parent households. Furthermore, it constitutes an attempt to blame contemporary social problems on the structure of the nuclear family instead of on the social and economic circumstances under which families must operate. But neither argument begins to address the central issue that lies beneath ghetto culture and permeates the lives of the underclass—dependency. Economic dependency engenders psychological dependency rooted in the failure of children to internalize parental authority, a process in which the family plays the essential role.[24] The relative strength of the ghetto family is directly relevant to the problem of dependent poverty— not primarily because a pathological cultural inheritance passed on to new generations of blacks in the ghetto renders them unable to take advantage of social and economic opportunity (as Moynihan and others argued), but rather because of the much more recent legacy of discrimination and economic oppression, which has largely denied poor black males the opportunity to sustain themselves as family heads and wage earners.

Proponents of the culture-of-poverty theory, along with many of those who studied black families in the ghetto, ignored the historical roots of urban dependency and paid no attention to the work of Myrdal, among others, who had painstakingly demonstrated the process whereby many black male household heads became obstacles to obtaining relief. Understandably, this fact made unemployed males even less likely to remain at home.

Social scientists who tried to examine the culture of poverty and the demise of the black family as phenomena somehow separate from developments in American culture and society as a whole missed the opportunity to see and understand the connection between ghetto life and the social and political economy of modern America, to which they are inextricably linked. Just as the culture-of-poverty theory exaggerated the distance between the "present-oriented" world of the black ghetto and the ethos of immediate material gratification that permeates American consumer culture, the Moynihan report exaggerated the distance between the erosion of ghetto family ties and the increasingly tenuous situation of the middle-class American family. Both the exploitive material self-interest common to ghetto culture and the demise of personal relationships within the broken ghetto family can be seen as the exaggerated and premature fulfillment of the slow decline of the family now taking place in mainstream American culture, a process often rendered invisible to the ahistorical world of the social scientist.[25]

The debilitating effects of dependency and unemployment are exacerbated by social values that place so much emphasis on one's ability to procure and provide material services. Those who would go about restoring the self-respect of ghetto residents might begin by conceiving the strategies to provide, in the words of William J. Wilson, "respectable jobs at reasonable wages" for ghetto residents, while, at the same time, rejecting the therapeutic approach to social action that relieves ghetto residents of the responsibility for their own fates and their own futures.[26] Such a development would do more to enhance the quality of ghetto family relations and to break the spell of dependency than any conceivable amount of social work or therapy.

WAR ON POVERTY—A POST-AUDIT

By mid-term in the Johnson presidency, the Vietnam War had displaced plans for the Great Society as primary concerns of the president and his policy advisers. The flow of appropriations for the Office of Economic Opportunity (OEO) and its related agencies began to dry up as the president's congressional opponents sensed Johnson's waning interest in the War on Poverty. Steadfast critics of the Great Society programs stepped up the level of their harangue, while many others in Congress who had supported the program in its initial stages paused to reassess their own position. In addition, by 1966 the movement of civil rights had broken away from its earlier commitment to nonviolence. The first sporadic outbreaks of violence had already ripped through the nation's cities. The possibility that the War on Poverty's program for community action was stirring up violent protest added to OEO's growing list of political liabilities. As the watershed of urban violence in 1968 approached, political support for the War on Poverty declined.

The struggle over basic policy issues underlying the War on Poverty continued well beyond the end of the Johnson presidency, but Richard Nixon's election victory in 1968 spelled the end for OEO. The Nixon administration began systematically to dismantle the Kennedy-Johnson antipoverty programs in favor of its own proposed Family Assistance Plan. But the War on Poverty's unseemly demise could not alter the fact that, successful or not, it had marked the most significant new effort since the New Deal in the struggle against poverty in America. From its inception until long after its formal end, critics on both the right and the left assessed the implications both of the War on Poverty itself and of the "welfare explosion" that was its principal legacy.

Some of the stiffest resistance to the War on Poverty's effort to include the poor in policy decisions through "community action" came from traditional political constituencies in the liberal camp—the big-city politicians and professional social workers. The predominantly Democratic political machines in major northern cities saw the community action program as a threat to their own political power, precisely because much of that power derived from the ability to control local welfare networks. Chicago's mayor Richard J. Daley observed that allowing poor people to determine how antipoverty programs were administered would be "like telling the fellow who cleans up to be the city editor of a newspaper." In June 1965 two Democratic mayors, John Shelly of San Francisco and Sam Yorty of Los Angeles, offered a resolution to the U.S. Conference of Mayors accusing OEO of "fostering class struggle."[27] Johnson and his advisors had miscalculated the level of opposition that would arise from within their own party. Resistance from such influential Democrats as the big-city mayors above helped to hasten the demise of the War on Poverty and suggests that the Democratic party's commitment to improving the lot of the poor was tempered by political expediency and the immediate self-interest of party regulars.

Meanwhile social workers, trained to take charge of the lives of poor people, resented the implication that given the opportunity the poor could fend for themselves. "You can't go to a street corner with a pad and a pencil and tell the poor to write you an antipoverty program," observed one member of New York City's antipoverty board; "they wouldn't know how."[28] Indeed, community action threatened to undermine the entire rationale behind the social services approach to fighting poverty—that professionals should fight the battle for poor people instead of equipping them with the means and resources to fight it themselves.

Even as the failure of the War on Poverty became progressively more evident, many observers on the left remained convinced that it could have succeeded if only more money had been spent. Michael Harrington, whose work had done so much to bring about the War on Poverty in the first place, leveled a stinging attack against the Johnson administration in a *Saturday Review* article in July 1968. Calling the War on Poverty a "skirmish," Harrington excoriated the administration for being unwilling to commit enough resources to make more than a dent in the poverty problem. Significantly, in this piece Harrington made no mention of the culture of poverty—instead he focused relentlessly on the issues of distributive justice and employment opportunity. "It is not enough to simply provide *a* job," he wrote, "there must be a decent job." Harrington emphasized the political struggle taking place over America's antipoverty policy and declared, "America knows how to abolish poverty but doesn't want to do it."[29]

By 1968 the bankruptcy of the therapeutic, cultural approach to poverty had become clear, even to the many liberals and leftists who had been among its earliest proponents. But the lesson—that poverty is finally a political and economic problem—was learned at the cost of wasting the nation's all-too-hesitant commitment to solving the problem. By the time the truth about the culture-of-poverty approach became apparent, it was too late to salvage the initiative.

Even as many liberals became disillusioned with the cultural critique of the poor, conservative critics seized the cultural battleground originally occupied by those proponents of the War on Poverty and pressed their own case for a halt in government attempts to ameliorate poverty. The War on Poverty had erred, they argued, not in assessing poverty as a cultural problem but in asserting that any way existed—therapeutic or otherwise—to cure the massive cultural deficiencies present in the "lower class."

Among the most prominent of these manifestos was *The Unheavenly City* (1970) by Harvard political scientist Edward Banfield. Banfield identified the "radically present-oriented" cultural values of the lower class as the primary obstacle to attempts at improving the lot of America's poor. No amount of economic aid and no range of government rehabilitation programs, he argued, could alter the worldview of the behavior of the lower class, since its members had been "permanently damaged by having been assimilated in infancy and early childhood into a pathological culture."[30] Banfield shared with War on Poverty ideologues the notion that the poor suffered from cultural problems, but he argued that the very failure of the War on Poverty to reform or alter the culture of poverty was proof that the poor existed beyond the pale of any attempts to influence their values or behavior.[31]

Of course, Banfield dismissed out of hand the possibility that economic strategies to combat poverty—such as providing either jobs at decent wages or the training to find them—would be successful. In his view, the "tastes" and desires of lower-class people were so different from the cultural mainstream that they had no desire to succeed or to take advantage of social or economic opportunities that might become available to them.[32]

Another conservative response to the aftermath of the War on Poverty was based more on interpretation of economic data than on assessment of cultural change. It held that the poor, especially blacks, had made significant progress during the 1960s. Because of the welfare explosion and the beneficial effects of continued economic growth, they argued, far fewer Americans were poor and those who remained poor were much more likely to be receiving aid.[33] This partially accurate assessment led many conservatives to the conclusion that social programs like the Great Society were no longer necessary, since those who had not responded by now to the new opportunities allegedly made available during the 1960s were unlikely ever to be helped. These observers further contended that liberals refused to recognize that significant progress toward eliminating poverty had taken place, since many liberals depended on the continuation of antipoverty programs for their economic and professional livelihoods.

An excellent example of this type of assessment of the War on Poverty's results appeared in Ben Wattenberg and Richard Scammon's 1973 article, "Black Progress and Liberal Rhetoric." By focusing on the status of non-Southern blacks who lived in two-parent families and attributing middle-class status to virtually anyone who worked, Wattenberg and Scammon were able to make a good case for the proposition that most blacks were now in the middle class.[34] But by leaving out the growing number of poor, single-parent ghetto families and ignoring Southern blacks who still worked in agriculture, the authors simply discounted that portion of the black population most likely to be poor. They also unwittingly focused attention on one highly significant effect of the civil rights movement and the War on Poverty on America's black community—that is, that both helped produce fissures along class lines. This development led to the speedy demise of the Black Power philosophy as a viable political strategy.[35] It also opened the way for class analysis of poverty, black and white.[36]

As might be expected, most ex post facto observers of the War on Poverty agree that it had a powerful immediate impact on the American welfare system and on the lives of America's poor people, but critics differ sharply over the long-term implications—the ultimate legacy of the War on Poverty. Two general themes emerge from the literature on this subject. First, because of the so-called "welfare explosion" and the expansion of the benefit distribution apparatus, the connection between poverty and welfare has become stronger and more universal. On the positive side, this means that some (although not necessarily sufficient) aid now reaches most poor Americans who need it. On the negative side, expansion of the welfare system has only exacerbated dependency among the poor.

Second, the continuing deterioration of economic and social opportunity in the nation's cities—due to recession, slower economic growth, and maldistribution of the benefits of economic growth—has strengthened the chains linking poverty and urban residency, essentially completing the "urbanization" of poverty and destroying any vestigial liberal or conservative faith in cities as the frontier of imagination and innovation. Today, we recognize that in the absence of a national urban policy, the cities "ill suited to today's industrial processes" are "in trouble—losing people, jobs, and fiscal solvency."[37]

The War on Poverty failed to defeat poverty. Its only lasting success came in improving and expanding the relief system. How shall we assess this development? If one takes a generally dim view of the prospects for structural change in the American political economy, then expansion of the relief system appears to constitute a substantial victory. This is the view put forth by Piven and Cloward, who write, "In the absence of fundamental economic reforms . . . we take the position that the explosion of the relief rolls is the true relief form and should be defended."[38] Needless to say, such a position represents a substantial retreat from the early prognostication offered by proponents of the War on Poverty.

But the weakness of Piven and Cloward's position—as a long-term approach to the problem of poverty in a political economy based on wage labor—lies in its failure either to address the damaging effects of prolonged dependency or to suggest what can be done about the increasing demand on the nation's resources by a growing dependent poor population. It appears unlikely that this dependency can be arrested by any means available to the welfare system as currently conceived. In Philadelphia, for example, the number of welfare recipients in 1960 stood at approximately 100,000, roughly 5 percent of the population. By 1980 that number had reached 334,000, or an astonishing 20 percent of the city's population. This rapid rise in the welfare population has been accompanied by a steady decline in employment. Between 1970 and 1980 alone, Philadelphia lost 130,000 jobs, 110,000 of them in manufacturing.[39] As the living standard of the often underemployed working poor declines and the relative status of the dependent poor improves, the near-convergence of the two groups is likely to create further disincentives to work at entry-level and low-paying jobs. Not only does this make an escape from dependency all the less likely, it also possibly opens the way to a new round of benefit cuts that can be justified as a method of increasing the "motivation" of the unemployed poor to seek work.

It is unconscionable for any advocate of the rights of poor people to abandon them to a life of dependency that wastes the resources of society as well as the potential of individuals to live a decent life. Since the problems of dependent poverty, urban decline, unemployment, and the growth of the underclass cannot be separated, the conclusion is inescapable: opponents of poverty must advocate and work for structural change in the American system for distributing opportunity and resources, no matter how unlikely the prospect appears in the short term.

The Programmatic Legacy

Did the Great Society and Subsequent Initiatives Work?

SAR A. LEVITAN
AND CLIFFORD M. JOHNSON

Two decades ago, on May 22, 1964, President Lyndon Johnson urged the nation to strive toward the establishment of a Great Society. "We have the opportunity," he stated in the memorable commencement address at the University of Michigan, "to move not only toward the rich society and the powerful society, but also toward the Great Society [that] demands an end to poverty and racial injustice, to which we are totally committed in our time."

Nineteen years later President Ronald Reagan urged the nation to abandon Johnson's faith in the potential of collective action and the benefits of government intervention. "It's time to bury the myth that bigger government brings more opportunity and compassion," he argued in August 1983.

Is President Reagan's harsh and negative assessment justified? How much truth is there to the currently prevailing view that the Great Society simply threw money at problems? Did the Johnson initiatives to build a better society indeed fail?

What is obvious is that our welfare system has expanded dramatically over the past two decades, with the cost of our efforts rising accordingly. Federal outlays for social welfare legislation, broadly defined, totaled $393 billion in 1984 compared with $164 billion (adjusted for inflation)

This essay is based upon *Beyond the Safety Net: Reviving the Promise of Opportunity in America*, by Sar A. Levitan and Clifford M. Johnson (Cambridge, Mass.: Ballinger/Harper and Row), published in October 1984.

two decades earlier. The more difficult question is whether the proliferation of federal social programs was the product of fertile bureaucratic minds in Washington or a response to real societal needs.

THE FRUITS OF THE GREAT SOCIETY

The development of the nation's welfare system, shaped and greatly accelerated under the Great Society, has improved the lives of millions of Americans by expanding opportunity and reducing deprivation throughout the life cycle. Federal initiatives have sharply reduced destitution among the aged and orphans, provided a cushion for those forced into temporary idleness, and extended support to poverty-stricken families with children and to the permanently disabled. Due to a dramatic expansion in public and private pension benefits, the elderly today are less likely to suffer economic hardship than younger Americans and the great majority are guaranteed adequate health care in their retirement years. Within fifteen years the proportion of the poor among the population was cut by two-fifths, falling from 19 percent in 1964 to nearly 12 percent in 1979.

Federal programs that bolster opportunities for advancement and self-sufficiency now span all stages of life. Some components of the modern welfare system preceded the Great Society, while others are more recent innovations. Yet the Great Society provided the impetus for creation of a comprehensive welfare system in America, one that seeks to bring all groups into the mainstream of American life. The evidence suggests that these initiatives have made a difference, offering no panaceas but yielding brighter prospects at every age.

In tracing federal interventions throughout the life cycle, wide variations in the size and scope of social welfare programs are unmistakable. If measured in terms of federal expenditures, by far the greatest share of social welfare resources have been devoted to income transfers, including social security, unemployment insurance, and Aid to Families with Dependent Children. In-kind assistance programs such as food stamps, Medicare, and Medicaid have also dwarfed other social welfare initiatives in federal budgets over the past two decades. Still, the impact of efforts to expand opportunity and promote self-sufficiency cannot be gauged in terms of dollars alone. By offering hope for a productive life and an escape from poverty, even relatively small investments in health care, education, employment, and training can make an important contribution to the nation's well-being.

The following review of the Great Society's legacy is not intended as an exhaustive survey of the modern welfare system. Focusing on attempts to broaden opportunity throughout the life cycle, relatively little attention is devoted to large and essential programs that provide income support to meet basic needs. In addition, the survey's emphasis on human resources programs precludes discussion of economic development initiatives such as the Model Cities program that complemented the Great Society's social welfare initiatives. However, the life-cycle approach vividly illustrates the remarkable extension of the modern welfare system, while at the same time documenting both the fruits and the potential of federal efforts to fulfill the promise of opportunity in America.

At the beginning of life. Recognizing that large families and unwanted births increase the probability that households will be destitute, the federal government supports family planning services for low-income individuals. Fertility control lowers maternal and infant mortality rates and reduces the incidence of mental retardation, physical defects, and premature births. In addition, children in smaller families tend to receive better care and support, becoming less likely candidates for a life of poverty than children from large families.[1]

Nutritional deficiencies can widen disparities in opportunity even before birth. The federal government has sought to mitigate barriers to advancement at the beginning of the life cycle through a special supplemental food program for women, infants, and children (wic). Low-income mothers, infants, and children suffering from poor nutrition are eligible to receive food or vouchers that can be exchanged for milk, cereals, juices, and other selected food items. In 1984, 2.3 million women received wic food packages with an average value of $378.

Federal provision of balanced diets, nutritional education, and health services to low-income pregnant women, nursing mothers, infants, and young children has significantly increased the likelihood of normal deliveries and healthy children among poor families. The wic program has been credited with marked reductions in the incidence of low-birthweight infants, with resulting savings in hospital costs for extended care estimated at $3 for every $1 spent in the wic prenatal component.[2]

The federal government continues its food assistance efforts for older children through the school lunch, school breakfast, and special milk programs. The largest federal child nutrition effort, the school lunch program, served 23 million youngsters in fiscal 1984 at a total cost of

$2.2 billion. In conjunction with the breakfast and special milk programs, these programs in many cases provide the sole nutritional meal each day that poor and nearly poor children receive. While the absence of narrow targeting of benefits in child nutrition programs has drawn criticism from some quarters, relatively broad eligibility requirements have responded to the need for economies of scale in program administration and have contributed to a solid base of political support for child nutrition efforts.

Beyond nutritional assistance, the federal government supports preventive medical services for mothers, infants, and children through grants to states for maternal and child health and through Medicaid. In 1981, 17 million pregnant women and children were served by the maternal and child health block grant program and Medicaid paid for the health care of more than 10 million poor children. The results of specific federal interventions in preventive health care have been impressive. A Texas study found that the state saved $8 in avoided medical costs for every $1 spent on preventive services, and a North Dakota analysis showed that Medicaid costs for children who received preventive health care dropped by one-third.[3]

In more general ways federal initiatives have sought to expand availability of health care in regions heavily populated by low-income Americans and underserved by private medical practitioners. Federal policy has encouraged health care personnel to reside in impoverished rural and urban areas through providing incentives of medical education scholarships and loan deferments. A targeted approach yielding dramatic results can be found in the record of the Indian Health Service, created to meet the acute health needs of isolated and poverty-stricken native Americans. As a result of this targeted federal effort, Indian life expectancy increased 5.1 years in the two decades following 1950 and the infant mortality rate dropped from 61 to 14.6 deaths per 1,000 live births between 1960 and 1980.

All these federal initiatives are based on the premise that equal opportunity can exist only when basic nutritional and health care needs are met in the formative years of development. If nutritional deficiencies or other health problems stunt intellectual and physical development in early childhood, compensatory programs are unlikely to erase the scars of initial deprivation. In this sense, the failure of free markets to guarantee equal opportunity for all members of American society is visible at the very beginning of the life cycle, imposing a cumulative burden on the least advantaged that often grows to insurmountable proportions.

Compensatory education. By the time children enter kindergarten, differences in family backgrounds have already been translated into a head start for some and a handicap for others. Repeated studies have found that children who come from low-income families or have parents with low levels of educational attainment are likely to begin school with fewer cognitive skills than their more fortunate counterparts. Thus the promotion of equal educational opportunity must reach down to preschool ages, lest those from the most adverse home environments fall hopelessly behind before the race for individual achievement formally begins.

At the preschool level the primary federal program designed to remedy educational deficiencies associated with poverty has been Headstart. Providing a comprehensive set of educational, medical, and social services to poor preschool children and their families, local Headstart agencies seek to raise the basic cognitive skills of disadvantaged youngsters to the norms for their age. Headstart served approximately 430,000 children at a cost of $958 million in 1984, reaching roughly 29 percent of the four- and five-year-olds from low-income households who were eligible to participate in the program.

Since its creation in 1965, research has provided substantial evidence that Headstart has a positive influence on nearly every aspect of early childhood development. Like federal interventions in child nutrition and preventive health care, early remedial efforts have been shown to be cost-effective because they inhibit the development of more serious educational and behavioral problems, thereby leading to a net reduction in public expenditures.[4] Longitudinal surveys have found that Headstart children are less likely to enter special education classes and more likely to be in the correct grade for their age than those in control groups.[5] It has also been shown that cumulative improvements in cognitive skills are linked to Headstart participation, and that the most disadvantaged children enjoy the most positive effect.[6]

Evaluations of Headstart have not been universally positive. However, in perhaps the most thorough analysis of early childhood programs, researchers found that Headstart children were nearly 20 percent more likely than children in control groups to graduate from high school, almost twice as likely to enroll in college or post-secondary vocational training, and about twice as likely to be employed. These preschool children were also found to be 20 percent less likely to be arrested, about half as likely to register for welfare benefits, and almost half as likely to become pregnant while teenagers. Based on these findings, the investigators estimated that taxpayers save nearly $3,100 for each preschool child in reduced crime alone, and that society's return on its investment ranged from $3.50 to $7.00 for every $1 spent on preschool compensatory education programs.[7]

For children already in school the most significant federal support for compensatory education is provided to local school districts under Chapter I of the Education Consolidation and Improvement Act (formerly Title I of the Elementary and Secondary Education Act, a program initiated in 1965). Federal funds for Chapter I programs are distributed to local educational agencies according to a formula based on the number of children from low-income families living in each school district. Limited federal aid is also provided to states for programs serving handicapped, migrant, neglected, and delinquent children. Congressional fiscal 1984 appropriations for Chapter I provided $3.5 billion for remedial instruction and related services at the primary level to school districts enrolling large numbers of poor children.

The magnitude of federal expenditures for compensatory education ensured that the program was among the most carefully evaluated social welfare initiatives. Evaluations of compensatory education efforts for the U.S. Department of Education found significant gains in achievement and educational attainment among low-income children over time.[8] Other studies have credited the program with eliminating over 40 percent of the difference in reading achievement between nine-year-old black and white children since its inception in 1965.[9]

Because local administrators had considerable discretion in the use of compensatory education funds, however, effective monitoring of expenditures has proved difficult. The extent to which aid was targeted to low-income children was frequently challenged, especially in the early years of the program. Tension between the goals of targeted assistance and broad provision of service has been heightened as a result of the 1981 revisions, which allow states greater flexibility in the use of federal funds intended for compensatory education.

Basic skills and youth employment. A few years later in the life cycle, teenagers with cognitive skills and educational attainments lagging well behind those of their peers face a compounded set of problems. The underachievers have been identified by educators as "slow" or unmotivated and find little positive reinforcement in academic settings. The primary challenge in promoting opportunity for disadvantaged youth is to keep them in school for a period sufficient to establish their basic competency to qualify for jobs.

The importance of educational attainment, and more specifically of a high school diploma or equivalency certificate, to occupational advancement and economic self-sufficiency has been clearly established. Years of schooling correlate positively with wages, earnings, income, employment rates, and occupational status. Employers use educational attainment as a basis for screening job applicants, even in cases where skill requirements are not directly related to completion of a high school education. For these reasons government interventions designed to promote equal opportunity among youth have sought to keep the disadvantaged in school and to bolster the development of their basic skills.

Federal initiatives suggest that even the most disadvantaged youth can acquire basic skills and work experience if careful attention is paid to program management and implementation. The strongest evidence of such potential can be found in the record of the Job Corps, operated directly by the federal government since 1965. Focusing primarily on school dropouts, the Job Corps is designed to remove youth from disruptive environments by placing them in residential centers with highly structured remedial programs. The combination of basic education, occupational training, and an emphasis on more general living skills necessitates a substantial commitment of federal resources: in 1983 annual costs per slot averaged $15,000.

Because Job Corps serves the most disadvantaged of low-income youth rather than selecting the most employable among eligible youth at the outset, the rate of attrition in the program is high. A 1977 profile of Job Corps participants conveys the magnitude of the challenge: five of six were school dropouts averaging below sixth-grade reading and math levels; only one-half came from two-parent families; the typical family size of enrollees was nearly twice the national average; and the per capita family income of participants was less than one-third that of the mean for the total population. Four of ten participants had previous arrests (of those, three-fourths had prior convictions), and more than one-third of all 1977 participants had never held a job with at least twenty hours per week for longer than a month. Not surprisingly, only a portion of this trouble-plagued client population is willing and able to complete the Job Corps program: for every ten entrants only three have managed to complete vocational training.[10]

Participants who complete training enjoy considerable gains in postprogram employment. Males who finished the vocational program in 1977 earned $1,250 more annually than experimental controls twelve to eighteen months after termination; the annual increase in earnings for females averaged $1,500.[11] These gains resulted almost exclusively from higher postprogram employment rates rather than from higher wage rates, and overall earnings for completers were enhanced by substantial increases in military enlistment among participants as compared to control groups. The Job Corps program generally has heightened the attachment of disadvantaged youth to the labor force while also raising their ability to meet entry requirements of private employers and the armed services.

Unlike many nonresidential supported work programs, Job Corps also has produced distinct behavioral shifts among participants. Studies show that self-esteem increased and family relations improved for those who remained in the program for at least ninety days. Reduced child bearing and out-of-wedlock births, increased mobility, and more frequent matriculation in college and postsecondary education have been linked similarly to Job Corps participation. Most important for taxpayers supporting the program, participants have proved far less likely to engage in criminal activities than their nonparticipating counterparts. In the first year following completion of the program, the arrest rate for participants was 35 percent lower than that of control groups. These salutary effects of enrollment in Job Corps contributed societal benefits at least equal to the value of gains in earnings derived from classroom training.[12]

The remedial instruction that is an integral component of the comprehensive Job Corps approach provides further testimony to the importance of self-paced educational programs for disadvantaged youth. Notwithstanding their demonstrated difficulty in traditional classroom settings, participants respond more positively to individualized instruction with standardized competency-based testing. Entering with less than a sixth-grade average reading level, participants gain an average 1.5 years of competency in 90 hours of instruction and 2.2 years in 150 hours.[13] This success in strengthening the basic educational abilities of poor school dropouts offers encouraging evidence that self-paced programs with clearly measured standards of progress can motivate the most disadvantaged students and facilitate their educational achievement.

Equal access and advancement. Not all low-income teenagers are candidates for remedial education and occupational training. Quite the opposite is true. Despite their relative deprivation many poor youth find the support, guidance, and motivation necessary to succeed in school and compete effectively with their more affluent peers. Others have the potential for sustained academic achievement, but need modest encouragement and support in order to develop their innate abilities.

Federal initiatives have sought to enhance the upward social mobility of low-income Americans by increasing access to higher education. Several programs—including Upward Bound, Talent Search, and other special services for disadvantaged students—have served potential college students from poor households since 1965, offering remedial instruction and tutoring, personal counseling, and career development services. To be eligible for TRIO services participants must be from families with incomes not exceeding 150 percent of the federal poverty threshold ($10,200 for a family of four in 1983), and neither parent may be a college graduate. Over 500,000 students were enrolled in these federal programs in fiscal 1984, for a total expenditure of $165 million.

Hampered by budget restrictions that enable them to serve only a small fraction of the eligible population, TRIO programs have nonetheless produced some encouraging results. Nearly six of every ten Upward Bound high school graduates have entered college. More important, at least 60 percent of those who enrolled in college in 1976 were still attending two years later, indicating that Upward Bound students are as likely to remain in college as students from more affluent backgrounds. Talent Search and related projects have been similarly successful, often placing between 75 and 90 percent of their students in postsecondary institutions.[14] The House Committee on Education and Labor estimated that 20 percent of all college minority freshmen in 1982 were placed by federally supported projects.[15] Despite the inability of these programs to overcome large educational deficiencies from earlier years, they are effective mechanisms for bolstering student motivation and providing the extra support necessary to guide many poor youth into postsecondary education.

The success of the TRIO programs must be shared with federal student assistance programs. Federal grant, loan, and work-study programs for low- and middle-income students have dramatically reduced financial barriers to a college education, reaching over 5 million students in 1984.

The cornerstone of federal support for low-income students in postsecondary education is the Pell grant (formerly the basic educational opportunity grant) program. Of the 2.6 million college students receiving aid up to $1,900 in 1984, 70 percent were from families with annual incomes below $12,000 and 57 percent were minority students. Between 1972 and 1982 there was an 85 percent increase in the enrollment of black and other minority college students. Federal student aid played a key role in boosting college attendance by low-income youth from 3 to 5 percent of total college enrollment between 1974 and 1981, even though an increasing proportion of aid flowed to middle- and upper-income students during this period.[16]

Skill training and work experience. For disadvantaged youth with the poorest educational prospects and for low-income adults, skill training and work experience emerge as the most promising strategies for boosting future earnings and self-sufficiency. The potential gains from such interventions are significant but far from overwhelming. Federal training and work experience initiatives can facilitate entry into the labor market, enhance the likelihood of steady employment in subsequent years, and generate marginal increases in future earnings. Yet the conservative ideal of equal opportunity provided through free markets is irrelevant for most disadvantaged adults, as their chances for career development and advancement have already been smothered under the collective weight of prior deprivations. At best, federal employment and training programs can mean the difference between poverty and modest incomes, between dependency and a firm attachment to work.

Though limited, the effectiveness of federal training programs has been well documented. Exhaustive longitudinal surveys of participants in federally supported training programs have found that on-the-job training raised postprogram earnings by 18 percent over those of comparison groups. Classroom training resulted in a 10 percent increase in the first year following participation. Participants in public service employment experienced a 7 percent increase in their postenrollment earnings compared to a control group's. Every dollar invested in on-the-job training returned an estimated $2.55 in social benefits, and a similar investment in classroom training returned $1.38 to society.[17] Because federal taxpayers bear the cost of training and earnings gains accrue directly to participants, the benefit-cost ratio for training from a narrow taxpayer's perspective is considerably lower, accounting in part for the tenuous political support lent to these activities.

Supervised work experience can provide some aid even to low-income adults for whom lack of a prior work record poses a major obstacle to employment. In the national supported-work demonstration project conducted between 1974 and 1979, individuals with poor employment prospects were placed for twelve to eighteen months in jobs in which their performance was closely supervised, work standards were gradually increased over time, and peer group support was emphasized. The demonstration focused on four target groups: women with a history of welfare dependency, ex-addicts, ex-offenders, and young school dropouts.

Supported work offered no training to participants and limited the duration of subsidized employment regardless of whether individuals had been placed in other jobs. With an elaborate experimental design, the program was structured explicitly to test the impact of a supportive work experience on future employability.

For those with limited work experience, lacking the discipline, work habits, or record of employment necessary to compete in the labor market, supported work demonstrated that provision of a supervised job in itself can reduce barriers to employment among some disadvantaged groups. The clearest successes were achieved in projects serving women with dependent children who had long records of welfare dependency. After an average stay in supported work of nine months, welfare mothers worked more and earned higher wage rates than controls who had not participated in the program. The long-term social benefits of increased employment and reduced dependency outweighed the costs of this government intervention, including day care services, supervision, and peer counseling, by an estimated $14,000 per AFDC program participant (1984 dollars) over a twenty-seven-month period.[18]

Supervised work experience is by no means a panacea for the employment problems of the disadvantaged. Although relatively successful in facilitating the entry of welfare mothers into the labor market, supported work had little effect on the employment and earnings of ex-addicts, ex-offenders, or school dropouts. The program did lead to reductions in the criminal activity of ex-addicts, but similar shifts were not identified among other target groups. The supported work approach appears most promising for low-income persons with the least amount of prior work experience and the fewest complicating behavioral problems.

Since the Great Society's heyday, efforts to open employment opportunities for disadvantaged adults have taken a back seat to income support initiatives. Income transfers and the provision of food, shelter, energy, and health care expanded rapidly during the 1970s in an essential response to unmet basic needs. For qualified jobless workers, unemployment insurance benefits provided an additional temporary wage replacement at a cost of $31.5 billion in fiscal 1983 and $20.7 billion in 1984. These income maintenance programs dwarf in size any federal efforts to broaden opportunities for employment and advancement through skill training or work experience, and constitute by far the most expensive component of the modern welfare state.

Public employment programs over the past decade have offered an alternative form of income maintenance, generally meeting basic needs

but contributing little to the skills and future employability of patici-
pants. If carefully administered, public service employment can serve
important goals, compensating for job shortages during periods of recession and fulfilling useful functions for local communities. As an alternative to welfare, public employment also gives able-bodied adults the
dignity of work and the modest benefits of sustained work experience.
Yet in the absence of structured training in basic or occupational skills,
job creation alone cannot be expected to yield lasting progress in opening doors to advancement and economic self-sufficiency.

Equality under the law. Job discrimination has long been one of the
major causes of poverty and one of the most obvious barriers to advancement in the labor market. Black and other minority workers suffer
higher unemployment rates and have lower labor force participation
rates than whites. When out of work they face disproportionately
longer periods of unemployment; when employed they are concentrated
in low-wage occupations. Beginning with the adoption of Title VII of
the Civil Rights Act of 1964 and the creation of the Equal Employment
Opportunity Commission to enforce its provisions, the federal government has played an important role in bolstering the economic prospects
of minorities and has prompted slow progress toward a society in which
opportunities for employment and advancement cannot be denied on
the basis of sex, race, color, or national origin.

The federal drive for equal opportunity spawned by the civil rights
movement of the 1950s and 1960s has brought significant progress in
ameliorating wage and employment discrimination. Between 1968 and
1983 the average income of black families with both spouses working
rose from 73.2 percent to 81.0 percent of that for comparable white
households.[19] Similarly, the gap between the median weekly earnings of
black full-time wage and salary workers narrowed from 74 percent of
white earnings in 1970 to 78 percent in 1982.[20] However, these gains
have not reduced income disparities between all black and white families, due to a disproportionate increase in the number of female-headed
black households in recent years. Adjusted 1980 data that control for
changes in family composition during the 1970s reveal that in the absence of such changes the ratio of black to white median family income
would have risen from 61 percent in 1970 to 66 percent in 1980, rather
than falling to 56 percent as it actually had by 1983.[21] This evidence
suggests that federal antidiscrimination efforts along with investments
in education and other social programs have contributed to a slow rise
in the earnings of black workers relative to their white counterparts.

Federal equal employment initiatives are also in part responsible for the gradually expanding access of black workers to better-paying occupations with possibilities for career advancement. Between 1972 and 1982 the proportion of professionals who were minorities rose from 7.2 to 11.8 percent. Among managers and administrators this ratio increased from 4 to 4.8 percent, and among skilled craft workers it rose from 6.9 to 9.0 percent.[22] Minorities continue to be underrepresented in these favored occupations. Yet these modest improvements in occupational distribution for blacks, representing increases in their share of employment in professional and skilled occupations ranging from 23 to 50 percent in the course of a decade, demonstrate the impact of equal employment and affirmative action programs championed at the federal level.

The gains of the civil rights movement have been most visible in advancing political participation among blacks. As a result of the Voting Rights Act of 1965, millions of black citizens have registered to vote, making them a powerful political force in many parts of the country. The number of black elected officials at all levels of government has risen from 1,472 in 1970 to 5,606 in 1983, including 248 black mayors representing over 20 million Americans. Another forty-seven United States cities, including San Antonio, Denver, Miami, and Tampa, now have Hispanic mayors. Although systematic efforts to deny minorities access to the polls persist in some areas, the outrage provoked by discrimination against black voters itself reveals the progress of the past two decades. Federal intervention has been instrumental in opening the doors to more equal political participation regardless of race or national origin.

Dignity in retirement. At the end of the life cycle, federal policy has long been directed toward the provision of income security in retirement. With the expectation to work largely lifted from individuals after age sixty-five, the federal focus on opportunity shifts from employment and occupational advancement to providing basic income for the "golden years." Though development of the Social Security and private pension systems, government interventions have been highly successful in breaking the link between old age and poverty during the postwar era. By 1982 older as well as permanently disabled Americans were less likely to live in poverty (14.6 percent) than were their younger counterparts—a sharp contrast to the situation a generation ago, when the national poverty rate for all ages stood at 22 percent, but 35 percent of those over sixty-five lived in households with incomes below the poverty line.

The effectiveness of federal aid to older Americans can be traced to the combination of income transfers and in-kind assistance to meet basic needs. Payments under Social Security have grown rapidly, and a steadily rising proportion of the aged population (nineteen of every twenty) receives retirement benefits. Pension benefits for indigent veterans provide additional income security in old age. Nonetheless, the dramatic advances toward fulfilling basic needs in retirement would not have been possible without health insurance coverage for the elderly through the Great Society's Medicare program.

The broad political consensus in support of aid to the elderly may never be achieved in other federal efforts to eradicate poverty. Posing none of the conflicts with work that plague direct assistance to younger persons, old-age benefits are generally perceived as earned and well deserved. Other groups especially vulnerable to deprivation enjoy neither the aura of deservedness nor the roots of shared experience that generate broad political support for aid to the elderly from all social classes. In this sense the substantial improvement of economic well-being after age sixty-five demonstrates both the efficacy of federal intervention and the potential for substantial progress against poverty at all ages if a more compassionate understanding of its nature and causes develops in American society.

PRAGMATIC CHOICES AND POLITICAL REALITIES

Many social problems have proved more pervasive and persistent than was originally thought, requiring more varied strategies for their amelioration and more realistic criteria by which to gauge success or failure. In addition, the process of change has sometimes generated unwanted side effects, posing new problems for policy-makers. Fundamentally, these problems are the natural by-products of any attempts to implement new processes and construct new institutions. They should not be allowed to obscure past gains and they should not be used as an excuse to abandon the struggle for social progress.

Nonetheless, in a political context the realization that there are no easy answers or quick one-shot solutions to problems of poverty and long-term dependency has created profound problems for the welfare system. Repeatedly, from the New Deal through the Great Society, policy-makers clung to the hope that the need for government aid to the poor would dissipate, if not within a few years, then over the course of a generation or two. The authors of the original Social Security Act in 1935 presumed that the need for public old-age assistance would wither away as younger workers became fully covered by social insurance—an expectation that was shattered by steadily expanding welfare rolls after World War II. Similarly, a central premise of the War on Poverty was that investments in education and training, civil rights protections, and community organization could dramatically lift this generation's poor out of deprivation and ensure their children a decent life. Poverty and dependency have proved far more intractable.

Because politicians and taxpayers prefer quick fixes and visible successes, comprehensive long-term approaches to welfare efforts have been extremely difficult to sustain or defend from political challenge. The legacy of the Great Society vividly illustrates the dilemma: federal initiatives in some cases produced little positive result due to an insufficient commitment of funds over too brief a period of time; in other cases promising strategies were misjudged as failures because they were slow in generating visible short-term gains.

Conflicts between long-term investments in social welfare and short-term political pressures are heightened by the complexity of barriers to economic opportunity and the difficulty of constructing effective approaches to social problems. The experience of recent decades suggests that the federal government must proceed on several fronts simultaneously if it is to be successful in alleviating poverty or reducing dependency. For example, training of low-income workers is not likely to have a significant impact on overall poverty levels or welfare caseloads if provided amid high unemployment or in economically declining geographical areas unless suitable employment and economic development programs are also initiated and the segmentation of labor markets overcome. Although income transfers address the immediate needs of the poor, they do not result in lasting improvements in the earnings capacity and self-sufficiency of beneficiaries unless they are complemented by public efforts designed to enhance the skills of the recipients and the institutions that trap them in poverty. As a result of the interdependence of federal strategies, individual initiatives viewed in isolation can appear to have failed because concomitant interventions necessary for their success were not undertaken. At the same time the interaction of these seemingly disparate programs can yield results far in excess of the potential of isolated efforts.

One of the clearest lessons of federal social welfare experience is that poverty cannot be eliminated solely through a reliance on income transfers. Income maintenance certainly must be a central component of any approach in aid of the poor, but a strategy relying on transfers alone cannot enhance self-sufficiency and irreconcilably conflicts with the functioning of the labor market. In a society where wages for millions of workers are too low to lift them out of poverty, the provision of adequate cash assistance to the nonworking poor, if unaccompanied by incentives to supplement assistance with earnings, inevitably raises serious questions of equity and generates strong political opposition within the working population. In addition, income transfers large enough to lift low-income households above the poverty threshold, if not tied to work effort, would trigger large drops in labor force participation or force massive public expenditures to the nonpoor in order to preserve acceptable work incentives. These political and economic realities have led to the demise of successive guaranteed income schemes during the past two decades and demonstrate the need for federal strategies that link work and welfare so as to assist both the working and dependent poor.

In the 1960s and 1970s federal policy-makers, regardless of party affiliation, partially avoided the conflicts of income maintenance by extending in-kind assistance to the working poor. Food stamps, school nutrition programs, subsidized housing, expansion of unemployment benefit coverage, and, in some states, health care coverage were made available to low-wage earners as well as welfare recipients, thereby raising the living standards of all poor Americans. Because in-kind aid does not provide the disposable income that most directly undermines work motivation, it has offered a politically acceptable means of supplementing the incomes of the working poor as well as the dependent poor.

In-kind assistance is an essential part of any comprehensive response to the needs of the poor. This fulfillment of basic needs not only arouses less public animosity than cash assistance but also responds to social problems arising out of specific market inadequacies. Cash assistance in amounts equal to federal expenditures on in-kind aid often cannot ensure the availability of supply or appropriate distribution of essential goods and services. When free markets would otherwise provide an inadequate supply of goods or services, public provision through the use of subsidies distributed to the poor for housing, for example, is more likely to raise rents than increase the supply of decent housing. Similarly, in the case of health care, where individual needs vary widely among those with identical incomes, in-kind assistance secures the necessities of life for all regardless of differing personal circumstances.

Success in reconciling conflicts between income maintenance and the functioning of the labor market will require greater ease of movement between work and welfare and new mechanisms for combining these sources of support. In the past, refusal to acknowledge that the meager returns of unskilled labor lie at the heart of the poverty problem has precluded adoption of policies that would reflect the need to combine work with welfare. Popular wisdom has preserved the traditional belief that work provides an escape from dependency and a path to self-sufficiency, despite conclusive evidence that work effort brings no such guarantee, particularly for large families. Hence the federal role in social welfare repeatedly has been based on sharp distinctions between the employable and the dependent poor that mask the reality of millions who can work—full-time, part-time, or intermittently—but cannot earn enough to escape from poverty. As already noted nearly half of the adult poor are in the labor force at least intermittently.

Future approaches that seek to integrate work and welfare will require a reexamination of society's definition of the deserving poor and of appropriate federal roles in social welfare. Sound approaches for combining work and welfare already can be found in rudimentary form in the federal earned income tax credit, supported work and other wage subsidy experiments, health care coverage for the medically needy, and AFDC benefits for households with unemployed fathers. However, opposition to the expansion of wage subsidies and in-kind assistance to the working poor is likely to be strong—a reflection of the belief that earnings are and should be based on an individual's market worth.

Federal social welfare initiatives operate within broad political and economic constraints. The experience since the 1930s clearly indicates the inherent tensions between targeting of benefits and the political acceptability of government programs. Without question, universal provision of basic services engenders broad public acceptance and a strong base of political support, as illustrated by the evolution of Social Security, Medicare, and college loan programs. Yet the extension of aid regardless of income necessarily increases the cost of government interventions, diluting their impact on the most needy and subjecting federal roles to challenge as inappropriate or extravagant. On the other hand, as a major architect of social legislation, Wilbur Cohen, has observed, efforts for poor people inevitably become poor programs. The conflict between targeting and universality can never be fully resolved; the challenge in the development of federal social programs is to strike a balance that gives every American a stake in the modern welfare system while focusing the necessary resources on those who need them most with due regard to the dignity of recipients.

The Reagan administration's attempt to focus federal aid on those with greatest need has some appeal and even superficial legitimacy. Although judgments regarding the appropriate degree of targeting are always difficult, a strong case could be made by 1980 that too large a share of scarce federal resources were being diverted into benefits for the non-needy. The tragedy of the Reagan program is that this criterion of more narrowly focused aid has been applied in a highly selective rather than a comprehensive and equitable fashion. To be sure, eligibility in means-tested programs has been restricted, targeting aid to the poorest of low-income households. Yet in a broader context the Reagan administration has not made a serious effort to curtail federal aid to the non-needy through a host of special-interest subsidies and universal entitlements, and its spending reductions have fallen most heavily on exactly those programs designed to serve the truly needy.

A MATTER OF PRIORITIES

Even in the most affluent of societies, difficult and unpleasant choices must be made among a multitude of public needs and goals. The willingness to invest resources in welfare initiatives is a reflection of its relative importance among broader national priorities. Although it appeared that the nation had made a commitment to eradicate poverty during the Great Society period, support for the drive has not been sustained.

In the mid-1980s it is difficult to predict how many additional resources our society will be willing to commit in support of the welfare system, particularly when the problems of the poor have such a relatively low profile in the American consciousness. Antipoverty efforts have fared poorly in the competition for national resources in recent years. But who can say that our priorities will not change? Who would have predicted in the 1950s that poverty and hunger would be powerful issues in the following two decades, or that the hippies of the 1960s would turn into the yuppies of the 1980s? One can always hope that the noble goal of the Great Society to expand opportunity to all Americans will again raise to the forefront of the national agenda. Only then will the nation meet the challenge voiced by Samuel Johnson over two centuries ago: "A decent provision for the poor is the true test of civilization."

Creating Jobs for Americans:
From MDTA to Industrial Policy

PETER B. EDELMAN

Twenty years after the Great Society it appears that the revisionism of the last decade is beginning to thaw, and perhaps before long the Great Society will begin to receive the credit it deserves. That is critically important for the future of social policy, as well as for purposes of putting the record of the past in proper order.

This essay evaluates efforts during the sixties and seventies to help people move into the labor market, improve their position, or make a transition, in circumstances where an imperfection or barrier in the labor market impedes their mobility. Job "creation" is also discussed. But full exposition of policies to promote a healthy economy is beyond the scope of the essay.

THE CURRENT SITUATION

Perhaps a Great Society issue exists that is now only a matter of historical concern, but employment is not such a one. Efforts to fight chronic joblessness among the historically disadvantaged have not caused the problem to disappear, and in the last four years that problem has been not only exacerbated but also joined by another: the plight of people displaced by the flight of jobs abroad and by automation. The former group—the "old" poor—tends to be concentrated by race or ethnic identification, while the latter group is associated with particular regions in the country.[1]

The combined numbers are large. The overall unemployment rate, hardly satisfactory in itself as it continues at well over 7 percent, tells only part of the story. Despite all the news about recovery and the number of jobs created by it, about 15 million people are still either unemployed, "discouraged" and no longer seeking work, or working part-time only because they cannot find a full-time job.[2] A million and a half people have been unemployed more than half a year.[3]

The problems of the "old" poor have become measurably worse over the past four years. Black teenage unemployment is regularly over 40 percent, compared to around 18 percent for all teens, and that again is not the whole story. Employment of black teenagers has deteriorated to the point where fewer than one in four black teenagers has a job of some kind, compared to a figure of nearly 50 percent employment for white teens. Fewer than one in ten black teens has a full-time job.[4] Female-headed families are disproportionately beset by poverty. One in three female-headed families lives in poverty, and over half the children living in female-headed households (56.6 percent, to be exact) are poor.[5] This is due to low-wage employment and unemployment of the household heads as well as to unduly low income-maintenance payment levels. The situation for black and Hispanic female-headed households is even worse.[6] Further, the so-called feminization of poverty has a male counterpart. Only 54 percent of adult black males are working, as opposed to 78 percent of adult white males.[7]

The numbers suggest that the problems of dislocated workers—the "new" poor—are not just a phenomenon of the business cycle. The share of manufacturing employment in the economy had declined before 1980, but the number of manufacturing jobs had not decreased. It has, since 1980. Sixteen of the twenty sectors where employment is now increasing most quickly are in the service sector where average wages are 60 percent of average manufacturing wages. The twenty fastest-growing sectors had an average weekly wage of $210 compared to $310 for the twenty sectors where employment is declining most rapidly. During the 1981–82 recession, 2 milllion of the unemployed were living in areas of declining employment. Nearly 400,000 of the total number of unemployed had at least ten years of job tenure and a slightly larger number were over forty-five years of age.[8] Time will tell how much help will flow from further recovery and other developments such as a softening of the dollar.

Most economists would say the current mix of fiscal and monetary policies does not augur well for employment prospects. Continuation of the huge deficit, effective in stimulating recovery over the past two years, will become inflationary or at least will be regarded as such. Consequently, interest rates will rise, whether as a result of conscious Federal Reserve policy to ward off inflation, competition in the credit markets between the need to finance the deficit and people who want credit for other purposes, demand by lenders for higher long-term interest rates to compensate for expected inflation or uncertainty, or a combination of these factors. Such a tightening on the monetary side will most likely mean another recession and thus more unemployment. This is why employment policy-makers need to pay attention to general, or macroeconomic, economic policy. Reduction in the deficit in the immediate future would have a salutary effect in preventing unemployment and, by allowing the recovery to continue, in stimulating increased employment as well.

At the same time it is amply clear that even the best macroeconomic policy will not make a sufficient dent in the problems of the "old" poor and it seems quite likely that the "new" poor will still have some problems as well. These are structural problems—problems in the structure of the economy that need to be addressed with specific tailored strategies. The history and future of such efforts are our concern here.

MAJOR THEMES—WHAT WE HAVE LEARNED

The current situation is a paradox. We know more than we ever have about what works programmatically and what doesn't,[9] and structural unemployment is worse than ever. It appears that we are not making use of what we know.

If we have learned that policies affecting the health of the economy should be a matter of interest to employment experts, we have also learned that "job creation" in the sense of government spending to create temporary jobs is not a complete or sufficient strategy in and of itself to deal with structural unemployment. Perhaps no one ever thought it was, but in the late sixties and through most of the seventies we heard a great deal about the government as the "employer of last resort," as though the only problem was finding enough money to spend under that banner.

Some brief history is in order here to show how we have come to the knowledge that dealing with structural unemployment must involve a multidimensional employment and training strategy. The "employer of last resort" or public-service employment advocates were reacting to a different mistake of oversimplification. The Manpower Development and Training Act of 1962, or MDTA,[10] was a training program not a job-creation program,[11] and as such it quickly became the object of criticism as an effort that trained people for jobs that did not exist, or at least jobs that did not exist in places near or accessible to the clients of the training programs.

Antipoverty advocates, further stimulated by the riots in Watts, Newark, Detroit, and elsewhere, therefore began talking about public jobs rebuilding the inner cities or providing needed services.[12] Yet with the Vietnam War draining the country's resources, no additional major investment occurred during the Great Society period.

Nonetheless momentum was building. To ration available funds and avoid attack for being even more profligate than they already were accused of being, the proponents of job creation pressed for temporary jobs, assuming that the larger economy would absorb the workers after their temporary work experience on a public or nonprofit payroll.

This momentum culminated in CETA, the Comprehensive Employment and Training Act of 1973,[13] which contained a full-fledged public service employment program. The act continued a large investment in training as well, including enlargement of the Job Corps, which was by then receiving strongly positive evaluations.

While the investment in training was therefore real and continuing, further enlargement seemed not to be a major agenda item for liberals, who perhaps had in mind that training by itself had not been a great success in the sixties. In the mid-seventies the job-creation rhetoric was about all one heard from the advocates, who were in effect saying that a bigger program of temporary public service jobs would tide the chronically unemployed over long enough to enable them to find jobs.

The Carter administration represented the best balance we have had. It greatly expanded public-service employment as part of its stimulative package in 1977, but it also gave public recognition to the fact that young people in particular routinely needed serious help on basic reading and mathematics skills and on other aspects of transition to the job market. By 1980 it was proposing a youth initiative that was sophisticated and sensible.

Public policy has now turned 180 degrees away from job creation. The Job Training Partnership Act (JTPA), our current statute in this general area, is a training initiative with no job creation component at all and without financial support for those undergoing the training.

Public policy has gone from the mistake of providing training without jobs to the mistake of providing jobs without training and back again. Students and analysts of the issue, as well as many advocates, now appreciate that policies and programs must be multidimensional and must be offered in combinations that will differ depending on the age, skill gaps, and other characteristics of the client group involved.

These insights are paralleled by an emerging awareness that the actors involved in an intelligent employment and training policy need to constitute a larger and more varied cast. The pattern of the seventies was a partnership mainly between the federal government and local governments in the shape of manpower agencies called "prime sponsors." States were not much involved; neither was the private sector nor the schools. Each, we have learned, has an important role to play in an appropriate effort.

Would that our problem had only been the necessity to learn the foregoing facts. Clouds are gathering on our economic horizon. International competition is a fact. Robotics and other forms of technology that reduce the need for workers are increasingly prevalent. The pressure to compete internationally may well accelerate the pressure to automate at home if it does not induce a firm to relocate to the source of cheaper labor.

The current "industrial policy" debate is important. While the phrase actually covers a multitude of areas ranging from changes in antitrust policy to government support of research and development, its premise is that the best macroeconomic policy will not produce enough jobs, and that what we might call structural efforts at economic development in order to create more jobs are essential as well. This is another dimension of the observation that what we have learned is that the problem is much more complicated than we thought. The good news is that the industrial policy debate is taking place, because a problem appears to be emerging that industrial policy initiatives could address. The bad news is that it is very hard at this juncture to tell whether the solutions proposed thus far have any real promise.

In this context, I hope we have learned not to trust economists too much. Some economists, for example, have contributed to the jargon the Orwellian phrase, " 'natural' rate of unemployment." As far as I am concerned the only natural rate of unemployment is zero, or as the jargon has it, "frictional"—the rate where the only people out of work are the ones who are between jobs for a brief period. Unfortunately, the fact is that too many people want jobs who are not in the right place geographically to get them, who lack the necessary skills, or who are victims of discrimination. These people still are not hired when employers run out of available workers and start bidding up wages in an inflationary way. The rate of unemployment at which this point is reached is called by some the "natural" rate.[14]

Apart from the inappropriateness of this terminology, it is important to understand that this so-called "natural" rate is not immutable. If people who are in the wrong place get to the right place and if people who are not prepared become prepared, the "natural" rate will fall and inflation due to labor shortages will not occur until a lower level of unemployment is reached. There are economists who have pointed this out clearly and helpfully.[15]

My complaint about some economists is that they imply an immutability to the "natural" rate. Hence we learn that full employment now is really 6 or 6.5 or 7 percent unemployment. This is simply wrong, and it does the nation a great disservice. Economists rightly complain that job advocates ignore macroeconomic policy, a point addressed above, but the economists have been less than helpful themselves. Some simply brand as inflationary all steps to reduce unemployment below the "natural" rate. Others agree that structural policies are appropriate but say they do not know anything about the specifics, implying that no one really does. This stance effectively denigrates such policies. This is not a blanket indictment, to be sure, but it captures the flavor of too many discussions that have occurred in high places and elsewhere in recent years.

Economists are by no means the only ones in error here. Employment policies have missed the point completely in major respects since right after World War II. Here I am not talking about the particular details of programs but rather about the mix between cash-transfer and employment programs, which has resulted in an unfortunate and unhappy growth of the former in relative terms. Unemployment of black young people began to climb precipitously and disproportionately in the fifties. I find it impossible to believe that the appropriate combination of education and training, placement efforts, antidiscrimination policies, and assorted family services could not have kept that from happening. Instead, the only legal source of money was the Aid to Families with Dependent Children (AFDC) program or, as it is colloquially known, the welfare system. It is palpable to me that this imbalance pushed young people toward welfare. Behaviorally, it meant that when children were born, marriages did not occur and families did not form. The problem was not just welfare.[16] Psychologically, a young man without a job found it hard to take on a family obligation, and the young mother found it hard to have him around. I am oversimplifying somewhat but not to a significant degree.

Certainly most welfare supporters did not believe welfare would come to be the sole and continuing support of large numbers of people. The legislative history of the Social Security Act in the 1930s suggests that Aid to Dependent Children, as it was then called, was envisioned as a residual program which, when the Great Depression came to an end, would shrink to providing assistance to a relatively small number of children whose mothers were widows or divorcees in difficult circumstances.[17] The chronic inner-city, rural, and now regional unemployment that ensued were not foreseen. Without going through the entire history since World War II, it is evident that those minority young people at the back of the jobs queue have found millions of others entering the labor market and gaining positions ahead of them in line. Women, the "baby boom" generation, and even illegal aliens have all done better. While I do not mean to suggest that minority young people are without a fair measure of responsibility in the matter, public policy until the late seventies did virtually nothing to redress the inequity of their position, and the limited effort then undertaken was essentially ended by the election of President Reagan. Welfare and later food stamps have been the only recourse, limited as it is, for these young people, and this has helped to produce a chronic dependency that is degrading and debilitating.

I began this point with a jab at economists because they among others have argued at times for policy initiatives involving exclusive reliance on more cash transfers. More adequate cash assistance is needed, but if it is provided without corresponding attention to the job side of the equation it stands to reason that such assistance will, among other things, produce more dependency. A full, three-dimensional anti-poverty strategy must involve attention to both employment and training policy and income maintenance, among other factors. Historically, while we have certainly not made adequate provision for income assistance, we have failed even more dramatically on the jobs side.

If we do not act we stand to lose another generation, at great cost to ourselves as a country as well as to the direct victims. It is true that the number of young people entering the labor market is decreasing, but the proportion of blacks and Hispanics among young workers is on the increase.[18] We face the absurd and tragic irony that later in this decade jobs may be exported for lack of skilled workers while an army of the unemployed awaits here, unskilled and untrained.

I know we have learned, all too well, that what needs to be done costs money and that severe fiscal constraints exist at least at present. We do have to understand that curing the deficit is critical to pursuing Great Society objectives. Funds to pursue those objectives will not be available in adequate measure otherwise. Indeed a key element of the Reagan strategy has been to assure a deficit large enough to make renewed investment in domestic social programs difficult. The deleterious effects of that strategy with which we are now living must be reversed, and the only way to do that is to act with the courage and commitment necessary to reduce the deficit, while making clear that a commitment to equity cannot be postponed until sufficient progress is made in closing the deficit.

I suggest as a major theme the importance of viewing our activity in all of this as an investment in human capital. Such activity will produce benefits for the country greater than its cost. Furthermore, the investment will reduce costs that would otherwise occur when large numbers of citizens are unproductive and requiring expenditures for government transfer payments, imprisonment, and extra social services. Whatever the validity of past appeals to morality and decency, the fact now is that we must see our reasons for acting in concrete investment terms. Such a view is not only correct but may also help to cut through some of the political difficulty in which such initiatives have found themselves in recent times.

SPECIFIC POLICIES FOR TODAY AND TOMORROW

We might divide the areas for policy prescription into roughly four: (1) improving access to jobs for those having trouble getting into the labor market in the first place; (2) improving income for those in low-wage jobs; (3) ensuring help for dislocated workers; and (4) implementing employment-related policies to preserve and create good jobs for Americans now and in the future.

The question of access at the outset of a working career is of course an old problem, but despite its complexities we now know more about what we should try to do. Clearly, young people are a major target group for policies to improve initial access.

The approach here begins with an education initiative: federal support for basic skills education in the high schools. The employment issue begins as an education issue. Far too many young people lack the skills to qualify for the jobs that are available.[19]

I begin with a suggestion of support—including federal support—for basic skills education in the high schools because, while the Elementary and Secondary Education Act of 1965 is one of the Great Society's successes,[20] it is a misnomer. It does not reach the secondary schools in any significant measure.[21] States are beginning to do so on their own, offering remedial assistance in tandem with somewhat toughened graduation requirements, but federal leverage and leadership would quicken the pace.

Of course, broadening our perspective to include education need not stop at the high school. Everything we do for children, from adequate prenatal care through good early child development programs and so on, produces more employable young people and prevents more young people from "falling through the cracks" in their late teens. All of these investments help reduce the size of the cracks, but cracks will still exist no matter what we do, and that is where the policies suggested here come into play.

Young people do not need a hodgepodge of items that would add significantly to the federal deficit. The appropriate strategies are rooted in technical assistance and information dissemination directed at involving the schools and business community more effectively. These include getting better labor market information into the schools; installing job-readiness curricula that teach students how to fill out job applications, perform well in interviews, and behave on the job; and involving the local business community in appropriate curriculum design and other relevant activities. These steps are already being taken in many localities. But enlightened and informed national leadership would help make things happen faster.

A major new strategy, tested successfully during the Carter years, would connect the schools more extensively to the world of work. It would involve offering part-time and summer subsidized work experience—preferably in the private sector in small businesses—to disadvantaged young people in return for their commitment to stay in school or, if they have already dropped out, their agreement to return to school or a high school equivalency program.

The Carter administration's multisite demonstration was called the Youth Incentive Entitlement Pilot Program (YIEPP). Evaluation by the Manpower Demonstration Research Corporation was on balance positive.[22] The idea was that young people already showing signs of being potential dropouts would be identified fairly early, perhaps in the tenth grade, and offered participation in the program. The most positive aspect of the evaluation was its finding that those who participated later had earnings of about $10 a week more, or about 40 percent higher, than those who did not participate.[23] Although they supplied only 23 percent of the jobs, 55 percent of the employers in the program were small private businesses.

A key element is that a significant portion of the work experience should be in the private sector. This is important because private-sector experience is a real credential for youths when they seek other jobs. The work would not be performed by someone else absent the subsidy. The subsidy is especially important because the young workers participating in the program were not yet fully productive. In many cases, employers found that the youths' presence was helpful; they continued employing the youngsters after the subsidy had run its course.[24]

The businesses involved should be small; this helps prevent abuse and encourages a mentor relationship between the employer and the youth.

The work-and-school proposal is an avenue to restructuring the summer youth employment program. Currently available summer job funds could be reprogrammed to give summer work to students working part-time in the winter. This would provide continuity and leverage that would help keep students committed to finishing school. A high school diploma is still the most powerful statistical variable in labor market success. It means less for blacks than whites, to be sure, but blacks with high school diplomas are far more successful than blacks who have dropped out, even if white dropouts continue to do better than black graduates.[25]

In another area, we should focus antidiscrimination policies on the racial disparities facing young people trying to penetrate the labor market. There has been an entry-level employment equivalent of redlining going on in major cities for years. The graduates of certain high schools located in certain parts of a city are simply assumed to be unacceptably prepared and are not considered by some employers at all. Improving inner-city high schools will help encourage employers to behave differently, but the application of legal tools to ensure that the qualifications of individual applicants are considered may be necessary as well.

Another initiative—based on the same insight that schools and the world of work need to be more closely connected—would be a significant effort at reform of vocational education. While there are numerous exceptions, vocational education tends to be classroom-based, sometimes even training people for jobs that no longer exist and sometimes serving mainly as a dumping ground for youths not doing well in academic settings. Federal vocational education funds are for the most part dispensed without strings. Since they then enter the state funding stream on a fundable basis, it is impossible to know precisely how the federal funds are actually spent. A sensible direction for reform would be to target a larger share to specific client groups and purposes, with particular emphasis on cooperative education that combines and integrates classroom teaching with actual work experience. If the linkages are strong, academic credit can appropriately be offered for the work experience. Experience shows cooperative education is effective, yet it is an underutilized tool.[26]

While it is not, strictly speaking, an employment policy, I think it is also timely to consider a voluntary, stipended community service initiative.[27] Fiscal considerations dictate that its scope be much smaller than serving all who would want to apply. Regardless of its size, if half its slots were reserved for disadvantaged young people such a program would have an employment impact during the stage in young people's lives when they have the greatest difficulty finding jobs.

The idea of community service can, of course, be pursued in many different ways. School districts can adopt it as a part of the curriculum, requiring a certain number of hours of community service by young people as a prerequisite to graduation, or at least strongly encouraging it. Perhaps we have erred in the past by assuming that the only way to encourage young people to help out was to involve them for a whole year on a stipended basis, as we did in VISTA. Shorter, less extensive experiences could also prove useful.

The foregoing is certainly not a complete youth employment policy. Young people with more serious problems need a greater investment and, if they have already dropped out of school, a different mix of agencies delivering the services. Not surprisingly, programs for dropouts have a lower success rate than interventions with less problematic clients. The only such program that is a clear success in national terms is the Job Corps, which is a residential program and is very expensive—about $14,000 per slot per year. The Job Corps should be expanded, but nonresidential analogues should be pursued as well. Experts agree that while there is no clearly successful community-based model for dropouts, many individual intensive efforts—involving competent leadership and combinations of work experience, classroom training, and supportive service—have had measurable impact.[28]

Another set of clients that should be targeted is young women with children. Too many discussions of adolescent pregnancy begin and end with prescriptions for education and family planning. It is abundantly clear that employment prospects are a demonstrably and dramatically relevant factor for both the young women and the young men involved. Improving access to the labor market has an importance even beyond the economics of self-sufficiency. It is a vitally important aspect of family policy.

The proposals to connect school and work more closely can be applied usefully as part of what might be called a pregnancy prevention strategy. Moreover, once a child has been born, these approaches can be adapted by the addition of day-care, counseling, and supportive services. Many communities have begun demonstration programs of this kind.

Female single-parent heads of families constitute a major target group for labor market access policies. Here we are often talking about women who are already working but are still in poverty because of low wages as well as women who would work if adequate day care, necessary training, and actual jobs were available. Public discussion on this subject tends to take the form of talking about forcing welfare recipients to "work off" their benefits. This concept has come to be known as "workfare." I propose that we start talking instead about converting welfare benefits into wages for real work. I call this turning welfare upside down. I pointed out earlier that over half the children in female-headed families are poor. Perhaps even more to the point, over half the poor children live in female-headed families.[29] Adequate welfare, food stamps, and other transfer payments are of course critically important to these families, but so is work. Why do we persist in talking about "working" 17.6 or 19.4 hours a week to work off a welfare payment? That smacks of punishment. Why not spend the extra money to create real jobs, with full application of fair labor standards and, where necessary, provision for day care? Why not do that in a context that includes job search assistance, creation of "job circle" peer support groups, and referral to stipended training when that is the better route for the individual involved? The client group I am talking about here—or at least the older members of the group, namely women on welfare in their late twenties and thirties—were the most successful participants in the supported work demonstrations studied by the Manpower Demonstration Research Corporation.[30] They are a most promising group for a targeted employment effort specifically designed to address the feminization of poverty.

Policy should not overlook the male counterpart of the feminization of poverty, or ignore the horrifying statistics about black adult male employment. Here success regarding jobs and training would bring about reductions in the costs of crime and incarceration, among other things. As in the case of dropouts (and the clientele I am talking about here are older dropouts), there is no one program model that has a positive track record, except perhaps the Job Corps model. Again, however, individual community-based programs around the country that have effectively combined classroom training, work experience, and serious placement efforts do show good results.[31] Such programs will never look as good as programs that serve young people who have not yet dropped out of school, but they can show a clearly positive net impact.

Confining training to the disadvantaged is no longer possible or appropriate. We must also focus on improving income for people in low-wage jobs—the working poor. Well over half of all poor families are headed by a wage earner. Two general sets of policy are involved here, not mutually exclusive: policies that improve wages and policies that increase income in other ways.

Discussion in this area should begin with improving minimum standards in jobs—in other words, the minimum wage. It is certainly not politically popular to discuss increasing the minimum wage at this time.

Moreover, economists quickly point out that raising the minimum wage at a time of labor surplus will drive even more people out of work. But it is nonetheless important to understand that the minimum wage has lost 15 percent of its purchasing power over the last four years alone and that, for a family of four with one wage earner, it produces an income of less than 70 percent of the poverty line. In the 1960s the minimum wage averaged 55 percent of the average hourly earnings of production workers in manufacturing. It has slipped to about 35 percent today.[32] We should be discussing raising it back to its historical average of about 45 percent, in careful increments so as to minimize inflationary impacts and job reductions.

A more promising subject for immediate consideration is the impact of federal taxation on people in low-wage jobs. Because payroll taxes have risen and the threshold for paying federal taxes has not changed in nearly a decade, a family of four at the poverty line is paying $1,076 in federal taxes at the present time—10.1 percent of its income, as opposed to 4 percent just six years ago.[33] Both the Earned Income Tax Credit and the threshold at which the federal income tax begins need to be adjusted upward. Because Congress will surely deal with tax reform, there is a clear target of opportunity for action.

The levels of welfare and food stamp payments provided to the working poor are a critical income supplement. The Reagan administration essentially destroyed the "incentive" for welfare recipients to work, that is, the feature of the AFDC system that allowed low-wage workers to receive a welfare supplement.[34] Some thought this would end up costing the taxpayers more because low-wage workers would quit and go on welfare entirely. Instead, however, the major effect was to make many workers poorer, because they continued to work and lost their AFDC benefits. Some ameliorative action in this regard has been taken, but particularly if we are not ging to take steps with regard to the minimum wage, improvement of income maintenance must be coupled with the tax changes suggested earlier.

Labor law "reform" removing impediments to union organization (proposed by President Carter but not enacted by Congress) is another step that would improve incomes for the working poor. Similarly, we should pursue stronger antidiscrimination policies, especially with regard to women in the areas of pay equity and equal pay for jobs of comparable worth.

Problems of dislocated workers need to be addressed in future policies. This, of course, is a new problem in terms of its present magnitude. Here there are no clear solutions. The retraining programs in the past have not been enormously successful, nor has generous cash assistance containing no incentive for training and relocation. One solution that makes some sense is a loan program for dislocated workers. The payback would be geared to success in finding a job and the level of job obtained, so that ultimately the program would be only partially subsidized. This seems more feasible than the currently popular notion of individual training accounts for all workers, since that idea necessarily involves the creation of many accounts that in fact will never be utilized. The Individual Training Account notion also entails a need for taxation of all employees and possibly employers to finance the accounts, and raises a question of what happens to people who need assistance immediately but have not built up coverage in their individual accounts. A more specifically targeted loan program seems to make more sense on all counts.

Significant attention needs to be focused on restructuring the unemployment insurance program in order to respond to problems of dislocated workers and workers in declining industries where dislocation is a strong possibility.[35] Clear federal standards for unemployment insurance have never existed. The Great Society administration attempted to legislate such standards, but it failed. At present only 45 percent of the unemployed receive benefits, compared to a figure of 78 percent during the 1975 recession period.[36] The fact is that unemployment insurance coverage has gotten worse rather than better.

In addition to measures that would simply provide compensation to a higher percentage of the unemployed, we need to explore options that would allow the states to give employees some choices. We should consider stretching their benefits out over a longer period of time in conjunction with participation in certified training programs, or even allowing them voluntarily to quit a job in a declining industry and receive benefits if that step is coupled with participation in an authorized retraining program.[37] National debate and congressional action in this area are urgently needed.

The last area that requires discussion in the context of employment policy is the question of how we will assure enough good jobs in this country. We need to learn much more in this area. It appears that international competition and, consequently, related automation in this country are finally having the effect of permanently destroying manufacturing jobs. Service jobs replacing the jobs being lost seem on the whole to be less desirable.

This is the area where the so-called industrial policy debate rages. Some proposals contemplate cooperation between business and labor in developing proposals for restructuring their industry that could be presented to the government as the basis for receiving some limited trade assistance or other benefits. These do appear sensible. The key to such proposals is their consensuality and their partnership approach, as opposed to dictation of plans from a governmental body.

We are heading into a difficult period. There are great dangers for the future of employment. It is hard to know how to make the pie grow. The equity agenda is ever-present and should join strategic efforts to mix fiscal and monetary policy. At some point we will elect a more progressive administration. If this new leadership, with all the fiscal problems that it will inherit, suggests that equity must wait on better economic health, then we will have lost the legacy of the Great Society. I hope our effort here to remember and discuss the Great Society is a commitment that we will not let the legacy be lost.

Six Welfare Questions Still Searching for Answers

HENRY J. AARON

Rereading the declarations of war on poverty penned in the mid-1960s is a bit like coming upon dusty wedding photographs or baby pictures of one's grown children. One lapses into reverie, recalling bygone emotions and events. But one realizes that those times are gone and cannot be relived or recaptured.

And so it is with the War on Poverty. Two decades of frustrations with imperfect policies, critical analyses, and slow economic growth have left most of us with a sophistication and wary cynicism quite out of tune with the can-do optimism of the 1960s.

As far as emphasis on welfare in early statements of the War on Poverty is concerned, the most striking fact is that there was none. The 1964 State of the Union Address did call for medical insurance under Social Security, an expanded food stamp program, and more public housing. But there was no mention there, in the famous chapter in the 1964 report of the Council of Economic Advisers, or in the announcement of the War on Poverty of any cash assistance program.

I wish to thank Gary Burtless for constructive comments and suggestions.

In fact, welfare became a prominent issue only after it became clear that millions of Americans would remain poor despite the best efforts to add up to their human capital, to lower the barriers of discrimination, and to cultivate a strong economy. Welfare reform then emerged gradually as one of the most important if not the dominant instruments for combating poverty.

The story of this transformation has been told often, and I shall not try to do so again. Rather, I shall identify six questions whose answers will, I believe, determine future welfare policy. Welfare policy is shaped by social attitudes and prejudices but also by perceptions of its effects on behavior. Consequently, these questions deal with changing attitudes regarding the categorization of the poor and the effects of welfare on the behavior of the poor. In these changes may be read the achievements and failures of the effort to reform welfare and the rise and fall of welfare reform as a realistically achievable political goal.

The first two questions must be taken together. Should eligibility for aid be determined by income or by category? What is the effect of welfare on pretransfer income (in other words, on earnings)?

President Johnson's refusal to mention welfare in the same context as poverty stemmed from a political judgment about attitudes of the American people. The judgment reflected the perception that Congress would support programs to help people become self-supporting but would not provide cash assistance for people potentially capable of self-support. Hence, everyone who might gain should be eligible for training; all would benefit from removal of discrimination; and a rising economy would raise all ships. But cash assistance was to remain limited to those— the aged, blind, disabled, and single parents (which meant women even more than it does today)—who were not expected to work.

These expectations changed for a number of reasons. The first was a direct outgrowth of the philosophy behind the War on Poverty. If poverty could be substantially eliminated by education and training, by removing discrimination, and by a strong economy, then poverty arose from causes largely external to the poor. Expenditures to help the poor become self-sufficient could be justified either by compassion or by expected gain to the rest of society from the elimination of poverty. Cash assistance could be justified, then, either as an act of compassion or as a carrying cost until profitable investments began to pay out.

A second factor was that economists discovered the welfare system and found it a complex mishmash of rules and formulas. United by a common revulsion against messiness more than they were divided by ideology, academics of the political left and right joined in calling for the payment of income assistance according to simple formulas based on economic need.[1]

Two assumptions lay behind the attitude that economic status alone should determine eligibility for cash assistance. The first was that the causes of poverty are external to the poor. The second was that cash assistance would not adversely change the behavior of the recipients. I believe that the assumption that poverty among blacks was attributable to discrimination was far more widespread before the civil rights achievements of the 1960s and 1970s than it is today. The willingness to provide cash assistance to the poor without condition seems to have been an early casualty of the slow economic growth since the first round of OPEC price increases.[2] If American workers were to be buffeted by events over which they had no control, they were less willing to provide aid to a few, with or without conditions.

The question of how cash aid affects the behavior of recipients has been the subject of unprecedented research for the past two decades. The results of this effort were not anticipated by the original sponsors of the cash assistance experiments. The originators of the negative income tax experiments believed that eligibility for cash assistance should be based on income, not inclusion in some other category. The general public, they believed, thought that the poor would sharply reduce work effort if given cash; and they were confident that the general public was wrong.[3]

The designers of the experiments won this battle, but they lost the war. The experiments indicated that few men who were offered cash assistance actually quit their jobs and that the percentage of reduction in the number of hours they worked was under 10 percent. But the experiments also suggested that a large part—one-fourth to one-half—of the *extra* costs of extending cash assistance to male-headed families would have gone to replace lost earnings.[4] The proportionate effects of cash grants on the labor supply of female family heads was somewhat greater than the effect on males, and the effect on wives and young single adults was even greater. This leakage could be reduced by imposing effective work requirements; but that solution raised other questions, to be addressed below.

A crucial point had been lost, however; the extension of welfare to two-parent families adversely changed their behavior, and the changes were *enough to matter*. It was no longer possible to maintain that the behavior of the poor would not be adversely affected if cash assistance was provided until they could become self-supporting. Whether the dominance of the traditional American view that only certain groups among the poor deserved welfare was ever seriously threatened is doubt-ful. But clearly the idea that economic status alone should determine eligibility for aid flickered only briefly and fluttered out.

The next two questions also must be taken together: What obliga-tions do recipients of assistance owe to society? Can large-scale work re-quirements be made to work? (In other words, can they be made to do more than harass?)

Welfare recipients have rarely been given cash under neutral condi-tions. The workhouse was an early accompaniment of aid. Stigmatizing application procedures and the ministrations of a social worker became the condition for assistance in recent years.

No such conditions made any sense if poverty was a condition im-posed upon people by external circumstances. Indeed, if people are the victims of external circumstances, unpleasant side conditions to assis-tance are a gratuitous cruelty inflicted upon the already victimized. In that event, welfare is a right; indeed, it is a form of just compensation for a kind of casualty loss, the accident of poverty.

This view, or something very like it, lay behind the move that began in the mid-1960s and reached its culmination in the early 1970s to de-liver welfare payments in dignified settings, according to procedures fully protected by rights of appeal and assurance of due process, free of any elements of coercion, and without requiring from the recipient any-thing in return.

There were at least three elements to this movement. One was the simple insistence that normal legal procedures and constitutional safe-guards be followed. A second was the effort to save applicants from be-ing stigmatized by welfare and thereby compelled either to forgo bene-fits to which they were entitled or suffer degradation in getting them. A third was the belief that the poor have an unconditional right to cash assistance. Sometimes this right was asserted without qualification. Some-times it was acknowledged that conditions might be imposed but only if they were surrounded with incentives and protections so generous that what began as a condition ended up as almost another right. Some-times it was suggested that work requirements were simply inoperable in practice.[5] But these arguments all came to the same conclusion: that cash should be provided without strings on the basis of economic need.

But the view that cash assistance should be provided without strings never appealed much to the general public or to Congress. As the courts prohibited "man-in-the-house" rules and state residency requirements, Congress moved in with job-search requirements for AFDC recipients. But for opposition from the Johnson and Nixon administrations, Congress might well have gone further than it did. On its brief political journey to oblivion, President Nixon's Family Assistance Plan became encrusted with conditions and mandatory "services." President Carter's stillborn welfare reform plan was predicated on the behavioral assumption that cash assistance without work requirements would have unacceptable effects on labor supply, and on the political assumption that a plan promising aid without conditions would be unacceptable to Congress.

The problem, of course, was how to make a work requirement real. The Carter program was the first to acknowledge that a work requirement without a job guarantee was unworkable. Although there was no precedent for promising to employ large numbers of actual or potential welfare recipients, the Carter administration committed itself to creating more than one million jobs for people who were demonstrably among the least employable members of U.S. society. The logic was impeccable. But there was no credible evidence that the enterprise could be made to work. The promise was never tested, however, as the cost was so high—close to $10,000 per job per year or more than $10 billion in total—that Congress refused to fund it.

Advocates of noncategorical cash assistance had reached an intellectual and political dead end. In an effort to gain acceptance for this approach to welfare, they had tried to persuade a skeptical public that poverty was visited upon the poor and that a change in the environment would drastically reduce it. Pending the success of such efforts, cash assistance should be provided without conditions and without regard for family status on the basis of measurable economic need. Payment of such assistance would not reduce work effort enough to matter, they argued, and the provision of such aid was no more than a compassionate stopgap until more fundamental improvements took effect.

But the argument did not take, and the facts did not support it. The effects of cash assistance were certainly not overwhelming but they were large enough to matter. To deal with that problem, supporters of noncategorical cash assistance were forced to accept the idea that conditions would be placed on the provision of assistance. Recipients of aid would have to accept jobs, if available. The acknowledgment of the need for a work requirement created an insoluble dilemma, however. With a sufficiently coercive administrative system, potential welfare recipients could be required to accept existing low-quality, low-wage jobs in the private sector. If a sufficient number of private sector jobs did not exist, public sector jobs could be created at low cost. If the work requirement discouraged a sufficient number of people from applying for welfare, costs

might even be reduced. But the coercion that would be necessary to enforce such a work requirement violated notions of fairness and rights.
Alternatively, the public sector could create jobs with sufficiently attractive working conditions and wages to reduce greatly the need for coercion. But the size of the program would be unprecedented and the cost
would be prohibitive, particularly since many workers in unattractive
private-sector jobs would find it attractive to switch to superior public-
sector jobs. Trapped on this political Möbius strip, welfare reform went
nowhere.

A fifth question is to what extent the rising incidence of single-headed
families is traceable to increased assistance. The number of families consisting of a woman and her children has risen from 4.5 million in 1960
to 9.5 million in 1982. The proportion of the poor residing in such families has risen from 18.2 percent in 1960 to 34.0 percent in 1982. Only
part of this trend can be explained by the baby-boom generation reaching childbearing ages. Part, no doubt, can be explained by changes in
sexual and social norms affecting the entire population. There are many
explanations, no one of which is sufficient wholly to explain the event
but few of which can be dismissed.

Among those that cannot be dismissed is the welfare explanation.
Welfare, it is argued, contributes to the increase in the numbers of un-
married mothers in various ways. Girls with few economic or social prospects can achieve a measure of independence by having a child or in
some jurisdictions simply by becoming pregnant, thereby becoming eligible in their own right for welfare payments. Welfare, it is alleged, not
only discourages women from working (an allegation to which the income maintenance experiments lend some support), but also discourages them from remarrying (because married couples are generally ineli-
gible for assistance). The same line of argument suggests that welfare
encourages the breakup of two-parent families when unemployment occurs; by leaving a woman and her children, a man makes them eligible
for cash assistance and in most places for health benefits as well.

Noncategorical assistance would appear to relieve some of these problems. It would pay assistance to couples as well as single parents, so that
the presence or absence of an unemployed spouse would not affect eligibility. Even under a negative income tax, however, there would still be
incentives for a spouse eligible for unemployment insurance or with opportunities for sporadic market income to leave the family. Uncategori-
cal assistance would do nothing to discourage young girls from seeking
financial independence through pregnancy.

Although they were not designed to investigate the effects of cash as-

sistance on family stability, it was on this issue that the income maintenance experiments dealt the campaign for noncategorical aid a second
major blow.[6] According to the *Final Report of the Seattle-Denver Income Maintenance Experiment*, providing cash assistance according to
the plans used in that experiment increased the rate of family dissolution by 53 percent for whites, 57 percent for blacks, and by 1 percent
for Chicanos.[7] Despite doubts about its validity, this finding received
some attention when released and further cemented opposition to noncategorical cash assistance.

If attention is directed to families with children who received cash assistance only, the rate of family dissolution appears to drop by 16 percent for whites, 4 percent for blacks, and 26 percent for Chicanos. This
bizarre contrast seems to stem from a sharp increase in family dissolution among childless couples and among families with or without children who received job counseling or education subsidies.[8]

However this analytical debate is eventually resolved, the hypothesis
that welfare reform increases family stability remains unsupported by
empirical research. The contrary hypothesis, that noncategorical welfare
would increase family instability, has been given official if premature
approval.

The sixth and final question is, what reliance should be placed on assistance in-kind? Despite the attention lavished on reform of the cash
welfare system, only one lasting legislative change emerged. The state-
run programs of aid to the aged, blind, and disabled were consolidated
into a single program, Supplemental Security Income.

However admirable this reform may have been, it was overshadowed
by the transformation of in-kind assistance, much of which went to the
poor. Medicare and Medicaid vastly extended financial access to hospital and physician services for the aged, disabled, and poor. The number
of publicly subsidized housing units grew at more than 100,000 units
per year in the late 1960s and rapidly through much of the 1970s. The
food stamp program was transformed from a small outgrowth of com-
modity distribution into the broadest federal program of economic assistance to the poor. Other programs, such as Headstart, nutrition support for women, infants, and children, and the earned income tax credit,
took root and grew. The American people, it appeared, were prepared
to provide vastly more assistance to the poor in the form of identifiable
commodities than they would dream of doing through cash. They were
willing to do so without troubling themselves about possible effects on
labor supply or family stability.

Logically, these programs should have the same effects on economic behavior that cash assistance has. Yet although the total amount of aid provided through these programs dwarfs income-tested cash assistance, no one has closely examined their effects on economic behavior. The mystery is heightened by the fact that experiments to measure the effects of housing assistance and health insurance were begun at roughly the same time as the income maintenance experiments.[9]

The rapid growth of in-kind assistance and the sluggish growth of cash assistance contrasts starkly with the proofs, well known to every survivor of at least two years of economic instruction, that in-kind assistance is less valuable to recipients than cash.

The unpersuasiveness of economic arguments to everyone except economists is breathtaking. Politicians have long appreciated that support for aid for the poor increases if the aid appears to create jobs for the nonpoor, for example in the construction trades or on the farm. Food stamps for many years has been bundled with agricultural programs to enable a coalition of rural and urban representatives and senators to pass programs that might be defeated if they were voted on separately.

The American public has declared unmistakably that it is willing to provide such commodities as basic housing, food, and health care, even if it is unwilling to give the cash to buy them. This attitude has persisted for long enough to be taken as a constant on the welfare scene. Future efforts to modify the welfare system should treat this attitude as a reality rather than try to explain why it does not make sense.[10]

Ten years of weak economic growth and several years of tight budgets have shown that an ebbing tide lowers all ships (with notable exception of military ships). Welfare programs of all kinds, along with other domestic spending, have been scaled back.

The election of Ronald Reagan signaled general cuts in most cash and in-kind assistance. New AFDC rules directly restricted eligibility by removing from the rolls some recipients with low earnings. Food stamp benefits were lowered and the implicit tax was increased. New subsidized housing starts were drastically curtailed. States were encouraged to apply for authority to administer experimental "workfare" programs.

Taken together, these measures reversed the direction in which welfare reformers in the Nixon, Ford, and Carter administrations had tried to go. Categorical distinctions were strengthened rather than weakened. Benefit reduction rates were increased rather than reduced. "Workfare" programs were promoted rather than discouraged. Perhaps most important, the traditional attitude that welfare is a seedbed of sloth and dependency reclaimed dominance from the upstart view that welfare is a right of the poor.

The most important explanation for this shift is probably the difficulty of sustaining redistributional transfers when taxpayers themselves are living through hard times. But it is important to realize that the welfare reformers of the Johnson, Nixon, Ford, and Carter years were intellectually disarmed by the very experiments that they had initiated to prove the benignity of noncategorical assistance.

The welfare reformer's ship is intellectually adrift in harsh economic weather. The climate is unlikely to improve until and unless economic growth resumes and the chronic budget deficits created by the 1981 tax cut are ended.

When conditions do improve, the prospects are poor for a resurgence of calls for noncategorical assistance. The intellectual case for that kind of reform has collapsed. A case can be made based on compassion for raising the benefits paid by the least generous states. A case can be made for linking cash to work or to training and education; but past research suggests minimal benefits from training and jobs programs should dampen enthusiasm. A change in social attitudes toward poverty and the poor may occur with a change in the economic climate. But it is clear that the next generation of social policy-makers, unlike the last, will not have the luxury of relying on ideas from an inherited, unfinished agenda.

Random Reflections on the Great Society's Politics and Health Care Programs After Twenty Years

WILBUR J. COHEN

To lead into my comments on America's attempt to develop effective health policies, I wish first to relate an actual experience that occurred during the Kennedy administration. It indicates some of the problems we faced at that time. After the first defeat of the elementary and secondary education bill in 1961, President Kennedy called me into the Oval Office and asked me what we should do next. I recommended we press for a bill to provide for education grants to physicians and medical schools. It would reaffirm the principle of federal aid to higher education. He authorized me to go ahead full steam. The first opportunity I had to do this was my testimony before the Joint Economic Committee. I went before that committee with my young, idealistic, naive enthusiasm. I boned up for strong advocacy of our position. At the conclusion of my testimony, I was cross-examined by a Republican. He said to me, "Mr. Cohen, you seem to have a very strange idea of what you're proposing. Let me ask you a question: If you want more physicians trained and you want to subsidize their education, what is their median income?" I looked it up in my briefing book and responded, "The 1959 median was $25,000 per year." (It's substantially more at the present time as a result of Medicare and other programs.) So he said to me, "Now, what is the median income of the average taxpayer?" I looked that up and I said, "About $5,000 per year." He said, "You've a very strange idea for a Democrat." I said, "What is it?" He said, "You want to tax people who earn $5,000 a year to enable people who will receive incomes of $25,000 a year." I replied, "Mr. Congressman, you don't understand the objectives of the Kennedy administration. That isn't what impels us. It's the concept of excellence. It is the concept of self-fulfillment, of giving every boy and girl who is an A+ student who wants to get into medical school an opportunity to achieve their lifetime ambition to be productive, to contribute their skill to the American social and economic and health system." I looked in my black book and said, "In 1959, there were so many people with an A+ average who were not able to get into medical school." When I finished, he said, "Let me ask you what are you going to do for us C+ students who really run the country?" That little experience had an impact on me. I told President Kennedy it was going to take us about one year longer to get this bill passed than I had thought.

The reason I'm telling this story is that I think it illustrates how we completely overlooked the political aspects of trying to get a controversial program through the Congress. If anything, I see the political process today as being much more complicated than in the 1960s. The weakening, or the absence, of the seniority system, the fragmentation of committees in Congress, the whole congressional situation makes the possibility of enacting complex and controversial legislation much more difficult.

A CYCLICAL THEORY OF SOCIAL REFORM AND
MAJOR POLITICAL CHANGE

America initiates significant social reforms about every twenty-five to thirty years. There is a generational situation in the way the ethos and political process in this nation work to secure major social reform.

I am also a strong believer that you get some social reform every once in a while between cycles. We obtained disability insurance in the Eisenhower administration. Congress passed the Supplemental Security Income in the Nixon administration. I can point to other incremental improvements in various administrations; for example, the diagnostic-related group reimbursement passed recently.

But if you are looking at really big changes, if you are looking at ones like the negative income tax, national health insurance, or even national health insurance for mothers and children, they come only when the body politic is willing to accept big changes. As long as we have large deficits, and high interest rates, and frustrations with the political process, the attitude of the American people will inhibit major new social policies. But change will come, probably in the mid-nineties. This would be consistent with the twenty- to thirty-year cycle of social reform exhibited in the past. If I'm right, we should begin thinking of alternatives in social policy and public affairs for policy-makers in the next decade.

I think that what we've got to look at, as professors and academicians in the field of public policy and public affairs, is how and why ideas get accepted and how and why ideas get rejected. We should start now. I can think of at least ten things that we wanted to do during the Great Society that didn't come to pass at all. We were not ready. We really didn't have a long-range strategy with respect to implementation. Policy windows came and went quickly.

During the sixties there was no policy window open for basic redistribution of income in any striking way. President Kennedy and President Johnson were politically scared of using the term "redistribution of income" in any legislative situation. To the extent that there were modest elements of income redistribution—in tax policy, in income maintenance, health, and education—the redistributive element was not stressed.

MEDICARE AND MEDICAID:
GREAT SOCIETY ACCOMPLISHMENTS

The passage of Medicare and Medicaid in 1964 was a major accomplishment of the Great Society. Its greatest achievement was to provide Americans, including minorities and older people, with greater access to physicians and hospital care. This fact is firmly documented by data. With the perspective of hindsight, of course, one can argue that increased access is not always necessary or desirable. As Henry Aaron suggests in his book[1] about the British experience in rationing medical care, some medical care that is costly to provide has little social benefit. This is the case, for example, when elderly or infirm recipients never return to an active, productive life-style despite costly medical intervention.

A less frequently discussed aspect of health access is the impact of federal program initiatives on racial discrimination in health care. On the day before Medicare went into effect, in every hospital in the South, over every drinking fountain, over every bathroom, over every cafeteria, there were signs reading "White" and "Colored" for separate but presumably equal facilities. On the day that Medicare went into effect in the South, all those signs and separate facilities began to come down. This I think was a singular achievement of Medicare. In one day Medicare and Medicaid broke the back of segregated health services.

I would also argue that the Medicare program presented more equitable financing of health care than existed in the private insurance area. With private insurance you have flat uniform rates for people irrespective of income. If you buy a private health insurance policy and your income is $100,000 or $10,000 a year, you pay the same premium. Despite some regressive features, use of the payroll tax for hospital services and general revenues to cover physician services illustrates a fairer approach. Could it be made more equitable? Certainly; all we need to do is increase general revenue financing. Currently, 75 percent of Part B of Medicare is financed out of general revenues, with the individual paying the remainder. Financing for the rest of the program could move in this direction.

Another innovative feature in the Medicare program was its reliance on the private sector. Use of Blue Cross, Blue Shield, and the insurance companies as fiscal intermediaries brought the private sector into a relationship with the public sector in terms of administrative responsibility. While some people were doubtful about a partnership with the private sector, it was a necessary political decision. I see no objection to using the private sector if it is not the basic insurer or the underwriter of the program. Private companies get no profits or income from federal taxes. As administrative intermediaries they are paid simply a management fee.

Two incremental improvements have occurred in the federal health program since 1965. First was the broadening of eligibility in the late sixties to include the disabled. The other was the inclusion in 1972 of kidney dialysis and transplants. Both eligibilities serve populations with considerable needs. These incremental changes are important to note. While it may have taken the Great Society to enact a major reform, it is feasible once you have laid the basic foundation to secure incremental improvement even in relatively conservative administrations.

Six criteria should be used to evaluate or grade Medicare and Medicaid: efficiency, equity, adequacy, administrative acceptability by the public, ideology, and provider response.

Let's take Medicare Part A. On efficiency, it deserves a rating of about 75 out of 100 percent. I say 75 percent because some of the money that is spent for hospital or physical services is unnecessary and inefficient. Many people are in hospitals who don't need to be. Doctors often keep them in longer than necessary.

On equity, Medicare gets a 95 percent rating. Medicare has significantly increased older people's access to hospital services and extended the services available to the disabled and the poor.

On adequacy of benefits, I would say that Medicare deserves only a 50 percent score. It doesn't include diagnostic examinations, eyeglasses, hearing aids, or long-term care. Certainly as far as the objective of adequacy is concerned, it does only about half of the job.

On the criterion of administrative acceptability to the public, I would say it gets an 85 percent score. Americans seem to like the idea of paying for their health care over their whole lifetime as long as their payments are taken out of their pay week by week.

On ideology, I'd give it about 95 percent rating. Here again, most people like the idea of being "insured" against a major catastrophic risk by paying small amounts over a long period of time. Further, they like the program because it doesn't have an income test for eligibility.

On provider response, meaning hospitals and doctors, I'd give Medicare only a 50 to 60 percent rating. In other words, doctors and hospitals still believe the program would be better if it were operated by Blue Cross, Blue Shield, or the private market. They also don't like the paperwork.

Let's turn to Medicaid. It deserves a 90 to 95 percent rating for efficiency. All funds are targeted to the poor and low-income population.

For equity, I would say Medicaid rates about 99 percent. None of the poor pay direct taxes for it or its benefits.

When it comes to adequacy, I would say that Medicaid gets about a 45 percent rating. Benefits vary tremendously by state. For example, it is inadequate in states like Texas but reasonably adequate in states like California and New York.

On administrative acceptability from the public point of view, I would say Medicaid receives only about 25 percent rating. It's a welfare program. Generally speaking, as soon as people classify something as welfare, public acceptability goes down. On ideology I would give Medicaid only 25 percent for much the same reason. For provider response, I would say it gets only about 10 percent. Many physicians will not take Medicaid patients.

In conclusion, the Medicare program has a very good overall rating, and even Medicaid comes out better than most welfare programs.

A RETROSPECTIVE ON THE POLITICS OF INITIATION

I think we would have had a better Medicare program and a better Medicaid program if the American Medical Association (AMA) had brought up its alternatives to Medicare earlier. The AMA fought vigorously against Medicare and Medicaid. In a similar vein, I think the Republican suggestions came in too late in the political process to affect the basic structure and content of the whole program. However, they did influence the development of Part B of Medicare—that is, the extension of coverage from mere hospitalization to physician services as well.

The absence of a radical left-wing program really constrained the debate and our consideration of options. If the socialists had advocated something much more radical, it would have presented a counterbalance to the conservative point of view and generated a better middle-of-the-road position.

What do I base that judgment on? I base it upon my early experience in 1935 when I first came to work for the New Deal. I think the more radical Townsend Plan helped us get a solid program like Social Security through. There was a great deal of opposition in the Senate to the federal government getting into the social insurance business. On the other hand, the fact was that the Townsend Plan was out there promising $200 a month to everyone over age sixty. Having a radical idea on the agenda proved helpful in building a moderate-center coalition.

Clearly there were some disadvantages to the Medicare program passed in 1964. The biggest difficulty in retrospect related to the method of reimbursement. Under the program, the federal government agreed to reimburse for the "reasonable cost" of hospital care and physician services. This method has clearly contributed to inflation in health care costs. How do I explain the outcome? First, it was the only way to get the bill passed. Second, nobody had other good ideas at the time. In the fifties and sixties very few analysts were concentrating on health policy from an independent point of view. There simply weren't many individuals thinking about fundamental variations. The major alternative at the time was to pay providers their actual cost of doing business. That option, favored by hospitals, would have been even more inflationary.

SECURING CHANGE

Whether a President is an ideologue or a pragmatist, political reality requires *simple* solutions to problems. Our tendency as academicians and as people teaching public policy is always to think about alternatives that are complicated and have many facets. But that's not what political leaders look for. They look for a simplistic argument, a simplistic solution to a problem because that's the only way they can dramatize an issue to the American public. Americans don't want to hear a politician tell them why there are ten good reasons for the negative income tax or for a new health policy. They don't want to hear why we ought to abolish poverty by using the educational system and the health system in diverse ways. Politicians understand that it's got to be reasonably simple in the sense of having a single dimension even if the problem or proposal is really multidimensional. Further, there must be some mythology to support policies. By mythology I mean there must be some acceptable ideology in major social reform proposals that borders on faith, myth, or mystery. Social Security has been successful precisely because of the "myth" that it's insurance.

Good social legislation incorporates evaluation. Ongoing evaluation allows for periodic and comprehensive reassessments of program performance in light of environmental change. If we have learned anything over the last twenty years, it is that there will be changes in economic conditions and political positions. By including evaluation in the design of the program, we increase the likelihood of incremental changes occurring in the years intervening between periods of major reform.

By 1995 we may have a different kind of health care system than we have today. I doubt that it will involve a complicated rationing system designed by Congress. But given cost constraints it may well be a rationing system resulting from the dictates of the hospitals, physicians, and families. Whatever emerges will likely be a compromise between the public- and private-sector system: the public sector could cover, for example, mothers, children, and the aged and the private sector could cover everybody from age twelve to age sixty. I see that as a distinct possibility. What we have to do as analysts and policy-makers in the next ten years is to try to devise a health and medical care system that appears to meet efficiency objectives but is at the same time adaptable to the "acceptable" inefficiencies in the American health delivery system. The system must also meet reasonable standards of fairness or equity. Medicare and Medicaid provide good illustrations of what works and at times what doesn't work. I would like to be here in 1995 and see what changes have been made in both programs.

3

Restructuring the Urban Environment

Revitalizing the Cities:
From Great Expectations to a New Realism
MARSHALL KAPLAN

Since 1960 every administration has expressed concern over the health of American cities, particularly older central cities. Both the New Frontier and Great Society initiated programs, such as the War on Poverty, Model Cities, and urban renewal, aimed in part at the urban poor and in part at deteriorating urban neighborhoods. New Federalism, Nixon style, while generating a shift in the relative flow of aid funds to reflect its nonurban constituencies, increased the absolute volume of federal funds flowing into urban areas. President Carter promised the nation a comprehensive urban policy. His administration delivered something less—a set of federal programs and a cluster of activities tilted toward responding to the defined ills of distressed central cities. President Reagan links his perception of city problems to the failure of the broader economy to provide cities with taxes and jobs, believing that a rising economic tide will float all (city) ships and their (resident) crews. Specific policies and proposals aimed at cities as places, according to the president, while often well-intentioned, have been and remain inefficient or worse.

After twenty years or so of trying, the nation still does not have anything resembling a focused urban perspective or a comprehensive urban policy. For those of us who believe that severe urban problems remain and that government at all levels can and should play a role in responding to them, this fact is disturbing. Perhaps we can more effectively address urban difficulties if we reflect on where the nation presently is with respect to its understanding of and commitment to cities and if we develop a better understanding of still-evolving changes in federal responsibilities toward cities.

Absence of a comprehensive urban policy. The assumed need for a comprehensive urban policy to respond to city ills became the favorite battle cry of many public- and private-sector leaders as well as many scholars during the late sixties and early seventies. Most policy advocates, understandably, looked askance at the proliferation of federal programs and disparate nature of federal involvement in cities. Their answer was more rationality, more focus, and in some cases more resources. Regrettably, very few among them took the time to define their requests in operational terms consistent with the institutional needs of the federal government or the need for congressmen to get reelected. Jimmy Carter's flawed effort to develop a "comprehensive" urban policy clearly illustrates the difficulties.

After Carter's mandate to his agency heads to prepare a comprehensive urban policy, months were lost while senior White House officials, agency staff, and consultants debated what he really meant. Did the term *comprehensive* envelop all major federal activities that affect cities? Did the term envelop all places defined by the census as urban? Did the term *policy* mean the granting of special priority regarding federal resource allocation? Answers to these questions were not pure or absolute. Substantive concerns sometimes gave way to ideological, normative, and political ones. Resource limits denied coverage of much of America's urban areas; distressed cities could be acknowledged as a priority but not to the complete exclusion of nondistressed areas. Federal agencies, if they protested loud enough, could exclude their key activities from the urban policy-makers' pens and ultimately the administration's urban initiatives. Targeting of dollars was politically difficult. This all was reminiscent of the War on Poverty, the Model Cities program, the block grant programs, and the evolving enterprise zone proposal.[1]

Absence of a theory of city development. While low on prescriptions, Jane Jacobs's recent book—*Cities and the Wealth of Nations, Principles of Economic Life*[2]—appears on target concerning our need to develop a firmer theoretical understanding of the role cities play and a more precise set of hypotheses concerning their development or redevelopment. Succinctly, we lack a solid theoretical base concerning why cities grow or fail to grow. Few of the models put forward by urban scholars can consistently stand the test of empirical evidence. Almost none can help us anticipate the future of American cities or conversely explain current economic and social occurrences taking place in some but not all cities and in some but not all neighborhoods within cities.

Much of what we have to work with still stems from the primarily nonstrategic descriptive analyses of urban geographers and the useful but now dated base-service models of earlier urban economists. Although we acknowledge the increasing importance of international economic trends as well as the significance of technological and structural changes occurring in our economy, we have yet to focus on hypotheses linking each to the health and well-being of cities. In a similar vein, we have yet to generate appropriate models suggesting the relevance or irrelevance of governmental policies aimed at aborting or slowing down economic and population trends, increasing incomes of the urban poor, and developing improved urban services.

Absence of consensus regarding problems. Put two urban analysts in a room and even if they are of the same political persuasion you will likely get three definitions of the urban problem and four solutions. Some will even say that problems do not exist or that they are rapidly vanishing. Despite millions of dollars spent in research since 1964, we have yet to build up a consensus concerning either the status of American cities or the extent to which national commitments are crucial to their well-being.

To the Great Society participants, cities were laboratories in which demonstrations and experiments could take place. Great Society programs varied between focusing on the plight of the poor in their *specific places* of residence and focusing on *deteriorating areas,* irrespective of who resided in them. Objectives associated with Great Society initiatives were generally complex, rhetoric was often grandiose, and relationships between ends and means were rarely specified precisely. Resources were many times inadequate to articulated legislative preambles. Cities, newly created public and quasi-public organizations, and community groups were granted center stage. The recipe for "marble cake" federalism[3] became complicated, and the federal system became existential.

By and large, Nixon's urban policies maintained the geographic or place orientation of the Great Society. While the number of and money associated with categorical programs increased, the Nixon administration's most visible urban initiatives were associated with its ostensible efforts to "reform" the growing federal inventory. In part because of legitimate critiques concerning the proliferation of sometimes overlapping federal aid efforts and in part because of the understandable White House desire to extend federal aid to a wider, perhaps more Republican constituency, the president asked Congress to enact general revenue and special revenue-sharing programs. The ultimate passage by Congress of part of the package expanded the number of jurisdictions eligible for federal dollars and the absolute number of dollars available to state and local governments. Both efforts diluted the focus of Great Society initiatives on the urban poor and on the worst urban neighborhoods.

Interestingly, Nixon's successful proposals to restructure federal assistance to cities were preceded by a failed but historically unique attempt to secure important amendments to the then-existing welfare system. Nixon's Family Assistance Plan (FAP) proposal, if it had been passed by Congress, would have provided many poor households with something like a guaranteed annual income. But FAP was neither sold nor perceived as an urban initiative. Indeed, its primary beneficiaries would have been low-income households in Southern states. FAP's urban policy importance was lost in the debate surrounding its adequacy, in the misunderstanding concerning its objectives, and in the doubts raised about the president's motives. Regrettably, what could have been a useful urban policy debate concerning the wisdom of income versus service strategies and place versus nonplace strategies never really took place.

On balance, the Nixon-Ford administration failed to add much in the way of knowledge about how cities functioned. Its biennial urban policy reports were high on data and low on analysis and prescription. Nixon's own personal ambivalence about acknowledging city problems and the related work of friendly scholars such as Edward Banfield[4] concerning the irrelevance of government actions muted any sustained drive inside the federal government to develop a fuller understanding of cause-and-effect relationships concerning urban ills and federal policy options.

Jimmy Carter's policy focus on cities was premised more on commitments concerning distressed central cities than on a firm understanding of the relationships between past federal policy and the symptoms or causes of urban ills. While its 1978 and 1980 biennial reports for the first time attempted to relate varied, often disputed, distress indices to population and economic trends, the Carter administration never really took the time to develop precise linkages between articulated city problems and federal policy options. In other words, while the Carter administration disowned market equilibrium, it never really matched its view that federal actions could make a difference in the quality of urban life with a clear perception of what the difference was. Its key new urban initiatives, such as UDAG (Urban Development Action Grant), and its partially successful efforts to retarget the federal inventory toward cities and their poorer residents, appeared premised more on helping cities grow old gracefully—on helping cities and their residents adapt to change—than on aborting seemingly overwhelming decentralization trends. They were decidedly oriented toward place or geography.

Like administrations before it, the Carter administration was unable to develop agreement (inside and outside the administration) concerning the extent of and factors leading to city distress. It was subsequently unable to secure agreement on key policy options. Reagan, based more on ideology than fact or serious evaluation, has abandoned the place orientation of previous administrations. He argues that efforts to improve the national economy will respond to most city ills. Past efforts at providing cities with federal support, according to the Reagan administration, provided few benefits and many costs. In this context, people stuck in poverty should vote with their feet and move on to a better life.

At the present juncture the debate over how well or how sick cities are is still open more to opinion and ideology than to proof. Population movements, population settlement patterns, annexation or the lack of economic growth or retardation, race and poverty, poor management, the decline of American values, patriotism, God, etc., have been and are viewed at various times as benefit, cost, cause, and problem. Consistency is the hobgoblin. Absolute wisdom is absent. Few attempt the art of urban analysis as positivists.

Absence of political clout. Urban policy-makers are up against it. Cities, particularly large central cities, were rarely popular among intellectuals, at least up through 1960. When cities are expanding, however, a case could be made that good urban policy makes for good and successful politics. But many central cities have lost and continue to lose population. The aggregate reduction in central city population is significant. More relevant, the population left behind contains a proportionately large share of the poor and powerless. Urging extra attention to central cities, even if consensus could be achieved on their problems and the response to their problems, is risky for many politicians.

WHERE ARE WE TODAY?

The characteristics of federal urban policies and programs have changed significantly since 1964.

We have moved away from holistic to the strategic. Gone is the optimism of the sixties, the belief that we could mount integrated or multidisciplinary programs that would cure multiple urban ills. We just don't know enough yet about the how-to or the relationship of the pieces of the urban puzzle. Further, we now realize that exogenous, often unpredictable events or nonurban policy actions often swamp relatively minuscule public initiatives regarding urban areas (for example, a change in Federal Reserve policy, Arab oil embargos). Specific urban initiatives in the future, irrespective of party line, likely will be more limited in scope and boundaries and more and more focused on relatively narrow objectives.

We have moved away from citizen involvement and toward established institutions. Citizen participation in the local allocation of federal funds is less important today than it was in the sixties. Part of the evolution away from formal recognition of citizens as partners in the distribution of federal funds stems from a political and institutional reaction to the ostensible excesses of the sixties. Part comes from a feeling that efficiency should command more priority, perhaps more than equity, given limited resources. Part results from the assumption in many cities of formal positions of power by the leaders of citizens groups in the sixties.

While the citizen participation genie will never be able to be put back in the bottle, neither will it be nurtured extensively by future federal aid efforts. Direct funding of citizen groups to come to the resource allocation table likely will not be in vogue during the eighties and nineties.

We have moved back from marble cake to dual federalism. The Great Society fostered numerous direct relationships between federal agencies, cities, and community groups—much to the chagrin of state officials. Subsequently, Nixon, Ford, and Carter each voiced concern about the role of states and the congested, seemingly chaotic characteristics associated with federal-state-local relationships. None of them, however, could or would attempt to sort out relationships or contend with groups satisfied (often for good reason) with the evolving federal system.

The Reagan administration has moved to change the balance of power in the federal system between local government, states, and federal agencies. While its ill-conceived, shift-share or New Federalism initiatives[5] went nowhere, its efforts to pool categorical programs into block grants have met with reasonable success. In the process, states have assumed a more important role.

We have moved away from individual programs to basic structural changes or changes in ground rules affecting behavior. The tremendous growth of categorical programs unleashed in the sixties and seventies is over. While the number of programs remains significant, few new programs have been added recently and the real dollar value of all urban-oriented grants is relatively minuscule. Block grants now constitute close to 35 percent of total federal grant-in-aid funds flowing to state and local governments. The total in the last Carter budget was approximately 17 percent.

Substituted for the federal-program-chasing-a-problem approach to federal aid have been attempts to amend or change basic ground rules affecting the health of cities. While what we have done has not always been directed specifically at city problems, the impact on cities has been, or will be, real. For example, provisions in the IRS code (such as accelerated depreciation) may speed up industrial relocation from cities and/or change the relative employment bases of city and suburb. Similarly, Reagan administration efforts to cut back means-tested programs and/or to contain hospital costs could exacerbate social overhead costs faced by many cities. Finally, the administration's relatively weak enforcement of fair housing laws combined with a refusal to use the stick (the cut-off of federal funds) on communities that do not open up housing opportunities to minorities could well intensify the concentration of minorities and poor people in cities and older suburbs.

We have moved away from a focus on city-specific economic develment to a concentration on broad economic policy. Urban Development Action Grants and Community Development Block Grants still exist. The Economic Development Administration still maintains marginal activity in cities. But the administration's heart and muscle are not in city or place-oriented economic development efforts. Right or wrong, its bet is that through combined fiscal and monetary policy the economy will return to health and all cities will benefit.

In a similar vein, even Democratic leaders appear to have disowned city-specific economic development options. Contrary to the administration's general reliance on the marketplace, some speak of the need to develop broad industrial policies. Such policies would aid and abet likely economic winners across broad industrial sectors, as well as help industrial losers adjust (or help their employees adjust) to economic decline.

We have moved from predominant focus on the public sector's role in urban problem-solving efforts to at least a willingness to foster innovative public-and-private-sector relationships. Our history is replete with public-sector efforts, not always cheap or successful, to seek private-sector involvement in nation and community building. But with the recent cutback in federal leadership and money has come the need for, and state and local government willingness to consider, new and extended examples of public- and private-sector collaboration.

ECONOMIC TRENDS AND ALTERNATIVE POLICIES

Trends in the national economy since the late 1960s have not been entirely unkind to many older central cities. Of note in some cities are two factors: The emergence of a "service economy" has led to increased employment in sectors such as finance, insurance, real estate, and business services; and corporate offices with expanding administrative and development functions have found many downtowns, particularly those with strong financial institutions and those close to producer services, a strong locational draw.

Some central cities registered major increases in office space. For example, Denver more than doubled its office space during the 1970s. Atlanta, Detroit, Newark, Pittsburgh, and Seattle showed increases of more than 50 percent.

Complementing expansion of office growth and office-related jobs was a modest revival of inner-city living for both middle- and upper-income residents. Later marriages, smaller numbers of children, and the increased likelihood of two-earner couples helped increase the demand for housing in some central-city neighborhoods.

But all is not rosy. While the data are not always conclusive, a strong case can be made that many American central cities and older suburbs still are in need of much and lack significant help. For example, as pointed out in a recent Joint Economic Committee of Congress report, a relatively large number of large and medium-sized cities still face significant fiscal constraints—constraints requiring often either counterproductive tax measures or inequitable cutbacks in services. Similarly, many continue to provide a home to relatively large numbers of minorities and increasing numbers of the poor.[6] Indeed, cities remain the only jurisdictional entity that witnessed a significant increase in the number of households and individuals in poverty during the seventies and early eighties.

Finally, the much-heralded urban revitalization, noted above, has manifested itself unevenly. Primary beneficiaries appear to be down-towns and nearby neighborhoods attractive to more affluent households. Left behind are blue-collar workers unable to find jobs in the new offices and the chronically unemployed unable to match the skills required by the expanding service economy. Also sometimes hurt are poorer, often minority households living in deteriorated neighborhoods who cannot compete with more affluent groups for scarce housing.

Regrettably for rising-tide advocates, evidence that better economic times significantly improve the health and well-being of cities, particu-larly older central cities, remains inconclusive. We do know that many central cities did reasonably well during the recovery part of the na-tional economic cycles of the seventies. But the data are complicated and cause-and-effect relationships elusive. Availability of (now reduced) federal aid apparently helped older central cities weather economic storms and facilitated their economic growth during upturns. Equally relevant, the migration of cyclically prone manufacturing firms to the suburbs—a real economic loss for most central cities—resulted in making many suburbs more sensitive to cyclical changes than their contiguous central cities. But for some older central cities this was a mixed blessing. Their economic base was lower, and economic activity within them was unable to cushion the impact of bust cycles, particularly for their low-income inhabitants.[7]

Current data illustrate increased, not reduced, economic and social disparities between central city and suburbs. For the chronically unem-ployed and the very poor—two groups increasingly and disproportionately concentrated in central cities—recovery from recession appears to matter very little. They were hard-pressed before and remained hard-pressed after national economic improvements.

Advocates of industrial policy offer only minimal hope that their ap-proach can help cities. Picking the industrial winners, given our mar-ginal capacity to predict and project, will resemble a crapshoot, and success, at best, likely will abet the fortunes of growing not declining areas. A focus on declining industrial sectors, would at most postpone the inevitable. We can hope that it would assist firms and workers to adjust and accommodate change.

Admitting that the urban problem is still with us and questioning the wisdom of the urban relevance of the "rising tide" and industrial policy does little to provide ready answers to what comes next. Clearly, budget and political constraints limit expectations concerning bold or significant new federal urban initiatives.

Urban policies and programs in the current political environment will

likely be limited to protecting and making better use of what we have
that appears to work well (such as the Urban Development Action
Grant program).[8] They will also rely more on our ability to figure out
how best to *co-opt* likely nonurban options that if structured appropriately will offer cities a better break (tax reform and new programs to
aid America's deteriorating infrastructure). In this context criteria of
equity as well as *efficiency* mandate attention to the special problems
of the urban poor and to the related difficulties faced by central cities
left in the wake of unfavorable national economic and demographic
trends.

————

Downtown Shopping Malls and the New Public-Private Strategy

BERNARD J. FRIEDEN
AND LYNNE B. SAGALYN

Urban programs of the Great Society era have much to do with the
current successes of city governments as initiators, financers, and managers of their own rebuilding efforts. The urban renewal program, enacted originally in 1949, prompted cities to go far beyond their earlier
regulatory role by undertaking complicated projects to clear and rebuild older areas. Although the program was plagued with troubles in
its early years—by 1964 cities had completed only a hundred projects
but had abandoned three times as many[1]—the Kennedy and Johnson
administrations expanded it greatly, supplemented it with related measures to help rebuild cities, and made it the largest of their urban development programs. By 1968, despite problems, federal urban renewal

We are indebted to a number of organizations whose support made our research
possible: the Office of Policy Development and Research of the U. S. Department
of Housing and Urban Development, the MIT Center for Real Estate Development,
and the MIT-Harvard Joint Center for Urban Studies. Case studies of retail development were prepared with the support of the Ernest W. and Jean E. Hahn
Foundation and the MIT Department of Urban Studies and Planning. Several research assistants contributed to this project, including Christie Baxter, Nancy Fox,
Jacques Gordon, and Allison Hall. We are also indebted to many colleagues for advice and critical comments, especially Robert Einsweiler, Robert Fogelson, Marshall
Kaplan, Martin Levin, Gary Marx, Francine Rabinovitz, Deborah Stone, and Raymond Vernon.

authorizations reached a total of $10 billion and some two thousand renewal projects were under way in more than nine hundred communities.[2]

Since urban renewal was an entirely new activity for most cities, federal administrators gave high priority to technical assistance and developed very detailed procedures for cities to follow, spelling out everything from the studies needed for initial project planning to procedures for land acquisition and resale to developers. Federal officials in regional offices in Washington monitored local programs closely. While their supervision was counterproductive in same ways, it was helpful in building a network of local agencies whose staff members had the capacity to carry out renewal programs.

The Great Society left its mark on subsequent rebuilding projects in other ways as well. Reacting against an earlier emphasis on large-scale clearance projects that evicted thousands of people from their homes, Secretary of Housing and Urban Development (HUD) Robert Weaver shifted the emphasis increasingly often to projects that rehabilitated existing housing instead of demolishing it. At the same time, federal legislation made available more generous relocation assistance and required cities to provide additional relocation housing.[3] The projects that later succeeded in transforming downtown areas generally followed the same strategies of minimizing clearance and avoiding relocation problems.

At about the same time, federal officials during the Great Society era anticipated more recent trends by giving fresh emphasis to efforts at involving the private sector in their urban programs. Low-income housing had been an important item on the federal agenda since the New Deal, but the federal government relied on local public agencies to build and manage the housing projects. By the mid-1960s HUD began encouraging local housing authorities to privatize all or part of their operations by purchasing or leasing housing built by private developers and contracting for private management of projects. Then in the Housing Act of 1968—one of the last major legislative achievements of the Johnson administration—Congress authorized new housing assistance programs that relied on private sponsors to build homes for sale or rent at below-market prices and what low- and moderate-income residents could afford to pay.[4] Although these programs generated too much scandal and too many defaults to serve as models for the future, they reinforced the belief that the private sector could produce impressive results if the public sector could find the right combination of incentives and controls.

Urban renewal provided the Great Society warriors with a cumbersome system for handling public-private relations. They failed to make any major improvements in it. Local government agencies took the lead in planning and starting renewal projects. Development companies were responsible for rebuilding cleared areas. Operating under federal rules that excluded developers from the early stages of planning, city officials had to figure out in advance what projects would be feasible for private developers to build. After the land was assembled and cleared, however, many renewal agencies were unable to find a developer willing to buy it or willing to build the type of project the city had planned for it. After years of costly and complicated planning, followed by more years of politically controversial land acquisition and relocation of people from the site, many cities had nothing to show for their efforts but fields of rubble. In short, the public-private relationship often failed.

THE IMPLEMENTATION PROBLEM

The delays and frustrations of urban renewal were characteristic of a broader group of community development programs undertaken in the 1960s and early 1970s. Even though federal aid flowed freely at that time, the cities had enormous problems trying to complete the projects they started.

One program, "New Towns In-Town," offered surplus federal land at low prices plus other federal assistance for large developments that would include some housing for the poor. The land not only was cheap but came in large tracts and was unoccupied, so that cities could bypass the usual delays, costs, and protests of relocation and clearance. Even so, four years after the program began three of the seven participating cities had abandoned their projects and others were stalled indefinitely as a result of local controversies or development problems.[5]

In late 1965 top officials of the federal Economic Development Administration (EDA) began to put together an ambitious public works program to create jobs for unemployed workers in Oakland, California. Their program included construction of an airport hangar, a marine terminal, an industrial park, and access roads; and they expected to attract private businesses that would provide work for more than two thousand of the hard-core unemployed, most of them members of minority groups.

Despite widespread local support for the program among Oakland's decision-makers, particularly at the outset, the obstacles were numerous and progress turned out to be painfully slow. Five years later the aircraft hangar, which was supposed to provide more than half the promised jobs, was still not built and the industrial park had created only thirty jobs instead of an anticipated 420. A well-known study of Oakland's implementation of the EDA program attributed failure to the extreme complexity of decision-making and to use of the wrong incentives with the private sector.

A reversal of past experience. Since the early 1970s the federal government has terminated the urban renewal program and cut back the flow of federal aid to local governments. Perhaps out of necessity many cities moved toward closer, more productive development relationships with the private sector. The most striking demonstration of city progress in managing complicated public-private projects is the wave of new retail centers built in downtown areas across the country.

The new retail projects are important to the cities for several reasons. Most are big, typically providing space for more than a hundred stores with the potential to generate substantial sales and property tax revenues. The successful ones are focal points of downtown activity, drawing crowds of 10 to 20 million visitors a year—like regional shopping malls in the suburbs. They mark a break with the long-term movement of retailing away from downtown.

The development of more than a hundred downtown retail centers since 1970 suggests that growing numbers of cities are finding ways to compete effectively against the suburbs for a share of retail sales. By 1983 one of every four new shopping centers in the United States was a downtown project.[6] The downtown centers follow several different retailing strategies. Some, such as Plaza Pasadena, are regional shopping malls offering a wide variety of goods aimed at the middle of the market. Others, such as Boston's Faneuil Hall Marketplace, are specialty malls that draw people by offering unusual foods and a festive atmosphere. Still others, such as Town Square in St. Paul, are mixed-use projects that combine stores with hotels, offices, convention centers, or other activities. Some are intended to appeal especially to tourists, conventioneers, and business visitors, while others have a shopping mix geared to nearby residents and in-town workers.

The earlier decline of downtown retailing was rooted in a major shift of population and jobs from the cities to the suburbs. These underlying trends have not changed: in fact, the central cities lost people and jobs at an accelerated rate during the 1970s. Nor has there been a reversal of the long-term trend in retail sales. While sales continued to expand strongly in the suburbs, the central business districts of major cities recorded even greater losses in real dollars in the 1970s than they had in the 1960s.[7]

What has changed is that for the first time in thirty years central cities have found ways to gain a competitive edge on their surrounding suburbs for certain kinds of development. This turnaround resulted in part from limited changes in the central-city economy and in the make-up of city neighborhoods. But it resulted much more from changes in public policy than it did from changes in real estate markets.

A new style of joint action for cities and developers began to work effectively for downtown retail centers. The new relationships are an important advance in the management of city-building. This essay focuses on why and how several new retail centers were built, how the new public-private relations differ—for better or worse—from earlier approaches, and how this recent experience is likely to affect cities in the future.[8]

MOTIVATING CITIES: PRESSURES AND OPPORTUNITIES

Federal policy changes. The basic pressure motivating mayors to search for new development strategies was a growing reluctance in Washington to continue funding annual increases in federal aid to cities. Yet the fiscal problems of the older cities grew worse in the 1970s. Hard-pressed to keep costs down, raise additional taxes, or increase bonded debt, several cities—most notably New York, Boston, Cleveland, and Philadelphia—reached the brink of default and bankruptcy. Many cities cut municipal services but continued to bear high tax burdens.[9]

Despite this ominous turn, the political alignment that had supported earlier federal aid programs lost much of its strength. Both the news media and the Congress grew increasingly indifferent to the pleas of the mayors. By 1978 *Harper's, Newsweek,* and the *New York Times Magazine* were declaring an end to the urban crisis.[10] A restless public and elected officials trying to bring the federal budget under control were inclined to agree for different reasons. The federal aid budget for states and local governments peaked in real dollars in 1978, midway in the Carter administration, and declined further during the Reagan administration.[11] The message to cities was clear: with less outside aid they would have to do more to help themselves.

The federal government made it easier for cities to commit available urban aid funds for downtown development by relaxing its controls. Of nine major community development programs in 1970, only urban renewal and historic preservation grants could be tapped easily for downtown revitalization. Several other programs were intended for residential areas, and the one that received greatest attention—the model cities program—had to be used to improve low-income and minority neighborhoods. In 1974 Congress merged these nine separate programs into a single community development block grant that cities could use flexibly to meet their own priorities, with a minimum of federal review and supervision.

The cities lost no time in changing their pattern of spending on development projects. In just the first year of block grants, cities cut their spending in low-income areas by more than one-third. The bulk of expenditures under the model cities program was for such public services as education, health, and job training. The block grant program set limits on local spending for service activities and required cities to use most of their aid for construction projects. Under the new arrangements, hardware expenditures, public works, and downtown development were soon back in fashion; and poor people and minorities were soon out of fashion.[12]

Further, in 1977 Congress enacted the urban development action grant program (UDAG) to fund local construction projects that stimulate private investment to create jobs and improve the tax base. By the second year of operations, three-fourths of the federal funds went for central-city projects and close to 60 percent of the central-city funds were for commercial developments.[13]

Other federal actions also had the effect of promoting downtown revitalization. Historically, federal tax laws greatly favored investment in new structures over investment in preservation and improvement of old ones.[14] Beginning in the mid-1970s a series of revisions introduced special tax incentives for investors who improved older and historic buildings and in 1981 equalized the depreciation benefits for new and existing buildings.[15]

New federal measures also made home financing more readily available in city neighborhoods. Regulations and laws of the mid-1970s directed against redlining required fuller disclosure of mortgage finance patterns and broadened the lending powers of thrift institutions in urban areas, thus helping home-owners to renovate older houses. Also, neighborhood housing service programs offered below-market loans and help with home renovation. These programs helped stabilize and improve many old neighborhoods and in doing so provided a middle-income market for downtown shopping malls.

Gentrification. An important but misunderstood change of the 1970s was the movement of relatively well-off people into old houses in what had been low-income city neighborhoods. For a series of loosely related reasons, enough newcomers invested in the older houses to make a visible difference in selected neighborhoods. These changes caught the eye of journalists and other trend-watchers who concluded that the urban crisis was over.

Yet this new commitment to in-town living remained a very limited movement—limited by the number of city-loving families able to put together an income package of $50,000 or more, by the number of neighborhoods with the right combination of charm and access, and by the fact that house prices in popular locations soon climbed out of reach of all but a few people. In a survey of the thirty largest cities, Phillip Clay found some upgrading in almost all of them, but he also found that declining neighborhoods greatly outnumbered those enjoying a revival. Contrary to popular impression, he and other researchers found no sign of the long-awaited back-to-the-city movement from suburbia: most of the renovators turned out to be families moving from one city residence to another.[16]

Still, the gentrification trend was a positive one for the cities. Housing renovation dovetailed with retail growth and with the expansion of downtown office districts. It raised the prospect that all three activities might be mutually supportive in encouraging people who worked in the expanding service and professional occupations to live and shop in the central city.

Shifts in taste. A final factor encouraging these new urban developments was an unexpected shift in public taste. The 1970s were a time when many Americans rediscovered the past and found they enjoyed it. Nostalgia was in and it was marketable. (A scrap dealer who handled salvage from the New York City transit system advertised old subway handstraps mounted on wood with the slogan, "Hang on to a piece of the past.") If the latest fashion called for renovating a Victorian townhouse rather than living in a contemporary deck model, the central cities had a corner on that market. If tourism and convention visits were emerging as important economic activities, the old buildings of central cities acquired new value as charming reminders of bygone days.

Other factors. A combination of other circumstances helped make downtown sites more attractive in the 1970s than they had been earlier. As suggested earlier, changes in family life were creating new marketing opportunities. The same changes that encouraged young people to live in the city—late marriage, shared incomes, few children—enabled them to indulge their taste for entertainment, restaurants, boutiques, and specialty retail items for the home.

The increasing number of workers in central-city offices were potential customers who would shop for clothes, fashion accessories, books, and other small items in stores near their jobs. As a result retailers considering a new or expanded downtown location were not completely dependent on bringing the suburbanites back to the city.

Meanwhile, retail development opportunities in the suburbs were no longer as promising as they had been. A network of regional shopping centers was already well established in the suburbs of most major cities, and finding good sites for more malls was getting harder all the time.[17] Compounding the search for sites was a rapid buildup of suburban growth regulations during the early 1970s. Prompted in part by the environmental movement and in part by local opposition to further growth, suburbs across the country were putting into place a network of new and demanding review and permit requirements for proposed developments of all kinds.[18] These had the effect of stretching out the development process and making it more costly, while also giving opponents of shopping centers easy and repeated chances to block them. Further, the mood of local citizens and their representatives was turning increasingly hostile to development, particularly in areas that had experienced high growth in the recent past.

On top of local regulatory snags, the newly created federal Environmental Protection Agency posed an even more direct threat to suburban mall development. In an effort to prevent automobile emissions from lowering air quality in places that already met pollution standards, it drew up plans to restrict the construction of major new parking facilities in the outer suburbs.

The high cost of building the infrastructure necessary for regional shopping centers also detoured many developments. In the past, suburban governments had been willing to pay for some of these costs or to use local bond issues to finance them. By the early 1970s the suburbs were increasingly often transferring these costs to the developer.[19] City sites, in contrast, were more likely to have the infrastructure in place and, to the extent they did not, the cities were more willing to use tax-exempt financing to pay for it.

Department stores, considered the indispensable "anchor tenants" that would draw customers to large shopping malls, were generally committed to suburbia for their new branches. But as retail trade became increasingly competitive, some department store chains recognized that specialization to serve a particular segment of the market could be an effective strategy. A few department store executives, at least, were willing to consider locating a new store downtown as a way of capturing a share of the market that the outlying malls had bypassed.[20]

NEW DEVELOPMENT POLICIES

In the 1970s the cities began moving away from the social agenda of the 1960s and returning to earlier concerns with revitalizing the central business district. The earlier political upheavals around urban renewal efforts had taught them to avoid clearance projects that pushed out large numbers of people, and they looked for smaller-scale projects, new public financing tools, new funding sources, and negotiated risk-sharing relationships with private developers. As these development initiatives progressed, several features of earlier city development practice began to reassert themselves: an involvement of downtown business interests in setting the redevelopment agenda; a preference for construction projects rather than public services; a predominance of commercial, governmental, and industrial projects over housing; an emphasis on projects that interested the broad middle class rather than the poor; a search for projects likely to stimulate additional development; and a strategy of creating conditions to attract private enterprise into ventures that served the city's purposes.

These redevelopment efforts built on several legacies of the urban renewal experience, literally as well as programmatically. First, newer downtown projects often filled in long-vacant parcels cleared through urban renewal; others made use of buildings that were rehabilitated with renewal funds. Both types of projects commonly benefited from outlays for site acquisition and preparation that had been financed earlier at lower rates and by large federal subsidies. Second, city officials inherited procedures and experienced staff from the urban renewal program.

The earlier urban renewal strategy focused on removing two key obstacles blocking private redevelopment: the difficulty of assembling construction sites out of parcels held by many separate owners, and the high cost of urban land. The more recent strategy expanded the public role well beyond site assembly and land subsidy, to include risk-sharing and help with financing some of the private components of the project.

The new approach gave high priority to establishing market acceptance of a project as early as possible and nailing down commitments from developers and investors before the city made major outlays of its own. By the mid-1970s the federal government also shifted its stance. Federal regulations for the new urban development action grants (UDAGS) called for legally binding commitments from private participants in advance. Program rules gave local governments discretion over how to use federal funds to attract private investment, but the private dollars had to be "live," ready to commit; hence the term "action grant."

As in urban renewal, public sector money continued to be an important ingredient in recent downtown retail projects. In a sample of thirty-two projects for which information was available, the public share ranged from as little as 3 percent to as much as 81 percent, with a median of 30 percent. In some early projects, such as Faneuil Hall and Pike Place, federal grants supplied most of the public funds, but in more recent projects local financing either complemented or substituted for federal sources.

CITY ROLES

City governments have been heavily involved in numerous ways, innovative and often entrepreneurial, to bring major retail activity back downtown. Some limited their activities to traditional roles of planning, grantsmanship, site assembly with a write-down of land costs, and provision of support in utility and street improvements, sometimes adding public financing of parking structures to the package. Others did more to increase the financial feasibility for private development by leasing the land buildings, making loan commitments, and sharing operating as well as capital costs. Many helped work out regulatory problems, improved the administration of city functions, or created a special public development organization to assist the project. A few even became developers and owners of retail property.

Political protection. One way city officials helped these new retail development projects was by insulating them from political pressures. Local governments almost always face pressure to spread available funds throughout the community and not to concentrate them on a few large projects. In many cities strong mayoral leadership and commitment was necessary to safeguard downtown retail projects against other claims on local and federal resources.

Regardless of the strength and commitment of the mayor, city officials had to search for politically feasible ways to justify concentrating funds in a single project. One strategy was to make use of a defined project area as the only place eligible for the funds in question. Applying for federal UDAG assistance, for example, tied the city to spending the funds on a specified project and allowed no diversion to other places. Similarly, setting up a carefully drawn tax district as a redevelopment area limited the possible spread of project funds.

Cities also assisted retail projects by limiting or restricting competition for a few years until the new shopping developments were well established. In California public revenue bond-finance legislation required cities to avoid sponsoring competitive projects.[21] Elsewhere cities acted without a legal requirement in order to protect their own interests in new shopping malls. In St. Paul, city officials used their influence with the metropolitan planning agency for the Minneapolis-St. Paul area to block a suburban shopping mall that threatened to compete with their Town Square project.

Financial incentives. Cities commonly provided supporting facilities for new shopping malls: utility relocations and replacements, street improvements, connecting walkways above street level ("sky-walks"), and parking facilities. Some built parks or other public open spaces to increase the attractiveness of projects.

Cities used their skill to write persuasive proposals and their political contacts to get outside grants. They found federal aid in many places, particularly in the urban renewal, UDAG, urban mass transportation, economic development, and historic preservation programs. And they were creative in the ways they used this aid. In Philadelphia, for example, an urban mass transportation grant financed direct access between a renovated subway station and the first anchor department store, meeting one of the store's basic conditions for participating in the mall. City staff also brokered contributions from business interests, historic preservation groups, and private foundations. In St. Paul, downtown businesses contributed $400,000, or nearly a quarter of the city's direct costs for project planning and management.

Another way some cities have helped with project financing is by assuming a long-term share of project risks through lease agreements with the developer. Leasing the land, building, or garage structure offers the developer certain advantages over ownership. It lowers the required front-end investment, reduces the costs to be financed privately, and can increase the equity return after federal taxes. Leasing potentially offers the city two main advantages: the ability to control the site through continual ownership, and a share in future profits through rental income and appreciation of the property value. Leasing may also

tributes to management costs for pedestrian ways throughout the entire retail area.

Summary: the new relationship. Academic analysts of implementation problems in the early 1960s and 1970s pointed to complexity of decision-making as the main reason for delays and failure, and urged simpler projects as the solution. Downtown retail projects did not get simpler, however. Some must be among the most complex ever constructed. Milwaukee's Grand Avenue, for example, consists of six historic buildings connected by a series of skywalks and shopping arcades and served by two new and two old parking garages. The maze of property interests and legal agreements is so intricate that a large insurance company spent more than two years working on the title insurance for the center. The underwriter in charge remarked, "I have been involved in the business thirty-five years and I have never seen a title this involved and probably never will again."[22]

These projects did not survive the problems of implementation because of their simplicity. They survived because unlike the 1960s and 1970s: (1) cities and developers worked together to establish project feasibility in the early stages; (2) both parties were willing to consult and revise agreements when circumstances changed; (3) both became increasingly committed to the project as they got in deeper and deeper; and (4) both showed great flexibility and ingenuity in coming up with solutions to unexpected problems.

ASSESSING THE RESULTS

The spread of downtown shopping malls is evidence that city governments are capable of generating major new development when economic circumstances provide even a limited and uncertain opening. If the cities had sat back and waited for development firms to recognize the investment opportunity and come forward with construction plans, they would still be waiting. Public action was required, but it had to be something more than the traditional approach. If city officials had organized typical urban renewal projects, they would now be trying to explain to angry voters why, after much trouble and expense, they had not yet found developers for the rubble-filled sites they were holding downtown.

The cities have found a better way than relying either on the invisible hand of the real estate market to revitalize downtown or on planning and urban renewal projects to do the job. What they have done is to restructure traditional relationships between the public and private sectors to make development more of a joint venture than ever before. The results are not all in, but the record so far is promising. The time needed to complete a project is shorter than it was under earlier arrangements. A few, such as Detroit's Renaissance Center and Atlanta's Omni Center, have failed economically, but most of the projects are attracting large numbers of people downtown and returning tax revenues to the cities.

Whether the downtown retail projects live up to all the cities' expectations for them will not be known for some time. Cities have promoted retail malls for several different reasons. Most often, local officials talk in terms of economic development when they describe the ripple effects they expect the retail centers to generate. Yet many also regard them as public amenities, much like an attractive park or zoo. Still others see them as necessary components of a campaign to create a new image for their city, as symbols of a healthy downtown and a well-managed community. To others, they are a way of restoring some of the traditions that make city life enjoyable and interesting: street activity both day and night, shopping, food markets, and open-air celebrations. These traditional elements take on special importance as the cities try to replace their traditional functions of manufacturing and shipping with a new function of service and entertainment.

Most retail projects are too new for their effects to be demonstrated convincingly—particularly those effects that result from their value as symbols of investor confidence and community well-being. While there is evidence of ripple effects in a number of cities, it is hard to judge how many of the ripples were created by the retail centers and how many by other downtown projects built about the same time. As for the direct employment in the retail stores, there is a question of how many jobs are net additions to the local economy and how many are substitutes for other retail jobs that are being lost.

In short, the early evidence suggests that downtown retail centers are helpful for economic development; but it is not yet clear how helpful they are, or how the benefits compare with the substantial public costs. At the same time, it is clear that they do not have the negative impacts of many earlier urban renewal projects. City governments have learned to avoid projects that threaten residential neighborhoods, and most of the current projects are located in downtown business districts, in port and warehouse areas, in areas specializing in pornography and "adult entertainment," or in similarly marginal locations.

The development process. For a city, learning to work with private developers in close, ongoing relationships is not trouble-free. The work of hammering out a complex development agreement that can run as long as 150 pages takes place behind closed doors. Since the city is sharing cost and risks, the final terms of the agreement become public information. But the details that are needed to understand the issues seldom come to light, and even with the best will in the world it is hard to imagine a way of keeping the public informed of the choices that must be made. Usually the issues are too complicated to lend themselves to a vote or a referendum; but once the agreement has been negotiated, elected officials are in the position of either rubber-stamping it or looking like enemies of progress.

City officials could become vulnerable to accusations that the public-private relationship is little more than a giveaway of public funds. The substantial transfers of city money that characterize these projects serve mainly to narrow the gap between development costs downtown and those in comparable suburban malls. Yet there are legitimate grounds for concern about giveaways. The risks of downtown projects are great enough to make developers ask for plenty of financial help, and city officials unfamiliar with development may indeed agree to give excessive aid for projects they are anxious to have.

So far the city record in creating staffs capable of analyzing the economics and finances of large private developments is uneven. The most typical safeguard has been city use of expert consultants who know enough about real estate to probe the claims of developers critically and to come up with their own estimates of what is needed. In the long run, a more reliable safeguard would be to have specialized city staff capable of keeping an eye on the proceedings and advising elected officials on the major issues that arise.

The problems of these joint relationships are not all one-sided. Developers are also put in roles that are new, involve additional risks, and require practical accommodation to the political situation. On major decisions they have a public partner who has to be consulted, which means that they are not free to decide and act alone. They have to share information that they used to consider confidential. They may get locked into a public-sector schedule and lose the freedom to time their moves, including even the ability to arrange their long-term financing whenever they consider interest rates most favorable.

From the point of view of public agencies involved in regulating city development, the new relationships with the private sector are potentially troublesome in other ways. They break with the long-established tradition that calls for uniform rules and procedures for everyone who does business with a city. The new style is one of negotiating special arrangements to suit each project and each developer. Administrators have more discretion than before, but they are losing the protection of established rules. Because the city acts increasingly often as both a financial partner and a regulator of development projects, administrators may come under great political pressure to compromise their regulatory standards for the sake of financial returns to the city. Or, when they agree to special arrangements for a project, they may become vulnerable to charges of favoritism. In short, the new relationships are likely to politicize decisions that used to be easier to handle equitably.

The first response of many administrators, however, has been to welcome the opportunity to operate in a more freewheeling style. Those administrators who negotiate development projects appear to attract many professional rewards, including recognition, high prestige, and high salary.

Will the public-private strategy spread? A question that remains is whether the new public-private relationship was simply a temporary expedient brought on by the special circumstances of the 1970s, or part of a learning process likely to continue in the future. With the threat of municipal defaults and bankruptcy during the 1970s, the cities were understandably willing to experiment with new ways of managing development despite the political and financial risks involved. Many cities still have serious fiscal problems, but with the mood of desperation gone city administrators may want to return to more traditional ways of handling development.

Our interviews indicate that city officials (as well as developers) who have made use of the new public-private management style see many advantages to it, and they are unlikely to give it up without compelling reasons—such as the emergence of scandals from these relationships. City staff members who have had personal experience with public-private developments are still a very small minority of their profession, and the details of the process are still not well known. Yet there is widespread interest in the entrepreneurial style of public administration, and by now similar methods have been applied to a number of other developments besides the downtown retail centers.

One type of project that combines public and private elements is the mixed-income housing development in which public funds are used to provide some apartments at below-market rents. Local examples have been numerous. A joint development strategy has also been proposed for public parks that contain commercial facilities. Recently announced plans for Bryant Park in New York, for example, involve a public-private combination in which the private sector will provide a restaurant, food kiosks, and a security force.[23] In Los Angeles, Washington, D.C., and several other cities, transportation agencies have made extensive use of joint development methods to promote the construction of private buildings on public land next to transit stations.[24]

There are also development situations where the public-private combination is either unnecessary or inappropriate. Many types of development—such as downtown office buildings—can be done privately with no special need for public assistance. Using public resources to share costs or risks for development of this kind would be wasteful. At the other extreme are projects that are unlikely to offer attractive profit opportunities without a level of public assistance that would be politically or economically unacceptable. This category would include many facilities serving primarily low-income populations.

The public-private process for downtown retail projects has four key elements that are broadly applicable to other settings: (1) assembling a mix of local and private resources to complement available federal funds; (2) establishing political and economic feasibility during early stages of project planning; (3) utilizing ongoing negotiation rather than arm's-length regulation of the private sector, with a continuing role for the city in decisions throughout the development process; and (4) trading public sector sharing of front-end risks for participation in future benefits.

Downtown retailing has been a good proving ground for these strategies, and many cities are likely to turn their attention next to other types of projects in other parts of the community. If public-private developments continue to spread as they have in the past few years, and if the cities can make their new managerial methods work for a broader development agenda, then the process that built the downtown shopping malls could turn out to be even more important than the malls themselves. We clearly have entered a different era of urban development than the one illustrated in the sixties in urban renewal projects. We have new opportunities, new problems, and new challenges.

4

Use and Misuse of Information

Random Observations on the
Role of the Media in Covering
the War on Poverty

IAN MENZIES

In February 1964 Charles I. Schottland, dean of the Florence Heller Graduate School at Brandeis University, commenting on the War on Poverty, remarked that, "the present interest in poverty throughout the country heralds a new social and political climate." Many agreed with him. His remark coincided with a report that one-fifth of all American families were then living in poverty—translated at the time as having a weekly income of less than $60.

What I would like to discuss from a media view, as we look back over the past twenty years, is Schottland's descriptive phrase. Was he right? Was there a genuine "interest," and even more to the point, if this interest existed was it "throughout the country," and did it portend a "new social and political climate?" Or was Schottland wrong? And if wrong, did this broadly accepted presumption subvert objectivity and compromise the War on Poverty? Further, were the media a party to the presumption and therefore a contributor to its failure, or, to put it more tactfully, its not "wholly successful" outcome.

From where I sat in the mid-sixties, directing the news operation of the *Boston Globe* in a city vigorously influenced by the ideas of academe, the challenge put forth by the War on Poverty had enormous moral appeal. Nor was interest lessened by the fact that the challenge came on top of the tragic death of an assassinated president, John F. Kennedy—a native son and a man whose ideals appeared directly associated with equal rights, equal opportunity, and a concern for the poor.

There is no question that in the early and mid-sixties newspapers, television, and radio endorsed the War on Poverty with little or no dissent. Also, I might add, with little or no analysis, and for good reason; there was nothing to analyze. The Great Society programs burst forth from task force and commission reports subject to little public review. Dialogue was preempted by speed.

Schottland argued that a "country-wide interest" prevailed. Did it? Was there a true public interest in the War on Poverty, or was the interest limited to a broad range of scholars and to those who saw in such a crusade an emotional penance for a murdered president. Did the press, television, and radio, at least in the East where the media's most influential policy-makers have long been a part of the liberal establishment, merely hear this moral drumbeat and march along?

Bernard Frieden and Marshall Kaplan raised this question of "interest" in their 1975 book, *The Politics of Neglect: Urban Aid from Model Cities to Revenue Sharing.*[1] They asked, was there ever a national commitment to the purpose of this program? It's a question that hasn't been examined very carefully, particularly from a media point of view.

Aided by the armchair of the time, I'd say no—there wasn't a national commitment and certainly there wasn't a media commitment. And I believe the answer was no even before the Vietnam War doomed the Great Society. Newspapers, television, and radio most certainly influence public policy but their interest, with certain notable exceptions—such as the Vietnam War and Watergate—can be just as fickle as public opinion.

The War on Poverty had an inherent weakness that the media failed to realize or chose to ignore—a latent grassroots opposition to its emphasis and direction. The nature of that opposition did not become clear to the supportive liberal Eastern media until the traumatic onset of school busing. Even then, speaking of my own city and my own newspaper, it was to a great extent disregarded.

I suggest that both liberal academics and the liberal press, despite their good-hearted intent, failed to understand the ethnic, social, and racial tensions that underlay both the War on Poverty and school busing. Those tensions centered not only on white lower-middle-income groups and working poor but on the more silent fears—prejudices if you will—of large sections of the urban middle class. This opposition, unjustified as it was, subverted both programs and diluted any ostensible sustained national commitment.

The fact is that the liberal press and liberal academics were out of touch with these groups in 1964, again in 1974, and I fear are still out of touch today. They show too little sensitivity to the hopes and fears of what is best described as working-class Americans, whether white or black.

There is, as there should be, some sensitivity in the upper echelons of most liberal newspapers for blacks—even though it doesn't extend to their hiring practices—but not for equally poor urban whites. The concerns of the former justifiably have earned a fashionable acceptance by top editors; the concerns of the latter have too readily been dismissed as merely racist. Yet any poverty program that hopes to succeed needs the support of both.

Had the *Globe*, my own paper, been more sensitized to the feelings of white working-class people as well as those of minorities it might have striven for a less traumatic, more balanced metropolitan answer to busing and might have provided more insightful coverage of the War on Poverty.

There is no question that the media have played a role in shaping public policy during the sixties and seventies. But covering poverty programs or poor city neighborhoods has never, since the slide to suburbia in the early 1950s, been high on the agenda of major newspapers; nor is it an assignment cherished by ambitious reporters, since it assures minimal attention.

Part of the problem is that the sons and daughters of working-class or poor Americans (whether white or minority) are seldom seen in newsrooms. Nor are there many reporters around who were born and bred in big-city neighborhoods. Street life and the struggles of the poor have difficulty penetrating the more collegiate tone of today's big-city newsrooms (a tone, however, that in other ways has improved newspapers).

I don't want to give the impression that newspapers did little or nothing during the War on Poverty years. Quite the contrary. We did try to expand coverage, but we had to be shocked into action, beginning with the racial tension in Selma. In 1966 the Celtic's basketball star Bill Russell warned *Globe* editors that Boston might burn if the establishment failed to face up to racism. That same year the *Globe* formed its first urban team of four reporters, one of them black. The Urban Team, rapidly expanded, covered not only the poverty programs but housing, city hall, and education. It could call on specialized reporters for assistance.

We did put reporters on the streets, to such an extent that when rioting struck the Grove Hall section of Roxbury in 1967, one reporter, a woman, was trapped for a time in the local welfare office during riots generated by inconsiderate and inefficient treatment of welfare mothers.

The *Globe* reporter was rescued by members of the Roxbury Multi-Service Center.

Following the rioting—exacerbated, some said, by police—*Globe* editor Tom Winship organized a weekend live-in between militant and representative Roxbury blacks and *Globe* editors and reporters at the Dublin School in Dublin, New Hampshire. Some friendships made then remain today. Winship also formed a Boston Media Committee that in fact gave blacks immediate access to top media executives.

In March 1968 the Urban Team produced an award-winning 36-page special magazine called "Poverty in Boston—the People, the Problems, the Programs," a unique effort unequalled in my view by any city newspaper as a combination commentary and guide.

After Nixon's election, newspapers, and I speak not only of the *Globe* but other major Eastern papers, changed their approach. The impact as I saw it was significant. Priorities changed. No one quite said it, but the poor were out; bottom lines were in.

In some respects, and here I speak only of the *Globe*, it was amazing that our effort to cover and support the War on Poverty, the Great Society, and the Model Cities program, as well as the civil rights movement, lasted as long as it did. Because in truth the *Globe*'s strongest emotional commitment during the sixties was to end the war in Vietnam. It was not easy in those years, as managing editor, to fight two wars—one in the streets at home, the other nine thousand miles away, both emotional and both traumatic.

In retrospect, from a media seat, it is clear that the War on Poverty never really got off the ground. It was covered but not really understood by the media. It failed to win the broad support of the white working poor and the working middle class.

I want to conclude by taking a broader look at the role of the media in shaping public policy. I believe the media have a major role, and that the nation's more powerful newspapers will play an even more critical role in the future than in the past. This is because the impact of other major communication outlets will be diluted with the development of cable stations, etc.

The ability of newspapers to relay domestic policy clearly and effectively depends in part upon an administration's ability to present it in those terms. It also depends on a newspaper's willingness to develop expertise. Washington bureaus, where they exist, are not noted for staffs either interested or familiar with programs in housing, education, Medicare, or manpower training.

The Role of the Media in Shaping Public Policy: The Myth of Power and the Power of Myth

CHARLES GREEN

"The role of the media in shaping public policy: 1964 to 1984" is, of course, an impossibly broad subject. It ranges from the flowering of the civil rights movement through the Vietnam War to the "Me Generation" era, and spans five presidents. There's an old author's trick that says when you're faced with an impossibly broad subject, the only safe course is to expand it still further. Thus, let's begin on 18 December 1917 by quoting a famous article published on that date in the *New York Evening Mail*:

A Neglected Anniversary
On December 20 there flitted past us, absolutely without public notice, one of the most important profane anniversaries in American history—to wit: the seventy-fifth anniversary of the introduction of the bathtub into these states. . . . Bathtubs are so common today that it is almost impossible to imagine a world without them . . . and yet the first American Bathtub was installed and dedicated so recently as December 20, 1842.

Curiously enough, the scene of its setting up was Cincinnati, [by] Adam Thompson. . . . [His] trade frequently took him to England, and in that country, during the 1830s, he acquired the habit of bathing.

The bathtub was then still a novelty in England. It had been introduced in 1828 by Lord John Russell and its use was yet confined to a small class of enthusiasts.

Moreover, the English bathtub, then as now, was a puny and inconvenient contrivance—little more, in fact, than a glorified dishpan—and filling and emptying required the attendance of a servant. Taking a bath, indeed, was a rather heavy ceremony, and Lord John in 1835 was said to be the only man in England who had yet come to doing it every day.

Thompson, who was of inventive fancy . . . conceived the notion that the English bathtub would be much improved if it were made large enough to admit the whole body of an adult man, and if its supply of water, instead of being hauled to the scene by a maid, were admitted by pipes from a central reservoir and run off by the same means. Accordingly, early in 1842 he set about building the first American bathroom in his Cincinnati home.

. . . In this luxurious tub Thompson took two baths on December 20, 1842—a cold one at 8 a.m. and a warm one some time during the afternoon. The warm water, heated by the kitchen fire, reached a temperature of 105 degrees. On Christmas day, having a party of gentlemen to dinner, he exhibited the new marvel to them and gave an exhibition of its use, and four of them, including a French visitor, Col. Duchanel, risked plunges into it. The next day all Cincinnati . . . had heard of it, and the local newspapers described it at length and opened their columns to violent discussions of it.

The thing, in fact, became a public matter, and before long there was bitter and double-headed opposition to the new invention.

. . . The noise of the controversy soon reached other cities, and in more than one place medical opposition reached such strength that it was reflected in legislation. Late in 1843, for example, the Philadelphia common considered an ordinance prohibiting bathing between November 1 and March 15, and it failed of passage by but two votes. . . .

. . . Dr. Oliver Wendell Holmes declared for the bathtub and vigorously opposed the lingering movement against it. . . . The American Medical Association held its annual meeting in Boston in 1859 and a poll of the members in attendance showed that nearly 55 percent of them now regarded bathing as harmless and that more than 20 percent advocated it as beneficial. At its meeting in 1850 a resolution was formally passed giving the imprimatur of the faculty to the bathtub. . . .

But it was the example of President Millard Fillmore that, even more than the grudging medical approval, gave the bathtub recognition and respectability in the United States . . . on succeeding to the presidency at Taylor's death, July 9, 1850, he instructed his secretary of war, Gen. Charles M. Conrad, to invite tenders for the construction of a bathtub in the White House. . . . This was installed early in 1851.[1]

Most of us are already familiar with most of these "facts" that were a staple of newspaper features and fillers for more than a half-century. Most of us also know that each "fact" was a total fraud generated by the beguiling mind of the article's author, H. L. Mencken.

As Mencken himself confessed in a 23 May 1926 article, his tongue-in-cheek article, buttressed by its rich if imaginary detail, lodged itself deeply in the popular culture:

> It was reprinted by various great organs of the enlightenment. . . . Pretty soon I began to encounter my preposterous "facts" in the writing of other men. They began to be used by chiropractors and other such quacks as evidence of the stupidity of medical men. They began to be cited by medical men as proof of the progress of public hygiene. They got into learned journals. They were alluded to on the floor of Congress. . . . Finally, I began to find them in standard works of reference. . . .
>
> I recite this history not because it is singular, but because it is typical. It is out of just such frauds, I believe, that most of the so-called knowledge of humanity flows. What begins as a guess—or, perhaps, not infrequently, as a downright and deliberate lie—ends as a fact and is embalmed in the history books.
>
> As a practicing journalist for many years, I have often had close contact with history in the making. I can recall no time or place when what actually occurred was afterward generally known and believed. Sometimes a part of the truth got out, but never all.[2]

Mencken's article is a legend among journalists precisely because it illustrates the staying power of misunderstanding—as well as the chronic inability of corrections to catch up with error, whether deliberate or inadvertent. Let a story contain an erroneous assertion and it will be faithfully clipped and filed in newspaper morgues and public libraries throughout the country—from which it is resurrected by diligent researchers and incorporated anew into more articles, which in turn are filed away to await a new generation of researchers. The correction, or in more serious cases the debunking article, seems in contrast always destined to lie below the fold under someone's birdcage, its nagging presence unseen, unwanted, and unquoted.

It's worth remembering Mencken's hoax today for reasons that go beyond comic relief. Today's media myths have lost none of their power to endure, although they often today assume less amusing forms. Today the prevalent myth is of the Imperial Media, an awesome force that somehow bestride the republic like a colossus, working their will and whim upon a passive populace.

I do not deny that the news media collectively played an important, even a vital role in the unfolding of public policy in the last two decades. But however important that role was, I suggest it was also primarily though not wholly passive. How can we be both powerful and passive? You need look no further than the nearest public address system for an analogy. The amplifier may increase the range of power of the speaker's words, but it has no control over what goes into it.

In a nutshell, we did our job, and generally, we did it very well. We recorded and sometimes catalyzed the great events of these two decades. But we did not cut them from whole cloth.

Let's begin with the most obvious myth, one that even sometimes finds adherents within the communications industry itself: that the news media drove President Richard Nixon from office. This is no place to recount in detail the sordid history of Watergate. But the belief that the news media were somehow the decisive actors in the events that by and large they faithfully recorded flourishes with a strength directly proportional to the believer's misunderstanding of the constitutional process.

It was, after all, federal judge John Sirica who struck the first decisive blow against the Watergate cover-up by sentencing the original burglary defendants to long prison sentences, then commuting them when they broke their conspiracy of silence about the instigators of their squalid caper. The next great acts were the hearings of the House and Senate judiciary committees. While these televised hearings made folk heros of the likes of Senator Sam Ervin and Representative Elizabeth Holtzman, they were not media events devoid of a broader power. They were acts of the most profound constitutional meaning, which the media were privileged to attend and report.

Finally, the U.S. Supreme Court cast the decisive blow by unanimously ruling against President Nixon on the question of the tapes. That set off the final act in this drama in which two of the coequal branches of the federal government, Congress and the judiciary, exercised their classic "checks and balances" role to terminate an unlawful act within the executive branch.

Admittedly, this is one occasion where the notion that the media's role is primarily passive seems contradicted by their own exertions. Obviously, the *Washington Post* exposed many of the early lies with which the White House had tried to sweep the burglary and cover-up under the rug. *Time* magazine and the *New York Times* reported on the wiretapping. The *Baltimore Sun* unearthed irregularities within the Internal Revenue Service. The Dita Beard–ITT connection received considerable attention in our own *Denver Post*, among other outlets. The television networks, while plowing little new ground themselves, did keep the nation's attention riveted on the unfolding events.

But all this activity only highlights the true power of the much-misunderstood "power of the press" on major public policy issues. The media do have power to focus public attention on a problem, to put a subject on the national agenda. But this is distinctly not a power to punish the wicked or to reward the just, save for what good or ill feeling the subjects of a story may privately derive from it. Such punishment or reward must come from other persons and institutions making their independent judgment upon those media revelations. We do not indict, we do not acquit. Newsrooms do not write laws, and paperboys do not enforce them.

Thus it is simply silly to say the media hounded Nixon from office. That gives us far too much credit. The truth hounded Nixon from office. The media merely reported the truth. Congress did not grovel before the pens of outraged editorial writers. It acted because its own investigations, however much they may have been spurred by media revelations, had stirred its own outrage.

The story of the news media and public policy throughout the rest of the 1964–1984 period is much the same—as indeed it was for centuries before and will doubtless be for generations to come. Our power, and it is a great one, is basically the power to put an issue on the public agenda. We are not the sole possessors of that power. But even when we do not initiate the discussion of an item on the public agenda, our decisions as to the reporting of that item can greatly shape its direction, amplifying or diminishing its importance.

That becomes clear if we turn back to the beginning of the era in question, when the great civil rights movement was stirring. The media did not instigate its seminal protest, the Montgomery bus boycott. That began when a black woman, Rosa Parks, had had enough of indignity one day and refused to move to the back of a bus. The media merely reacted, rather laggardly when one considers the scope and duration of the underlying social policies, to a great event already unfolding.

The institution most responsible for putting the question of black dignity on the national agenda was one with which we share the first amendment, the church. Beginning with black religious leaders such as the Reverend Martin Luther King but swiftly spreading to those of white Christian and Jewish groups, ministers and rabbis began denouncing a system of laws and customs violently at war with our Judeo-Christian tradition.

Obviously, the coverage in print and on television of the protests at Selma, Birmingham, and Ole Miss, of such martyrdoms as those of Goodman, Chaney, and Schwerner, and above all the impassioned dignity of King helped arouse the conscience of the American people.

But it's worth noting again that our role was essentially passive. However strongly we might sympathize editorially with their goals and however far we might spread their words, we did not create the Selma marchers. Moreover, victory was theirs only after the other great institutions of American public opinion—the church, the academy, business, labor unions, and political parties—had weighed their message, found it just, and marched by their side.

In debunking the myth that the media exercise awesome power in public affairs, I do not wish to belittle the role we do play. But it is quite clear that however effectively we may serve as amplifiers, and occasionally as catalysts, we are generally not leading actors in the dramas we report and have very little power to determine their outcome.

The contrast between the power to focus public attention on an issue and the power to influence the outcome of the resulting political process is vividly apparent in the very different outcomes of the black civil rights movement and the similar quest a decade later by homosexuals for equal rights. It can be argued that the media gave comparable and fairly respectful coverage to the demands of gay and lesbian leaders. But with the exception of a few scattered local ordinances, homosexuals have had much more limited success in changing their standing in either the law or public opinion than blacks did. In the latter case, our reporting and commentary have simply not convinced the other opinion-molding institutions of society or the public at large to embrace the gay cause. The media can lead the public policy horse to water, but we can't make it drink.

Oddly, the myth that the media somehow determine the outcome of the public agenda hides and obscures just how great our real power is in terms of forming that agenda itself. The power to put an item on the public agenda—or to keep it off—is more than enough power for any one institution in a free society.

Mussolini once mused, "If you give me the power to nominate, you can vote for whomever you please." We similarly tell our readers that we can't tell them what to think. But we have a great deal of influence in deciding what they think or don't think about.

That power is at its most absolute when exercised in the negative. Every day in the newsrooms of print and broadcast media in this country thousands of stories come in begging for a few seconds of airtime or a few inches of print. We select only a small fraction of them. You may disagree vigorously with the opinions or purported facts we do present—but you have little means of knowing about the more numerous items we did not transmit. The latter may well have been the more critical.

As a very simple example, consider the coverage given to the massacre of Moslem refugees in Beirut by Christian Phalangists. Much criticism was vented upon Israel for not acting more decisively to prevent such slaughter. The day the Israelis released their own official report on the massacre—one that sharply criticized their own government for its indirect complicity—our wire services at the *Post* bulged with nearly seventy different accounts of that report.

I don't think we really need to write editorials and columns saying that the Beirut massacres were bad. People in general don't like massacres and if the question, "Should we stop massacres in Beirut?" is put on the public agenda, then the answer is inevitable. But why was there no similar outcry over the massacres at Ad Judayl or Hama?

Ad Judayl is—or more precisely, was—a town in Iraq where, on July 11, 1982, someone made an assassination attempt on Iraqi dictator Saddam Hussein. According to a five-inch article in the London magazine *The Economist* five months later, Hussein responded much as Hitler did in destroying the village of Lidice, Czechoslovakia, after the assassination of Reinhard Heydrich.

The British newsmagazine reported: "There were about 150 casualties in the two hours of fighting that followed the attempted assassination. After that, 150 families simply disappeared. The remaining men were sent off to northern Iraq, the women and children were sent south. Bulldozers then demolished the town."

A check of *Post* wire services and a computerized data-base search of American newspapers and magazines produced absolutely nothing about this event. We did base an editorial on the *Economist* article and what little we were able to learn from our own independent sources about the Ad Judayl massacre. But it is clear that the general decision to regard the massacre in Iraq as non-news and the massacre in Beirut as news had a profound effect on U.S. foreign policy in the region.

Little more attention was given in American media to a far worse massacre in Hama, a city in Syria where the Moslem Brotherhood had mobilized opposition to the rule of Hafez Assad. Assad surrounded the city with troops and opened fire with artillery rather indiscriminately. Reports that reached us through Japanese newspapers later indicated that between 5,000 and 10,000 people died—mostly innocent people caught in the crossfire. Yet U.S. media paid very little attention to the event.

Such events are not suppressed as a result of a conscious conspiracy. But they do reflect a sense of what journalists think is important in selecting items for the public agenda, and those choices do influence the outcome of public policy. If every Israeli misdeed is to be analyzed in exhaustive detail and every atrocity of its most bitter foes is to be overlooked, it can be safely predicted that ultimately the U.S.-Israeli "special relationship" will be undermined.

Paradoxically, it is the fairly open societies, such as Israel, that receive the often unwelcome microscopic examination. Reporters can get into the country, talk to victims and survivors, film with only a minimum of censorship, and report in voluminous detail. Contrast that to the fact that it took five months for even the most minimum account of the Ad Judayl massacre to leak out of the tightly closed Iraqi society. When such facts do emerge, they are difficult to verify and have lost much of their timeliness.

Still, I think the media in general do a fair job of setting that public agenda. It is fortunate that the media in this country are quite numerous and diverse. Thus critical issues have a way of being thrust upon us by our own brethren. Much of the intellectual agenda actually comes from small journals of opinion, such as the *National Review, Commentary, The New Republic,* or the numerous outpourings of liberal and conservative think tanks such as the Brookings Institution or the Heritage Foundation. Their readership is small but highly concentrated within the mass media.

To a substantial degree the initiatives of the Great Society were a success. But because the media used its agenda power in a negative way, the public was left with an overriding impression that they failed. That, in turn, may have profoundly influenced the political climate to usher in the so-called "Reagan revolution" of the 1980s.

Let me quote from John Schwarz, associate professor of political science at the University of Arizona, in *The New Republic:*

> The War on Poverty decisively changed the living conditions facing the poor. Programs such as food stamps virtually eliminated serious malnutrition among low-income children and adults in America. Medicaid and Medicare greatly increased the access of low-income Americans to health care. In turn, the enlargement of both the nutritional and medical programs led to a decline in the infant mortality rate among minority Americans of 40 percent between 1965 and 1975, a drop that was eight times larger than the decline that had taken place in the ten years prior to 1965. The expansion of governmental housing programs helped to reduce the

proportion of Americans living in overcrowded housing from 12
percent in 1960 to 5 percent in 1980. Those living in substandard
housing declined from 20 percent to 8 percent.

If that's true, then how did the popular impression emerge that
the War on Poverty was a failure? That impression did much to aid
the success of Reagan's attack on what he called "the failed policies of the past."[3]

To a great extent, such success stories just did not make good copy.
Editors and reporters did not aggressively pursue them. The negative
side of our policy role showed its power because people were not made
aware of these successes.

Of course, it must be said that one reason the media did not declare
a victory in the War on Poverty is because its own generals were so busy
crying defeat. The Pentagon doesn't march into a congressional budget
hearing and loudly proclaim that the Red Army couldn't fight its way
out of a wet paper bag. The administrators of the War on Poverty were
no less canny in the bureaucratic infighting, trying to bestir Congress to
increase their budgets by focusing on the magnitude of yet unsolved
problems. Many minority leaders, fueled by a sense of frustration over
what remained undone, similarly belittled the genuine progress that had
been made. Once again we see the media's role in public policy being
essentially the passive one of transmitting the ideas of others—even
when exercising our greatest power of deciding what stories to ignore.

Let's close by discussing issues great and issues small: the tragedy of
Vietnam and Gerald Ford's tendency to bump his head. Taking the
latter first, we get a small glimpse of the fairly inadvertent exercise of
media power.

Ford was actually our most athletic president since Teddy Roosevelt.
It's a fact that even the best skiers fall down occasionally, let alone one
of his age. The rule that the exceptional tends to make news dictated
that those pictures would be given disproportionate play—and that the
public would pay more attention to them than to shots showing the
president gliding smoothly down a slope. Thus an impression was created
of clumsiness—which then led photographers and the public to watch
eagerly for more such inevitable incidents, which reinforced the erroneous stereotype. The image became a kind of metaphor for his administration.

The same rule applies, of course, to the verbal "faux pas." James
Watt actually did say some sensible things in his stormy tenure. But
his love for the vivid and polarizing remark soon had everyone waiting

to pounce upon further controversial remarks. A public figure who gets into too many controversies simply reaches a point where he can't avoid them because he's subjected to an intense scrutiny by journalists looking for a "there he goes again" story.

The power to stereotype and to ridicule has a potent effect on the course of public policy. Once again, however, a media image need not in itself be decisive to a politician who carefully tends his base. Jesse Helms has certainly received a generous dose of such treatment, yet he succeeded in his 1984 race for Senate reelection.

What then of the seminal media issue of this turbulent period: Vietnam. Its complex history shows evidence of all the issues we have discussed so far. Obviously, the news media didn't put the war itself on the agenda. Presidents Kennedy and Johnson deployed the troops. By and large, the media didn't begin the chorus of protest either, though that protest was often carefully crafted to attract the attention of the press.

But the power of setting agenda still showed at key points. The Viet Cong and North Vietnamese terror campaigns that killed thousands of local leaders and their families received scant attention in American media. But the picture of General Loan executing the Viet Cong suspect went worldwide. The My Lai massacre was intensely reported, as it should have been. But once again, a relatively open society found its warts displayed before the world while a closed one basically limited the message of its atrocities to those they were intended to terrorize. The power of stereotype and ridicule showed clearly in coverage of the inept South Vietnamese regimes, particularly in the era of frequent coups that followed the assassination of Ngo Dihn Diem.

In retrospect, it is clear that the Tet offensive of 1968 was an enormous military defeat for the Viet Cong, which lost so much of its cadre that it had to turn over the main battlefield role to North Vietnamese main force units. But it was a tremendous psychological victory for the National Liberation Front and North Vietnamese and broke the back of American public support for the war. Many media critics have used this as a key example of how ignorance of military history, sensationalism, and the rush to deadlines in the media can distort the path of public policy.

Even more basic, many thoughtful analysts argue that the U.S. defeat in Vietnam stemmed from its being the first war fought in the living room. Advances in technology made it very easy to cover the war and plaster ugly images across the nineteen-inch color screen.

Yet even the lessons of Vietnam are at least ambiguous. It's worth noting that even before the Tet offensive the United States had been involved in Vietnam longer than our entire fighting role in World War II. And Tet was hardly the first time we'd been caught with our pants down by a supposedly beaten enemy. Remember the Battle of the Bulge? Yet the Nazi Ardennes offensive only served to stiffen American resolve to destroy the Hitler regime. Why did Tet weaken our resolve in Vietnam?

One of the best analysts of that war, Colonel Harry Summers, Jr., has argued,

> Our failure in Vietnam mostly grew out of a lack of appreciation of military theory and military strategy, and especially the relationship between military strategy and national policy.
>
> By failing to mobilize the national will behind the Vietnam War, our national leaders ignored Clausewitz's precept that war is a continuation of national policy by other means.
>
> American leaders deliberately excluded people from their role in selecting the political object—the reason for fighting the war. Not only did the Johnson administration fail to declare war; it sought to commit American troops to combat as imperceptibly as possible, lulling the American people into forgetting that a war was on. It was not surprising that Washington's resolve collapsed after Tet-68. What is surprising is that it did not collapse much earlier. We must relearn that public support is critical to American military strategy.[4]

Former secretary of state Dean Rusk has stated that President Johnson deliberately forswore stirring up patriotic sentiment over Vietnam because he was afraid of arousing a conservative political tide that would hinder his liberal Great Society programs domestically. Whether that would have happened is debatable. What is not debatable is that the president called the people to arms with an uncertain trumpet. The media did not create this ambiguity in public policy. They could not and should not have avoided reporting it.

After all, technological flourishes aside, the media today aren't really so different from their predecessors in their power to inform and arouse emotion. Someone once quipped that "Marshall McLuhan says the printed word is obsolete. He wrote eighteen books to prove it."

Can it really be said that it took television to expose the horror and ugliness of war? Did Stephen Crane write *The Red Badge of Courage* for nothing? Didn't *All Quiet on the Western Front* and other works expose the stupidity and slaughter of World War I? Didn't Ernie Pyle and a generation of combat reporters expose all too vividly the horror of Guadalcanal, of Tarawa, of Omaha Beach? Yet the public bore the burden of those wars because the same media that reported their horror were used by their political leaders to justify their necessity.

In summation, I should say that as the Mencken piece shows an enduring myth takes on a kind of reality of its own. It is an overstatement to say that in politics the perception of power is power, because there can be power in the unperceived as well. But while the media's power in public policy is both misunderstood and overrated, the very fact that politicians and others themselves tend to believe in it tends to reinforce it. They may overrate our ability to influence public opinion, as distinct from reporting it, but they do assign some weight to our opinions.

But in the end, it is the broader reality that we try to report that decides the outcome of public policy, not reporting itself. Just ask President Thomas E. Dewey.

Social Science and the Great Society
RICHARD P. NATHAN

Science! True daughter of Old Time thou art! Who alterest all things with thy peering eyes.—Edgar Allan Poe, 1829

One of the by-products of the Great Society was the creation of the public policy research industry. It was well fed and grew large. Now, like the social programs of the same period, it is on a greatly reduced—some would say starvation—diet. There is, moreover, growing skepticism about the contribution of social science research in the field of domestic policy. Conservatives generally do not like social science research, yet they often use the results to raise sharp questions about social programs. On the other hand, liberals who generally like and support social science research are increasingly worried about its results and applications. In a December 1983 radio address, President Reagan said, "There is no question that many well-intentioned Great Society-type programs contributed to family break-ups, welfare dependency, and a large increase in births out of wedlock."[1] Although the president's radio

I have tried out the ideas in this essay on a number of wise and understanding colleagues. Appreciation is expressed to Charles F. Adams, Jr., Orley C. Ashenfelter, Rebecca M. Blank, Barbara B. Blum, Shepard Forman, Eli Ginzberg, Judith M. Gueron, Sar A. Levitan, Laurel McFarland, Gilbert S. Omenn, Robert D. Reischauer, Robert Solow, Steve B. Steib, George Sternlieb, and Raymond Vernon.

address did not specify the sources for these conclusions, most social scientists who work on domestic policy issues have a pretty good idea of the history and studies to which the president's comments refer.

As indicated, it is not just conservatives who have found fault with the Great Society. An important postmortem of the Great Society that focuses on social science research is the book by Henry Aaron, *Politics and the Professors: The Great Society in Perspective*. The book has on the cover a caricature of a pointing professor who looks quite a bit like the author. He is being inundated by what looks like waves of the Red Sea, which, to continue the metaphor, parted for a while but had rolled over the professors by 1978, the year in which the book was published. In his foreword, Brookings Institution president Bruce K. MacLaury says of Aaron's book: "He finds that faith and beliefs, not research, are the real basis for commitment to social reform. In his view, research tends to be a conservative force because it fosters skepticism and caution by shifting attention from moral commitment to analytical problems that rarely have clear-cut or simple solutions."[2]

Aaron in this book talks about "the corrosive role of research and experimentation."[3] In the final analysis, he says, the combination of external events (Vietnam, Watergate, etc.) and the failures of social programs as documented by researchers brought about "the demise of the simple faiths of the early 1960s."[4]

Henry Aaron's skeptical conclusion about the uses and usefulness of social science in the Great Society period are important to this inquiry. He is a distinguished practitioner. I use his book as the jumping-off point for this essay because the book is widely known (and rightly so) and because I want to contrast Aaron's quite pessimistic conclusion in *Politics and the Professors* with the more upbeat and hopeful view of the same subject presented here.

The major themes of this essay are (1) there are lessons to be learned from the application of social science to social policy-making in the Great Society period; (2) if we heed these lessons, there is reason to be more hopeful than Henry Aaron was in *Politics and the Professors* about the applications of social science to social policy-making; (3) the key to this brighter future is a greater emphasis on large, interdisciplinary evaluation and demonstration studies that link quantitative and qualitative research techniques and data; (4) we should view such major interdisciplinary social science research undertakings as agents for institutional change; and (5) we need to disaggregate when we examine the history and prospects for applied social science.

I begin with an organizational scheme for distinguishing among the various major approaches to applied social science. Some social science policy research is *analytical*—that is, researchers examine social and economic conditions and how they have evolved and can be understood. *Evaluation* studies examine how particular programs work. Still other studies are *demonstrations* to test new approaches to social problems. The disciplinary equipment, epistemological mind-sets, and political preconceptions of researchers also vary.

I have been thinking about the experience of social science researchers in the field of domestic affairs in a way that involves an H-shaped grid as shown in the following diagram.

Type of Study			Qualitative
Analytical Studies (Assessments of conditions and trends)	Type 1	}	Type 2
Evaluation Studies (Assessments of policy changes that have occurred)	Type 3	IMMUTABLE BOUNDARY	Type 4
Demonstration Studies (Assessments of policy changes that are proposed for wider application)	Type 5	IMMUTABLE BOUNDARY	Type 6

Analytical studies. The first line in the diagram represents analytical studies. I use this term to refer to domestic policy studies on conditions and trends. At research centers and schools of public policy, such studies are often seen as "defining the problem," the presumption being that policy analysts can then test (using simulations and demonstrations) various alternative solutions to the problem.

I have difficulty with this problem-solution metaphor. Social scientists who specialize in domestic policy studies not surprisingly tend to *believe in* government, though there are more exceptions to this generalization now than there were in the heady Great Society days. While they may not admit to this, or even think very hard about it, a subtle bias exists in an approach where liberal domestic policy analysts discover and publicize a problem as a way of building up a head of steam for solving it. Policy analysts are not without political savvy, and should

avoid being tied to a progovernment conception of their role. For domestic policy researchers particularly, the best strategy is to characterize
analytical studies as studies of conditions and trends, rather than as
studies of problems.

Type 1 studies. Type 1 studies in the diagram are those that are intended to produce systematic, objective statements about social and
economic conditions and trends. It is useful to divide these studies into
two subcategories—general studies by domestic policy analysts covering
a broad field or functional area and relying on secondary data, and
specific and more focused analytical studies that may involve the collection of original data.

The general kind of public policy writing burgeoned in the mid-
sixties. The most notable expression of this development was the plan-
ning-programming-budgeting-system (PPBS) applied in typically grandiose fashion by Lyndon Johnson when he ordered in August 1965 that
the entire federal government adopt the PPB system. This kind of broad-
gauged policy analysis writing by social scientists also emerged outside
of government. One prominent example is the work done in the Brookings budget books, the annual *Setting National Priorities* volumes that
began in 1970. The Brookings model of an annual volume of analytical
essays by knowledgeable, conscientiously objective analysts became a new
genre for think tanks, with similar volumes published by the American
Enterprise Institute, the Hoover Institution, the Heritage Foundation,
the Urban Institute, etc. In fact, this motif has been adopted so widely
that it has become old hat. There are only so many ways to write an
overview analysis of health, welfare, the environment, jobs, cities, education. After a while, the Brookings budget books and others like them
lose their attention-getting value. When the Brookings budget volumes
first came out, they were the subject of large press conferences and extensive media coverage. Now, fourteen volumes later, they have much
less impact. Considerable time and energy are devoted to this kind of
broad-gauged domestic policy writing by social scientists interested in
applied work. Some of these resources, I believe, could be more produc-
tively devoted to other types of domestic policy studies.

Specific policy analysis studies range from "cubiclized" social science
papers (one social scientist, one discipline, one terminal, one article) to
larger studies that cross disciplinary boundaries. The latter can involve
original data collection and observations and yield a number of prod-
ucts—some with important policy applications.[5] My concern applies to

studies in this group that have a highly theoretical focus and little relevance to real-world conditions.

Type 2 studies. The label of type 2 policy studies in the H-shaped grid above is "Analytical/Qualitative." This category, as in the case of the categories above, gets at a basic point about the way social scientists treat values and qualitative data. The predominant emphasis of academic social science, both in classrooms and journals, even for practitioners with applied interests, is on rigorous proof in a Cartesian fashion. (Descartes was a mathematician.) Qualities that cannot be defined and measured carry little weight.

In recent years, however, there has been a gradual but steady increase in writing by academic social scientists who are challenging these traditions. Economist Donald N. McCloskey argues that the actual behavior of economists differs markedly from their official methodology.[6] McCloskey says, despite the fact that the official methodology of economics is what he calls the "modernist view" or "the credo of Scientific Method," that economists

> in fact argue on wider grounds, and should. Their genuine, workaday rhetoric, the way they argue inside their heads or their seminar rooms, diverges from the official rhetoric, because they will then better know why they agree to disagree, and will find it less easy to dismiss contrary arguments on merely methodological grounds.[7]

A good way to nail down this point is to note that much type 1 policy writing (especially the general studies), as McCloskey points out, actually is highly qualitative. Although the type 2 category in the H-shaped grid may suggest to readers the work of advocates and polemicists using "impressionistic"[8] data, hard thinking and honest reflection about current practice, I submit, would result in classifying much of what purports to be type 1 policy writing in the same way. This is the subtle point expressed by the wavy line in the H-shaped grid above.

EVALUATION

The second main heading in the diagram denotes evaluation studies. This is an area on which, I argue, we should place greater emphasis in a manner that blends quantitative and qualitative techniques and data. It is in this section that the "Immutable Boundary" in the diagram first enters into our consideration. The war between the "crunchers" (column 1 of the diagram) and the case studies (column 2) has produced a no-man's land of intellectual and professional danger. Battles occur *between* disciplines and *within* disciplines. Two main categories of evaluation studies—quantitative and qualitative—are discussed below.

Type 3 studies. Einstein once said, "I have little patience with scientists who take a board of wood, look for its thinnest part, and drill a great number of holes where the drilling is easy."[9] The research that Henry Aaron wrote about so critically in *Politics and the Professors* consists in large measure of type 3 domestic policy evaluation studies in which the crunching is done where the crunching is easiest. Statistical variables (mainly demographic and economic variables) are used extensively and systematically. Political and institutional variables, because they cannot be measured and hence are qualitative, are left out or treated in a cavalier manner. Complaints about this situation are frequently made by noneconomists. Fortunately, a number of respected economists have recently been making the same point.

In a brilliant book-essay, *The Moon and the Ghetto: An Essay on Public Policy Analysis,* Richard Nelson reviewed the three main traditions of policy analysis (economic, organization, and "R and D") and his conclusion has important implications for evaluation studies.[10] Nelson found all three traditions wanting and said that domestic policy research at its best indicates the need for and often the best approach to *institutional change.* His emphasis on this institutional dimension in the conduct and use of policy research can also be expressed in terms of a *systems approach*—a focus for evaluation research that includes both analytics and institutional knowledge and blends the two in creative ways.

To do this—to take institutional factors into account—requires new kinds of research designs. They can work in a number of ways. One is to begin with a quantitative study and then interpret and use the findings in a manner that brings careful and thorough process and institutional (qualitative) studies into the picture. Another way this linkage can be made is to conduct a systematic qualitative evaluation and then examine and test the findings with quantitative techniques.[11] There are, of course, other ways these connections can be made, relating both to basic research design and the many details involved in the planning and execution of policy research projects.

The idea that we should make such linkages on an explicit basis is a more comfortable one for sociologists and political scientists, but it also has an important place in the history of economics. Beginning in the thirties, University of Wisconsin economist John R. Commons stressed the importance of institutions to understanding public-sector economics. Commons defined institutions as involving "collective action in control of individual action."[12] He further suggests that "this control of the acts of one individual always results in, and is intended to result in, a benefit to other individuals. . . . Or, the collective control takes the form of a tabu or prohibition of certain acts. . . ." Commons advocates understanding the institutional context—the "working Rules" which "indicate what individuals can, must, or may, do, or not do, enforced by collective sanctions."[13]

This failure to take into account the institutional dimension of public policy is a serious deficiency of many evaluation studies by social scientists. The major evaluation studies of the sixties in the field of elementary and secondary education, reviewed by Henry Aaron in *Politics and the Professors*, illustrate the point. Aaron criticized these evaluation studies (for example, Coleman, Rand Corporation, Jencks)[14] as too narrow; they were typically cross-sectional (point-in-time) studies based on existing available statistical data.

In a vein similar to Aaron's discussion in *Politics and the Professors*, Alice Rivlin in the early seventies criticized evaluation studies in the field of higher education. She said, "The higher education studies were weakened by an almost complete absence of behavioral information."[15]

Type 3 evaluation studies of the type discussed above use *strong* mathematical techniques to assess the effects of *small* treatments with *weak* data. This approach is inexpensive; such studies can be conducted by small groups of researchers or individual researchers. There is often no cost for data collection and (alas!) for field investigation. This kind of research inspired Wassily Leontief's famous lament. Leontief wrote to the editors of *Science* magazine in 1982 complaining about academic economics, saying, "the king is naked . . . no one dares to speak up." His point was that government statistics are too weak to be used for high-powered scientific research. Said Leontief, "Page after page of professional economic journals are filled with mathematical formulations leading the reader from sets of more or less plausible but entirely arbitrary assumptions to precisely stated but irrelevant theoretical conclusions."[16]

Type 4 studies. I use the term "qualitative" in this essay in a way that is conservative from the point of view of my argument. The category is not limited to discursive writing. It is defined to include studies that use *numbers* (dollars spent, people served, types of recipients and programs) as well as *words* (big, small, new, old). For my purposes here, the distinction between studies under this heading and studies classified as quantitative is that qualitative studies are not set up in a way that enables the researcher to use conventional statistical tests of probability to establish—or at least infer—causality and proof.

The bulk of research, beginning a dozen years ago at Brookings, fits the type 4 category. I refer to what we have termed "field network evaluation studies." These studies are in effect similarly structured case studies conducted by a group of economists and political scientists to evaluate the effects of major changes in the domestic policies of the U.S. national government.

In these studies we have modeled the counterfactual in that most powerful of all computers, the human brain. Independent field researchers observe how jurisdictions are affected by specific federal policy changes, comparing observed outcomes to what they (the field researchers) have determined would otherwise have occurred. Each study began when the new federal policy was adopted and has involved a representative (not random) sample of forty or more state and local governments. Our focus is on the *effects* of the policy changes studied on the sample governments and the people they serve. We have studied four types of effects—fiscal, programmatic, incidence, and institutional. In some instances we have had opportunities to change field researchers, to duplicate field observations, and to estimate the range of confidence the field researchers have in their impact assessments, but we have not used statistical techniques in the conventional way to assign probabilities to the results obtained.

Moreover, these field evaluation studies came up with what many politicians and interest group officials felt (or came to feel) were straightforward, credible, and useful results for the programs involved. The fungibility point mentioned earlier is a good illustration of this point. Many members of Congress, particularly liberals, wanted money from revenue-sharing to be used for "innovation" (whatever that means) and for "good" (whatever that means). They thought that the substitution of shared revenue for taxes that otherwise would have been raised was bad. One of the things our study of revenue-sharing did was to clear the air on this issue. We argued that U.S. Treasury Department data on the use of shared revenue (based on self-administered reports by state and local officials) were absurd. You have to wrestle with the concept of substitution to make any sense out of the use of revenue-sharing funds. Furthermore, this wrestling match is best waged at the local level, with researchers on the scene using local records and budget data and interviewing local officials. There are no data available from the U.S. Bureau of the Census or other federal agency that provide the kind of uniform and detailed information needed to answer the crucial questions about the effects of federal grant-in-aid programs. All of the researchers in the field network for the Brookings study of revenue-sharing were using the same conceptual apparatus to study substitution under revenue-sharing at the state and local levels.

The field researchers not only presented their conclusions about the impact of revenue-sharing, they also indicated the reasons *why* a particular state or local government responded as it did to the new revenue-sharing program. They identified the most important institutional and political factors shaping government behavior.

The complementarity principle as applied to field evaluations. These field evaluation studies do not represent the full agenda of the interdisciplinary group that conducted these projects. This research led to experiments with new approaches that suggest the potential for linking qualitative and quantitative research. One of the researchers, Steven B. Steib of the University of Tulsa, made the following summary points about the way we view this linkage.[17]

(1) To achieve scientific power, qualitative research requires a set of conventions for its conduct. Unfortunately, such a consensus does not exist; this set of conventions continues to evolve experimentally.

(2) In order to conform to the falsification principle, quantitative studies are limited to levels of generality and central tendency which are often uninteresting and usually omit important information subsumed in terms such as "error term" and "covariance."

(3) Qualitative studies, although lacking in scientific pedigree, are rich in content beyond the confines of the central limit theorem.

(4) Let the future be one in which qualitative studies provide the understanding upon which useful formal modeling can be done. Let qualitative research create hypotheses, lists of important variable, and tentative conclusions. Quantitative researchers can then attach this meat to their ever-changing skeletons and subject it to the falsification criteria.

Steib's fourth point is the most important one for this essay. We have applied this point about using qualitative studies as the basis for conducting large quantitative studies in our research. In two of our studies, after we had finished the field analysis, we used national statistical data and regression techniques, closely tied to the field evaluation studies, to check our findings—specifically about the impact of the new general revenue-sharing and CETA public jobs programs.

These "complementary" studies seek the best of both worlds. The essential rationale for this work is that a researcher is not likely to know how to use statistical data (for example, U.S. Census of Government data) to study revenue-sharing—to model the counterfactual and study the program's effects—unless and until he has been out there wrestling with this bear in his cave. Several field researchers, notably Charles F. Adams, Jr., Dan Crippen, Robert F. Cook, Arthur Maurice, V. Lane Rawlins, and Michael Wiseman designed and conducted complementary statistical studies of the revenue-sharing and CETA jobs program that used lessons and insights from the field analyses to devise a better statistical research design for econometric studies of program impacts. Fortunately for us, their findings were quite similar to what we found in the field evaluations.

The work done on the displacement effect of the CETA public service jobs program (at one time operating at nearly $8 billion per year) is the most interesting. Previous econometric studies on the actual and potential effects of federally aided public service job-creation programs had come to the conclusion that eventually all or nearly all of these federal aid funds become substitutive. That is, the recipient state and local jurisdictions eventually use all of this aid to employ workers who would have been employed anyway. We found a very much lower displacement rate (around 20 to 25 percent) both in our field study and in the statistical study linked to the field evaluation. We then went back and identified the assumptions used in the econometric models that caused the difference. We found the assumptions involved to be a function of a lack of understanding of governmental institutions and processes on the part of those conducting the econometric studies. The interested reader can refer to the literature on this piece of social science history.[18] The point, I believe, is that greater power was obtained by linking institutional and statistical studies.

DEMONSTRATION STUDIES

The term "demonstration studies," as used in this essay, refers to research projects where a given treatment is administered for the purpose of assessing its impact and learning about its costs and benefits. A demonstration research project is in effect a more elaborate study, typically with a randomly selected control group, that tests a new program or program idea; while an evaluation study assesses an ongoing program and may use comparison sites, but generally does not have a randomly selected control group.

Type 5 studies. During the early seventies a group of policy experts was assembled by Mitchell Sviridoff, then vice-president of the Ford Foundation, to wrestle with the challenge of how to conduct a large-scale demonstration study with random assignment to test the so-called supported work approach for aiding underclass groups. The supported work approach is a job-focused "treatment" characterized by graduated stress and peer-group support to aid severely disadvantaged persons in entering the labor market.

Although originally recruited as an advisory committee, the group found it necessary to become incorporated. In this way it could serve as an intermediary to receive funds from several government agencies and foundations to conduct the supported work demonstration.

Over ten thousand people participated in the treatment and control groups for this demonstration. They were divided into four groups—long-term female welfare family heads, ex-offenders, ex-addicts, and problem youths. There is a six-foot-long shelf of reports, books, papers, and articles on this demonstration.[19]

The Manpower Demonstration Research Corporation operates much like a university seminar in a way that is both useful and intellectually enriching.[20] Over the ten years of its operation MDRC has conducted seven major national demonstrations. It is now engaged in new demonstration projects with random assignment that in my view are very promising for applied social science.

MDRC's newest demonstration, the work-welfare demonstration, was initiated in 1982 to test the efficacy of "workfare" and related provisions included in the Omnibus Budget Reconciliation act of 1981. This Reagan initiative involves a fundamental shift in concept from welfare to so-called workfare for the Aid to Families with Dependent Children (AFDC) program, a shift that could not have been adopted in the Great Society period and was resisted under both Nixon and Ford. Qualified AFDC family heads in this MDRC demonstration are initially assigned to an intensive job-search program. If the job-search phase is unsuccessful for a particular recipient, it is then followed by mandatory assignment to a low-skilled public service job, usually for up to six months. Typically, participants work for the number of hours each week that equals their welfare grant divided by the minimum wage. Other qualified welfare family heads in the test areas are randomly assigned to a control group whose members do not receive either intensive job-search assistance or a mandatory public service job.

To date, MDRC has found based on interviews that both participants and controls *want* public service jobs and believe that it is "fair" to require welfare recipients to work. Other studies (for example, Goodwin) have made similar findings.[21]

Following John R. Commons's and Richard R. Nelson's point about the need to take institutional considerations into account in policy research, the design for the MDRC work-welfare project includes both intensive process and impact studies. We are interested in the welfare *system*. How could the welfare system be changed in ways that would reduce welfare dependency and enhance the public credibility and acceptability of these transfer payments? In this case the research target has been chosen on a basis that views the role of research as a potential institutional change agent in an area where basic systems changes are widely felt to be needed.

This demonstration is being conducted with large enough samples in several states that we can compare the way the programs and systems work or don't work in each area. The staff for process analysis at MDRC, along with on-site contract researchers, are collecting uniform information on the way these programs work—the participants, the jobs provided, the experience of participants on the job, the types of work involved, the structure and management of the job-search and job programs, to name some of the prominent areas of the process studies.

In short, this demonstration has been designed to take full advantage of the variation among the states in order to go beyond what has been done previously to *link* impact and process research. This study has other attributes that build on past experience with demonstrations. We are cutting costs (the supported-work demonstration was expensive) by using administrative reporting data in the research. The hope is that we will learn about welfare in both behavioral and institutional terms in a way that will provide valuable lessons for policy.

This work-welfare demonstration is important for the general point made at the outset of this essay that I am more hopeful about the uses and usefulness of applied social science—if we do the job right—than was Henry Aaron in *Politics and the Professors*. Other demonstrations now being planned by MDRC (notably, a youth initiative focused on alternative school institutions) build on the corporation's experience and draw upon the lessons discussed here.

The first large-scale demonstration conducted by MDRC—the supported work demonstration—was important in the same way as current efforts.

I believe, however, these kinds of large interdisciplinary studies can be even more successful if two conditions are met, conditions that were only partially met in the case of the supported work demonstration. The two conditions involve research design and strategy. First, more should have been done in the supported-work demonstration to link the process and impact studies. The second condition involves the selection of the demonstration research subject. In that case, the demonstration may not have had sufficiently deep roots in Washington and around the country.

To sharpen the point, it is my opinion that the subjects of large interdisciplinary demonstrations must be very carefully selected with the goal in view that "success" could attract enough political support to cause the generalization of the demonstration findings. The supported-work demonstration (highly successful for welfare mothers) has influenced state and local policy and the literature. But it did involve a relatively expensive program that because of its cost has not been as widely adopted as some of its advocates would have liked. In these terms, relating to the politics of the selection of major demonstration research targets, it is hoped that the current and similar MDRC work-welfare demonstration will have wider applicability, because the basic idea involved has deep and broad public support. This point, of course, depends on the results of this demonstration.

Type 6 studies. I do not have much to say about this final category ("Demonstration/Qualitative"). It makes me think of Woody Allen and the expression, "So what else is new?" Perhaps the reference is too obscure. The point is that the idea of conducting so-called demonstrations to learn about new programs and approaches has been abused for a long time. It has often been used as an excuse for inexpensive, politically focused programs that are not the least bit serious about anything even resembling research. Some may call this a qualitative demonstration; I would not do so.

The status of demonstration research. In the late sixties there was a flurry of activity and interest at the Brookings Institution in the conduct of large-scale demonstration studies led by Alice Rivlin, who directed the Brookings Studies in Social Experimentation. In this period, Rivlin wrote a book on social research, based on the 1970 H. Rowan Gaither Lectures, in which she argued that "systematic experimentation must be an important federal activity if we are to achieve breakthroughs in social service delivery."[22] Note Rivlin's references here to social ser-

vices. Most social experiments of this period, however, focused on income-maintenance or transfer programs (welfare, housing, health). Disillusionment with the results and uses of these studies cooled the ardor of practitioners for experimental studies. The MDRC demonstrations begun in the mid-seventies, based on Rivlin's comment quoted above, are focused on service programs. This in my view is desirable.

Despite the difficulty and expense involved, social scientists interested in applied work need to think again and very hard about the value of large-scale demonstration studies with random assignment that have a system's focus on critical social service areas.

Concluding comments on applied social science. Social science is one among many inputs to social policy. It was never otherwise. Yet there was a period of wistful expectation—a Camelot for social science—when many practitioners believed it could be more than that, a determinant in and of itself of new policy directions or, if not that, the input with a presumed special claim and higher standing than others in the policy-making process.

When we place research as an input to domestic policy in its proper perspective, the conclusion I draw is not so much that social science has an inherently conservative effect (Aaron's theme), as that we as a generation of social scientists have learned a great deal from our experience that must now influence our practice. Returning to the H-shaped grid used as the analytical scheme for this essay, my conclusion can be summarized as follows: Social scientists interested in research applications should put *less* emphasis on two kinds of studies—type 1a general analytical studies and type 1b specific analytical studies that are primarily theoretical. Likewise, they should *not* become involved in type 6 demonstration studies that are substitutes for establishing small and politically targeted programs and that use research as a guise for doing so.

More emphasis, on the other hand, should be placed on evaluation and demonstration research—specifically research done in (or at least close to) the critical boundary area between type 3 (quantitative) and type 4 (qualitative) evaluation studies. More emphasis should also be placed on type 5 demonstration studies that combine quantitative and qualitative research designs and techniques. The subject areas for these types of studies should be carefully chosen, with major attention given to their policy relevance and potential applications. As a general rule, subjects should be selected to focus on *systems* on a basis where applied social science has a potential for being an *institutional change agent.*

The task of bringing about such a shift in the targets of applied social science ultimately falls on the shoulders of the government agencies and foundations that pay for applied social science. Skillfully developed strategies on their part could have a positive effect on the industry— that is, on research universities and nonprofit centers for social science policy research. Major applied research projects, for example, could be organized to enable researchers to carve out pieces of the design and analysis in a way that would lead to coordinated, individually authored articles and books suitable for review and assessment in line with the standards of academic social science departments that award advanced degrees and tenure.

Although I believe we can be creative in these terms without being radical, I am fully aware that the terrain is difficult and that the job would not be easy or the process of institutional change rapid. The pay-off, however, could be appreciable for public policy and governance. There is reason to hope that research funders in the process of trying to do this would attract greater numbers of capable social scientists to applied work. Many readers of the mainline journals in the social sciences would agree that such an outcome—promoting a better balance between theoretical and applied work—would be desirable for its own sake.

In sum, the aim of this prescription is that applied social science would come to have a greater *impact*. Within the field of applied social science, more emphasis would be placed on empiricism and opportunities for replication, as opposed to policy studies undertaken by social scientists that in reality are very similar to the kinds of things politicians and their aides do in the normal discourse of politics in order to make an argument. This does not mean that social scientists should avoid becoming involved as participants or experts in government policy-making. My view is that the two roles—policy expert and policy researcher—can and should be distinguished, and that greater priority should be assigned to the role of social scientists as applied researchers on the bases indicated in this chapter.

At the end of *Gulliver's Travels* Jonathan Swift has a wonderful piece of satire, meant to apply to the British Royal Academy, that has an eerie relevance for modern social science. He describes a voyage to Laputa and a visit to its major metropolis, Lagado. Everything in the kingdom of Laputa is in a state of disrepair and decay. Meanwhile experts in the Grand Academy of Lagado are at work on projects so that "all the fruits of the earth shall come to maturity, at whatever season we think fit to chuse, and encrease a hundred fold more than they do at present; with inumerable other happy proposals."[23]

The author visits the Grand Academy, and among the academicians he meets there my favorite is a man "with meagre aspect, with sooty hands and face; his hair and beard long, ragged and singed in several places." The author explains that this academician "had been eight years upon a project for extracting sunbeams out of cucumbers; which were to be put into vials, hermetically sealed, and let out to warm the air, in raw inclement summers."

I shall spare readers an account of the other fruitless projects being pursued at the Grand Academy of Lagado. The moral of this story for me is that social science researchers need to get out of their laboratories and give more attention to real-world conditions. In particular, social scientists interested in applied work in domestic affairs need to give more attention to institutions and especially to the link between institutional change and behavioral change. It is not enough to study impacts if we do not have a deep understanding of the real-world nature of the programs and activities of government that produce or do not produce the impacts being studied. The analogy is not perfect, but there are more things than a knowledge of cucumbers necessary to an understanding of the wonder and power of sunshine!

5

The Impact on the Structure of Governance

Fiscal Federalism in the 1980s:
Dismantling or Rationalizing the Great Society

ROBERT D. REISCHAUER

The Great Society marked the beginning of an era of fiscal federalism that continued largely unabated for a decade and a half. During this period federal grant programs proliferated, and the fiscal interdependence between the federal government and states and localities grew both in complexity and importance. By 1978 this era had run its course, partially exhausted from its own successes and partially defeated by its excesses and the contradictions that had developed between the Great Society's premises and its changing reality.

The policy void that emerged after 1978 was filled by the Reagan administration's New Federalism proposal, a radical departure in intergovernmental fiscal relations characterized by devolution, disengagement, and decremental budgeting. Congress enacted some elements but not the core of the administration's initiative. But the period of change is not over. The huge structural budget deficits facing the federal government make it probable that there will be a further restructuring of the current system of intergovernmental fiscal relations.

This essay reviews the course of fiscal federalism over the past two decades in an attempt to shed light on whether the Great Society's grants policy will be dismantled, will be rationalized and reformed, or will find a new life and reemerge.

THE ROOTS OF THE GREAT SOCIETY GRANT STRATEGY

Both from the federal government's perspective and from that of the state and local governments the policy environment in 1964 was far different from that which exists two decades later. The international situation was fairly benign; the Bay of Pigs disaster and the Cuban missile crisis were behind the nation and Vietnam was still a country most Americans had never heard of. Defense spending was level in real terms, and the federal budget exhibited a small, $6 billion deficit (about 1 percent of the gross national product) that was entirely attributable to the fact that the unemployment rate exceeded full employment levels. The economy was relatively strong and was improving.

In short there was no resource constraint at the federal level. In fact the opposite was the case. The president's economic advisers warned of "fiscal drag," a situation in which economic growth and "bracket creep" would cause federal revenue to grow more rapidly than the built-in expenditure requirements of existing federal programs. The resultant surpluses would retard economic growth unless disposed of through tax cuts or increased government expenditures.

Into this environment catapulted a president with a limitless domestic agenda. When Lyndon Johnson looked at America he saw educational deprivation, poverty, decrepit housing, poor transportation, discrimination, rural economic backwardness, poor health, urban slums, and so on. While his enthusiasm, energy, and knowledge of the congressional system were undoubtedly enough to guarantee a major explosion of domestic policy initiatives, the new president's proclivities were buttressed by advisers who conveyed a sense of optimism about government's ability to intervene and solve domestic problems.

Of course, in 1964 the federal government's involvement in most of these problem areas was limited or nonexistent. To the extent that responsibility for these problems rested anywhere it was with state and local governments. Yet state and local governments were far from being wellsprings of innovation or engines of change. From the perspective of the Washington policy-maker, these governments suffered from three major weaknesses. The first of these was fiscal starvation. In 1964 states and localities depended heavily on regressive sources of revenue that increased only slowly with an expanding economy. Over 90 percent (93.3 percent) of the general revenue they raised from their own sources came from property taxes, sales taxes, charges, licenses, and fees. In short, states and localities lacked the wherewithall to address the pressing domestic needs.

The second shortcoming of state and local governments was one of technical and administrative capacity. From the perspective of the intellectual advisers of the post-Camelot era, the bureaucracies at the state and local level were poorly trained and badly paid. Administrative competence was undermined by political oversight from part-time legislatures, governors who served short terms, and a dispersion of authority among independently elected commissions.

Even if there had been the resources and the capacity, the will was lacking in many jurisdictions to undertake a major expansion of social policy. The agenda of state and local governments through the 1940s and 1950s had been limited. Traditional services, fairly narrowly defined (such as education, highways, cash welfare assistance, public safety, and sanitation), dominated the state and local menu. Rural domination of state legislatures together with machine and business control of city governments precluded innovative programs to help the disadvantaged.

A mismatch thus existed in which the federal government perceived that it had the resources, the technical and administrative capacity, and the will to undertake a major enrichment of domestic public services while the state and local sector had the traditional responsibility for such service delivery. This mismatch was bridged by a proliferation of categorical grant programs that enlisted states and localities as agents of the federal government.

The objectives of this federal largess went far beyond merely providing states and localities with the resources required to provide adequate services. The federal government wanted to dictate to these governments what specific services to provide, how much of these services to offer, the appropriate mechanisms and forms for providing these services, and the decision-making processes surrounding these services.

THE CHARACTERISTICS OF THE
GREAT SOCIETY'S GRANT STRATEGY

No single dimension of the Great Society's grant strategy was revolutionary or totally new. But taken together the shifts in magnitude, focus, mechanisms, and methods did constitute a policy break with the past.

Most notable was the spectacular explosion that occurred in the number, size, and relative importance of federal grants. The number of grant programs increased from 132 in 1960 to 379 by 1967 (see table 1). In three years—1964, 1965, and 1966 alone—a total of 198 new grants were authorized. Grant outlays grew from $8.6 billion in 1963 to $20.3 billion in 1969. Recipient governments became increasingly dependent upon federal aid as a source of revenue—federal aid as a percentage of receipts from state and local sources grew from 16.5 percent in 1963 to 21.6 percent in 1969.

Table 1   Federal grants-in-aid, 1960–83

Year	$ Billions	Number of federal grant programs	State-local receipts from own source (percentage)	Federal outlays (percentage)	GNP (percentage)
1960	7.0	132	16.8	7.6	1.4
1963	8.6	na	17.9	8.6	1.6
1967	15.2	379	20.6	9.6	2.0
1975	49.8	448	29.1	15.3	3.3
1978	77.9	498	31.7	17.3	3.7
1981	94.8	539	29.4	14.4	3.2
1982	88.2	441	25.3	12.1	2.9
1983	94.0	409	24.1	11.8	2.9

Source: Table 75, Advisory Commission on Intergovernmental Relations, *Significant Features of Fiscal Federalism, 1982–83 Edition*, January 1984, M-137.

Grants also became an increasingly important component of the federal budget, rising from 7.8 percent of federal outlays in 1963 to 11 percent in 1969. While a less spectacular grant explosion had occurred during the Great Depression, that surge was a temporary one that was reversed during World War II.

A second distinguishing aspect of the Great Society was the variety of areas for which grants were provided. Before this period grant outlays were heavily concentrated in the public assistance and highway areas. These two functions alone accounted for roughly two-thirds of all federal grant outlays. While small grant programs existed in most other areas, more often than not they helped recipient governments pay for traditional services that the recipient governments were already providing. In many cases the impetus for establishing these early grants had come from the recipient governments.

In contrast, many of the Great Society's grants were intended to encourage recipient governments to provide new and different services—ones for which a local constituency did not exist. These grants focused on providing services to the underprivileged, the poor, and areas of economic distress—in short, to the powerless and neglected. The result was that the Great Society's grants shifted the spending priorities of recipient governments to a greater extent than had been seen in the previous thirty years. In many cases this shift was accomplished by sweetening the pot; that is, by lowering or eliminating the matching funds that recipient governments were required to contribute. The federal government thus made an offer that even reluctant jurisdictions found hard to refuse.

The Older Americans Act, the Model Cities Program, Head Start, School Breakfast, School Desegregation, the Community Action Program, Grants for the Humanities and Arts, the Economic Opportunity Act, the Highway Beautification Program, Mass Transit Aid, and Title I of ESEA (Educational Aid for the Disadvantaged) were just some of the new grant initiatives that were undertaken during this period. Grant programs were also established in the areas of drug and alcohol abuse, family planning, migrant health, black lung, and bilingual education.

A third distinguishing aspect of the Great Society's grant thrust was the willingness of the federal government to expand the list of eligible recipients. With the exception of the temporary Depression-era programs and the public housing program, federal aid had been channeled almost exclusively to state governments. While much of this aid ended up in the local government's hands, states played an important role in determining and administering substate allocations. Under many of the Great Society's programs local governments became direct recipients of aid. Neighborhood and nonprofit organizations of various sorts, regional consortia of states or counties, and special districts also came to be recipients of federal aid.

The decisions to expand the list of eligible recipients and to circumvent the existing political institutions were not accidental. They were consistent with the negative view of state and local capacity described earlier. However, this aspect of the Great Society's grants strategy upset traditional political and administrative relationships and thereby destabilized the political environment. It is a paradox worth noting that at a time when Washington policy-makers had great expectations that government institutions could bring about significant change, they held state and local institutions generally in low regard.

A final distinguishing characteristic of the grants of this period was the degree of administrative and programmatic control exercised by the federal government. Old grants were not lacking in such restrictions but their regulations were not designed to control recipient behavior strictly. Moreover, the objectives of the federal government and the recipient jurisdictions were more compatible. Many of the new grants were project grants—a type of grant that maximized the interaction between the recipient and the federal agency. At every stage of a project federal approval was required. The Washington policy-makers also were infatuated with planning; hence numerous planning and regional coordination requirements were injected into the new grant programs. Process requirements, having little to do with the particular service being provided, were grafted onto the grants.

The patterns set during the Great Society era continued to dominate domestic policy-making for almost a decade after Lyndon Johnson left office. The emergence of each new domestic problem during the early 1970s was met by still another federal grant program. The number of grants increased from 379 in 1967 to 448 in 1975 and peaked at 539 in 1981. Grant outlays more than doubled every five years during this period. Grants grew to be an even more important source of revenue for recipient governments, rising from 21.6 percent of revenue from their own sources in 1969 to 31.7 percent in 1980. This growing dependence prompted Richard Nathan to characterize some local jurisdictions as "federal aid junkies." By 1977 $1 out of every $6 spent by the federal government was a grant to a state or local government, and grants had risen to equal 3.7 percent of the gross national product—two and a half times the ratio that existed at the beginning of the Great Society.

Grants continued to be used to push the federal government, states, and localities into new service areas such as environment, energy subsidies for the poor, and pollution control. However, the major thrust of the 1970s was to deepen and expand federal involvement in service areas that had been opened up during the Johnson years. Major grant programs were established in the areas of community development, income support, job training, housing, education, medical care, nutrition, and mass transportation. Overall, there was less emphasis during this period on aid to disadvantaged people or depressed geographic areas.

In the middle of the 1970s the grants strategy had its final expansionary burst when the federal government enlisted states and localities in what heretofore had been a singularly central government function—namely, economic stabilization. Through the local public works program, the countercyclical Comprehensive Employment Training Act (CETA), states and localities were asked to help pull the economy out of the 1973–75 recession. Like the programs of the great Depression, these grants were intended to be temporary. They disappeared by the end of the decade but not before serious questions had been raised concerning the efficacy of enlisting lower levels of government in stabilization policy.

As the number of new grants tapered off in the last half of the 1970s, emphasis shifted to the tax code. Programs were enacted or expanded that permitted states and localities to offer tax-free bonds to provide for economic development and housing finance.

Despite mounting complaints, administrative requirements and regulations were not relaxed during the 1970s; instead, new rolls of red tape were wrapped around existing programs. These new regulations more often than not reflected national goals not directly related to the particular services involved. For example, regulations aimed at the environment, the prevailing wage, antidiscrimination efforts, the handicapped, and citizen participation were added to the older program-related restrictions.

THE REACTION TO THE GRANT STRATEGY

The reaction to the excesses and contradictions inherent in the Great Society's grant strategy began to emerge even before Lyndon Johnson left the White House. By the early 1970s a fairly coherent critique of this dependence on categorical grants had developed. This critique had four key components. First, there were too many categorical grants. Grants congestion created needless confusion and duplication. It gave an advantage to those jurisdictions skilled at grantsmanship—to those who knew their way around the halls of Washington rather than to those who really needed the federal aid or who could best provide the service.

Second, grants had needlessly distorted the system of public service delivery. Tax revenues were siphoned out of states and localities and sent to Washington where priorities were set that were not in accord with the desires of the citizenry in the recipient jurisdictions. Moreover, many of the programs supported by the grants could not be justified as reflecting any national need. For example, programs to control neighborhood rats or to train local school bus drivers could hardly be justified as reflecting high-priority national problems. Rather, special interests that could not generate support for their favorite programs at the state or local level had successfully captured the attention of Congress.

Third, the grants system had undermined accountability and efficiency because the responsibility for raising the money was now divorced from the responsibility for delivering the services. Incentives for minimizing costs were lacking. Much aid was channeled through narrow categorical programs that bypassed the legislative allocative process or the political oversight of recipient governments.

Fourth, the regulations and rules of the federal government were counterproductive because they were too rigid, inflexible, and ephemeral. Federal bureaucrats had little understanding of the local conditions that needed to be accommodated if a program was going to work outside of Washington. Federally mandated standards were often too high for the conditions in particular recipient communities. Federal regulations precluded mixing the inputs in proportions appropriate for providing the services efficiently. Federal restrictions caused delays that raised costs. Moreover, the complex array of regional office structures and the constantly changing relationships between Washington and these regional authorities resulted in additional confusion, unnecessary delay, and wasted resources. Too much power and discretion was left with the federal bureaucrats, particularly in the case of project grants where they could use these grants as discretionary prizes to reward those local bureaucrats who responded most readily to Washington's whims.

The New Federalism initiative of the Nixon administration responded to these criticisms of the Great Society's grants strategy. This initiative encompassed the General Revenue Sharing program (GRS) as well as six special revenue-sharing proposals.

General Revenue Sharing provided states and some 39,000 general purpose local governments with a formula-allocated entitlement to federal monies. Recipients were free to use the money pretty much as they saw fit. Excepting the federal payment to the District of Columbia, payments made in lieu of taxes, and certain shared receipts, General Revenue Sharing constituted the first general purpose grant from the federal government to states and localities.

The program brought thousands of local governments into a direct grant relationship with the federal government for the first time. While the red tape, regulations, and restrictions associated with GRS were inconsequential when compared to those of the average categorical grant, for these newly involved governments they appeared substantial. At its peak General Revenue Sharing amounted to 13 percent of federal grant outlays and some 3.1 percent of the expenditures of state and local governments. Rapid inflation and a failure to raise the authorization substantially eroded the importance of GRS to the point that by 1980—the last year states received money from this program—this figure had dropped to 1.9 percent.

The Nixon administration's special revenue-sharing proposals fared less well legislatively. These proposals were modified block grants. They called for a consolidation of some 130 categorical grant programs into six special revenue-sharing programs. Recipient governments were to be given greater discretion over the use of the monies that were to be allocated by formula. Regulations, matching requirements, and maintenance of effort requirements were to be abolished.

Block grants were not a completely new concept. The Partnership for Health Act had consolidated sixteen categorical grants into a modified block grant in 1967. The Safe Street Act had established a new block-type grant in 1968. Of the original six proposals of the Nixon administration only two, the Manpower Training Special Revenue Sharing (1973) and the Community Development Block Grant (1974), were approved by Congress. The proposals for special revenue-sharing in the areas of Law Enforcement, Education, Transportation and Rural Community Development never progressed far through the legislative jungle. President Ford's proposal to create four block grants in 1976 struck an equally unresponsive chord in the Congress.

The special revenue-sharing measures that were enacted and a later effort (the Social Services Block Grant) represented only a partial retreat from the interventionist philosophy of the categorical grants era. While recipients were given a good deal more freedom to spend on projects of their own choice and reporting requirements were reduced, congressional modifications to the original proposals ensured that plenty of strings were left in place. There were mandatory pass-throughs to local governments and requirements limiting the recipient's ability to shift funds across broad categories of services. Overall, the Nixon initiatives enhanced the role of general purpose governments over special districts and nongovernmental recipients. But General Revenue Sharing supplemented, not supplanted, categorical aid. Thus general contours of the intergovernmental fiscal system were not changed drastically. It is also important to realize that while the reaction to the categorical system was being expressed through the enactment of these broad-purpose aid instruments, new categorical programs were being enacted and additional red tape burdens were being imposed, although at a slower pace than during the 1960s.

An important cause for this continued momentum was the interlocking network of groups that had grown up to support the categorical grants strategy. In each area of federal involvement a powerful network of interest groups had developed. First there were the representatives of the recipient governments. These included not only interest groups representing governors, mayors, city managers, county executives, state legislators, and the like, but also recipient agency organizations such as chief state school officers, public welfare directors, and highway commissioners. All told, some seventy-two different groups of this sort existed. A second element of the network consisted of the general providers of the services funded by the grants—organized teachers, builders of public housing, social workers, public employee unions, and so forth. The recipients of the services also formed an element in this network— ranging from welfare recipients to PTA organizations to automobile clubs. Private-sector suppliers of the inputs needed to provide the services also joined the effort. These organizations might represent the producers of library shelves, manufacturers of school buses, book publishers, or asphalt suppliers. The academics and private-sector consulting firms that made a living evaluating existing programs and planning and designing new programs also formed an element in the support group for the grants strategy.

Of course many of these groups existed before the Great Society began. But during this era their staffs grew tremendously and their involvement in legislative matters expanded. They became more focused on Washington and many moved their offices from New York, Chicago, and other cities to the nation's capital.

Washington contributed its own resources to the effort to perpetuate the categorical grants strategy. Federal agencies responsible for administering the various programs were effective advocates for additional initiatives as well as fierce defenders of enhanced appropriations for existing grants. More important probably was the proliferation of congressional committees and their staffs and the dispersal of congressional power that occurred during this period. From the mid-1950s to 1975 the number of committees and subcommittees of Congress increased from 242 to 385. Each new subcommittee that sprang up had a staff and a chairman to defend its grant programs from assault. Once established these subcommittees sought to gain political power and capital and to rationalize their existence by suggesting new ventures.

While Nixon policies represented one challenge to the Great Society's grants strategy, a second was provided by the economy and the havoc it wreaked on the state and local sector. The deep recession of 1973–75 and the high inflation that came from the first oil shock revealed the fragility of the finances of the state and local sector. The New York City fiscal crisis was the earliest manifestation of the problem. While some dismissed New York's difficulties as reflections of that city's clear fiscal peculiarities, the illness soon spread to Buffalo, Detroit, and other localities. High borrowing rates, wage demands pushed up by rapid inflation, and the recession's effect on local revenues soon led many jurisdictions to the conclusion that they were overextended. They were offering too many services to too many people and had become too dependent on uncertain federal aid.

If they needed any reaffirmation of this conclusion it was provided by the public's reaction to the economic circumstances of the mid-1970s. Slow wage growth, high inflation, and rising federal taxes resulted in sharply reduced rates of growth of real disposable personal income. Feeling the pinch, the public began to resist attempts by states and localities to raise taxes. A flurry of referenda and constitutional amendments was passed to limit spending and tax increases. The most widely publicized of these were Proposition 13 in California and Proposition 2½ in Massachusetts. Between 1977 and 1980 fifteen states enacted state spending or tax limitations and seventeen states imposed limits on property taxes or local expenditures.

A final development of the 1970s that contributed to the demise of the categorical grants strategy was the erosion of general optimism concerning government's ability to solve problems, an optimism that had been a hallmark of the Great Society era. The Vietnam War experience and the economic turbulence of the mid-1970s turned this optimism into bare cynicism.

THE REAGAN RESPONSE

Ronald Reagan inherited a grants environment that seemed ripe for major change. The dominant categorical grants strategy was being criticized from virtually all quarters. State and local governments realized they were overextended, needed to reduce their promises, and could not rely on the federal government. For its part, the federal government realized that some simplification was needed and that its capabilities were limited. The Reagan administration read this unsettled environment as one conducive to revolution rather than reform and proposed a radical New Federalism initiative.

This initiative had two distinct thrusts. The first was a block-grant thrust that was similar to Richard Nixon's special revenue-sharing plans. The Omnibus Budget Reconciliation Act of 1981 authorized seven new block grants and modified two existing block grants. Altogether some seventy-seven categorical grant programs were consolidated into these block grants. Four of the new block grants were in the health area— Child and Maternal Health Services, Preventive Health and Health Services, Alcohol, Drug Abuse and Mental Health, and Primary Care. The other five block grants were in the areas of Social Services, Low Income Home Energy Assistance, Community Services, Community Development for Small Cities, and Elementary and Secondary Education. In 1982 Reagan proposed and the Congress enacted a block grant for mass transit capital and operating assistance, and replaced the CETA program by the Job Training Partnership Act. The administration made additional grant consolidation and block-grant proposals in such areas as Nutritional Assistance, Older Americans Act programs, and Primary Care during 1982, 1983, and 1984 but none of these efforts received a sympathetic hearing on Capitol Hill.

The key characteristics of the Reagan administration's block grants were not unlike those of the Nixon era. Matching requirements were reduced or eliminated. The role of the states was enhanced while the roles of localities and nongovernmental agencies were reduced. Recipient jurisdictions were given greater discretion to use grant resources to fund services of their own choosing. They were also given greater authority to determine substate allocations. There were fewer mandates and regulations, and federal grants management was simplified. Recipient governments were freer to choose the method of providing particular services. Finally a sharply lower level of federal money was the price that had to be paid for this greater discretion. Not only were the block grants funded at levels lower than the aggregate of the consolidated programs, but some twenty-six other grant programs were not funded at all.

Overall, this thrust of the Reagan administration's New Federalism initiative represented reform reflective of agreed-upon criticisms of the Great Society's categorical grants strategy and the public's desire to reorder spending priorities. While the original block-grant proposals promised recipient governments a great deal of discretion, Congress limited the extent of this freedom just as it had done with the Nixon block-grant proposals. Restrictions were placed on the extent to which monies could be shifted across the program categories within each block grant, pass-throughs to local governments were mandated, and some key programs such as Title I school assistance for the disadvantaged were removed and protected from the president's block-grant proposal.

The second thrust of the Reagan administration's New Federalism initiative was the revolutionary proposal unveiled in the president's 1982 State of the Union message. This proposal called for a major reallocation of service responsibilities between the federal government and states and localities. The federal government was to assume the complete responsibility for the Medicaid program, and the states were to be given the full responsibility for AFDC and food stamps. In addition, there would be a devolution involving 40 programs and 124 separate grants. These program responsibilities would be given back to the states along with the resources from a trust fund. Roughly $28 billion would be put in the trust fund from federal excise taxes on alcohol, tobacco, and telephones, a portion of the federal gasoline tax, and part of the windfall profit tax on oil. States could either draw their share of this money as special revenue-sharing to use as they saw fit or receive a portion of the trust fund to finance continuation of the old categorical grant programs. The trust fund would be phased out over a four-year period as would the federal taxes used to support the fund. By 1991 states would be free to impose their own levies to support these services if they so desired.

The administration's proposal was motivated first and foremost by a desire to shrink the size of the federal government. But states and localities saw this shrinkage at the federal level as generating an unwarranted increase in their responsibilities. Many of the nation's most powerful and vocal interest groups would be sent from Washington to the state capitals. A secondary motive behind the administration's initiative was to increase the correspondence between the level of government that raised revenues and the level that administered services. However, many questioned whether there was much of a match between the geographic distribution of the responsibilities being returned to the states and the new revenue sources upon which these governments could rely. Finally there was the administration's desire to simplify, sort out, and rationalize governmental responsibility. However, the administration's plan revealed little logic in this respect. The redistribution function would still be split under the new plan with the federal government providing medical care for the low-income population, the states providing income support for the non-aged, and the federal government and the states sharing the responsibility for income support for the aged poor. Services for groups that had long been of national concern, such as migrant labor, were to be devolved. Programs aimed at dealing with problems that by their very nature extended beyond state boundaries (for example, runaway youth or environmental pollution) were to be devolved.

The administration's proposal lacked a constituency. The public, the states and localities, the interest groups, and Congress found it too radical. After a year of difficult negotiating with state and local government interest groups in an effort to come up with a modified plan, the New Federalism proposal died. A less radical version was proposed by the president in 1983 but it was ignored on Capitol Hill.

In some respects the Nixon and Reagan efforts to curb the categorical grants monster were successful; in other respects they left the terrain relatively unchanged. Although it had expanded steadily from World War II onward, state and local government spending stopped growing after 1975 relative to the gross national product and national income. This is

Table 2   State and local government expenditures as a percentage of GNP

	From own source revenues	From own source revenues and grants-in-aid
1964	9.1	10.7
1975	11.5	15.0
1980	10.0	13.6
1983	10.4	13.0

Source: Council of Economic Advisers, *Economic Report of the President 1984.*

true both for spending financed out of state and local revenues and for spending financed by federal grant-in-aid (see table 2).

Federal grants-in-aid measured in constant dollars peaked during the 1978 to 1980 period and then declined. By 1983 the level of federal aid had fallen to the levels of the mid-1970s. Relative to state and local revenues the importance of federal aid in 1983 had diminished to the 1971 level.

The number of different grant programs also decreased due to the actions of the Reagan administration. From a high of 539 in 1981, this number fell to 409 by 1983. Of course there has not been a moratorium on new grants. Even the Reagan administration has succumbed to the lure of the grant strategy in such areas as wetlands management and enterprise zones.

With the reduction in the overall importance of grants has come a shift in the purposes for which federal money is given out. Grants directed at individuals (AFDC and Medicaid) now make up close to half of the total just as they did in the pre–Great Society era. Noncapital, nonentitlement grants, which formed the core of the fiscal interventions of the Great Society and its aftermath, have receded rapidly in importance (see table 3).

While the fiscal importance, number, and broad objectives of federal aid have changed significantly since the early 1970s, there has been considerable constancy in certain other dimensions of the grants landscape. For example, the bulk of federal grant money still is disbursed through narrow categorical programs despite the consolidation and retrenchment of the Reagan administration. While the importance of general purpose aid has declined with the erosion of General Revenue Sharing, the proportion of aid distributed through block grants has gradually increased (see table 4).

Table 3   Percentage distribution of grants by type, 1955–83

	Grants to individuals	Capital grants	Noncapital, nonentitlement grants
1955	50.6	26.7	22.7
1960	35.3	40.1	23.8
1970	37.5	29.5	33.0
1975	34.9	22.0	43.1
1978	33.3	23.6	43.1
1980	37.3	24.6	38.1
1983	48.1	22.1	29.8

Source: Office of Management and Budget.

Similarly, overall recipient matching rates have changed little. While recipient governments had to put up 42 cents for each dollar of federal aid in 1972, eleven years later they had to provide 43 cents. This constancy has resulted from two conflicting developments. First, the relative importance of AFDC and Medicaid, with their high matching rates, has grown. Second, there has been a reduction in the matching requirements for other programs, but their relative importance has diminished.

TAKING STOCK OF THE GREAT SOCIETY'S
CATEGORICAL GRANTS STRATEGY

From the perspective offered by the passage of twenty years one would have to conclude that many of the general objectives of the Great Society's grants strategy were achieved, even if the particular goals of individual grant programs proved elusive. First and foremost, the scope of do-

Table 4   Distribution of federal aid by type of grant program

	1972	1974	1976	1980	1983
General purpose (Revenue-sharing, etc.)	1.5		12.1	9.4	7.0
Broad-based (Block grants)	8.3		10.4	11.3	13.9
Narrow (categorical)	90.2		77.5	79.3	79.1

Source: Office of Management and Budget.

mestic services was expanded tremendously. Today there is recognition that these new services are the responsibility of all levels of government, not just the federal government. None of the problems Lyndon Johnson tried to alleviate is being denied. These problems are receiving substantial rhetorical if not financial attention. Social services, housing, nutrition, the environment, health care, economic development, and services for the disadvantaged and powerless are now the admitted concern of cities, counties, and states. Of importance to the future is that the Great Society has built a constituency for these services that exists both in Washington and across the nation. This has ramifications for those who wish to dismantle the existing structure or to sort out functions and neatly assign each problem to a different level of government.

The corollary to the growth of service is that tax burdens at all levels of government are far higher than they were in 1963. State and local receipts from their own sources rose from 9.3 percent of the gross national product in 1964 to 12 percent in 1977, a level that remained constant in 1983. This growth was achieved by greater reliance on broad-based tax sources, particularly income and sales taxes. This has increased the elasticity of the state and local revenue system, making these governments better able to maintain services as the economy grows, without resorting to tax increases. The increased reliance on income taxes, the reforms made in state sales taxes, and the adoption of property tax circuit-breaker programs have improved the progressive nature of the state and local revenue system as well.

The Great Society has undoubtedly raised the quality of services and brought forth more uniformity of service quality across the states and the local jurisdictions of the country. The service standards imposed by the regulations accompanying federal grant programs put very high floors under many state and local services. Professionalism of service delivery at the state and local level has also been enhanced by the Great Society programs.

The Great Society programs also clearly affected the political dynamics at the state and local levels. Not only did new interest groups emerge, but new, more open decision processes became routine. Citizen or interest group participation became more prevalent—in short, state and local government procedures were rationalized and opened up a bit. Planning and evaluation became more common.

On the other side of the balance sheet, the experience of the Great Society left state and local governments overextended, involved in more areas than they could handle administratively or fiscally. In addition, the Great Society shattered the optimism about government's ability to intervene to solve domestic problems.

The experience of the Great Society era also taught the nation a great deal about the limits of the categorical grants tool. There is now a heightened awareness of the diversity of problems facing the nation and the multiplicity of solutions for solving these problems. Policy-makers are currently more willing to admit that programs designed and operated out of Washington may not always be the best solution to the problems facing a jurisdiction.

The experience of the Great Society era revealed that states and localities could not always be relied upon, like hired contractors, to carry out the will of the federal government. Because these governments are political entities subject to their own constituencies, their behavior often deviated substantially from that desired by the federal government. This independence was reinforced by the fact that few jurisdictions received anything close to the majority of their support from federal grants. Thus in designing programs that involve several levels of government, it is essential that the federal program's objectives are basically compatible with those of the state or locality that is being asked to deliver the services.

WHERE DO WE GO FROM HERE?

The economic and political environment of the 1980s clearly precludes a reemergence of the Great Society's grants strategy. The foremost roadblock is the fiscal problem confronting the federal government. In contrast to the conditions prevailing in the 1960s, the federal government faces huge structural budget deficits for the foreseeable future. Unlike in the 1960s the state and local sector is experiencing a period of general fiscal adequacy. Federal taxes no longer represent a dynamic source of revenues. Excluding payroll taxes, federal receipts are expected to rise less rapidly than the gross national product over the next half decade. Rate cuts and indexing of the income tax have reduced the elasticity and progressivity of the federal revenue system. Reforms and increased reliance on broad-based taxes have done just the reverse for the state and local revenue system.

On the spending side, federal outlays are dominated by entitlements, interest, and defense commitments that the political system appears unwilling to change. States and localities, in contrast, have shown a remarkable ability to curb spending to meet their available revenues.

The simplest manifestations of the nation's domestic problems (hunger, poverty, inadequate health care) have been addressed with varying degrees of success. The remaining problems appear more complex and the available tools of government intervention less likely to produce acceptable results. The limitations of intergovernmental grants are more clearly understood than they were two decades ago. With numerous actors, each affected by a different set of political forces and each with a different concept of the problem and the appropriate solution, intergovernmental grants have proved to be clumsy devices for coordinated efficient actions. Moreover, the congressional system makes it difficult to target grants effectively on problems that are as unevenly distributed across the nation's political jurisdictions as are the problems of the 1980s. All of this reduces the chances of a resurgence of the grants strategy.

While a renewed emphasis on categorical grants seems extremely unlikely, the prospect for successful implementation of major devolution or the sorting out of functions of levels of government seems equally remote. The radical geographic redistribution that would occur in tax burdens and service levels represents a major obstacle to this approach.

The nation's marbleized political and institutional structure represents a second reason why it is futile to tie each domestic policy problem to a single level of government. Responsibility has always been shared. The political system at all levels is inhabited by independent entrepreneurs looking for issues that will serve their constituencies and raise their personal visibility. This means that the president of the United States cannot be kept from proposing initiatives that deal with potholes in local streets, and the mayor of New York cannot be prevented from suggesting local income redistribution programs.

The structure of our institutions ensures that even if it is successfully devolved to lower levels of government, responsibility for dealing with pressing domestic problems will tend to gravitate to Washington. Without a major change in the committee structure, Congress will remain an echo chamber for the nation's unmet needs. The Great Society era underscored the multiplicity of rationales that exist for federal intervention into problems that seem local in nature. The complex interest-group structure that has emerged as a result of the expansion of government activity will also press in this direction. Most groups find it more efficient to operate primarily at a national level rather than to work separately in fifty states or thousands of local jurisdictions. Finally, the emergence of the national media through which most Americans obtain their information about domestic problems reinforces the tendency to centralize policy-making in Washington.

Federal budget pressures will undoubtedly reduce the relative importance of federal grants. The strengthened capacity of states and localities will call forth more relaxation in federal mandates and controls. Nevertheless, the significant reliance on categorical grant programs that emerged during the Great Society era is not likely to disappear soon.

The Nature and Systemic Impact of "Creative Federalism"

DAVID B. WALKER

Lyndon Johnson's impact on federal-state-local relations was more profound than that of any president since Franklin Roosevelt and in several respects it surpassed Roosevelt's. Though it was the offspring of "Cooperative Federalism" (1933–1960), Johnson's "Creative Federalism" differed both qualitatively and quantitatively from its parent philosophy. Both emphasized intergovernmental collaboration and the sharing of personnel, financing, and program responsibilities. Johnson's concept, however, involved a more panoramic approach to partnership, a greater urban thrust, a broader definition of national purpose, and much more federal funding.

Moreover, it conditioned both politically and programmatically the successor federalism—Nixon's "New Federalism," Congressional Federalism, Carter's "New Partnership Federalism," and Reagan's "New Federalism." While President Nixon campaigned in 1968 against much of the Johnson intergovernmental record, he furthered many of the managerial efforts launched in 1967–68 and signed into law various measures that expanded upon or added to the Johnson legacy. Meanwhile, the Democratic congresses throughout most of the seventies— with increasing Republican support—became the prime and expansive legatees of Johnsonian federalism. These later extensions of Creative Federalism will be probed in the middle sections of this analysis.

With President Reagan's New Federalism fiscal, programmatic, deregulatory, and devolutionary attacks were made on the Johnson, inferentially the Nixon, and clearly the congressional intergovernmental records. But despite some successes no wholesale eradication of major programs nor even overall funding reductions occurred. Finally, as the final section of this essay will demonstrate, the "Reagan reaction," which was partially a continuation of the "Carter reaction," can be understood only in terms of the fiscal, programmatic, and regulatory excesses of the seventies—some of which were enacted and heralded (erroneously in my view) as logical extensions of the Great Society.

THE CHARACTER AND BASIC TRAITS
OF CREATIVE FEDERALISM

Philosophically, Johnson's Creative Federalism represented a combination of four different political traditions: two were liberal (and in partial conflict with one another) and two were conservative. The first tradition, which draws on the thinking of Franklin D. Roosevelt, Theodore Roosevelt, and Herbert Croly (the "New Nationalist" philosopher of the Progressive era), incorporates the liberal nationalist reformist belief in the national government's capacity to solve basic economic and societal problems. Explicit in this, for Johnson, was the overriding national purpose of promoting the integrative, educational, economic, and redistributive goals of one vast commonwealth, of one Great Society.

Alternatively, Johnson shared a liberal federalist ideal that also harked back to Franklin Roosevelt but thence to Woodrow Wilson and Louis D. Brandeis. From this particular liberal perspective the states and localities take on greater significance—as partners in the system, as implementers of national and subnational programs, as indispensable components—albeit politically independent—of our federal system. Hence, grants-in-aid became a prime mechanism for promoting partnerships to achieve national as well as state and local goals.

All this is in contrast to the liberal nationalist view that focused more on direct national governmental action, regulation, and implementation. Put differently, the twin liberal themes in Johnsonian theory and practice were reflected in the contrasting though overlapping goals of his Great Society and his Creative Federalism.

Despite his predominantly liberal outlook, Johnson's pragmatism and fiscal and administrative conservativism should not be ignored. In his "concert of interests" approach to legislative enactments, in his distributional approach to parceling out benefits, and especially in his dealings with individuals and groups, the pragmatist in Johnson was rarely missing. With his efforts to keep the budget under the $100 billion mark in the mid-sixties, with his worry about deficits and about the conservative criticisms they would generate, with his hostility to welfare reform, and even with his antipoverty efforts, which after all were geared to producing "tax payers, not tax eaters," a strong streak of fiscal conservativism was clearly manifested. His heavy reliance on grants to achieve most of his program goals and his concomitant hostility to a heavily expanded federal bureaucracy reflected his administrative conservatism. These traits in part suggest again the influence of Franklin Roosevelt, but Johnson's heritage as a Texan also cannot be overlooked as a conditioning factor.

Latter-day Johnsonians frequently lacked both his pragmatism and his fiscal conservatism. Had these traits been better honored during the seventies, it would have been far different from the recklessly expansionist decade it was, and the scene would not have been set for the kinds of reactions that set in near its close.

Turning from the more philosophic to the systemic, the cumulative effects of Creative Federalism on the overall system were profound. Intergovernmental relations between 1964 and 1968 became bigger (in the dollars, programs, and jurisdictions involved), broader (in the range of governmental functions affected), deeper (in terms of intrusive grant conditions and of the expanding number of recipient local governments and nonprofit organizations), and certainly more complicated when compared to the relatively neat, narrowly focused, inexpensive, basically two-tier intergovernmental pattern of 1960.

SEVEN DIMENSIONS OF THE JOHNSONIAN REVOLUTION
IN INTERGOVERNMENTAL RELATIONS

Federal-state-local intergovernmental relations after Johnson would never return to the simpler days of Eisenhower and Kennedy. The marble cake metaphor that was used to describe what was presumably a complicated and convoluted network of federal-state-local relations was a good one to use for the earlier era—good in the sense of unintentionally describing the relatively clear (two distinct colors), largely federal-state (only two flavors), the narrow four-major-program-focused (the four to five chocolate and vanilla swirls in the cake) nature of the intergovernmental system of the fifties and early sixties. But Creative Federalism dramatically modified its Cooperative Federalism predecessor, and the marble cake metaphor gave way to one based on fruit cake.

Seven basic shifts brought about this transformation.

First, *grant-in-aid outlays nearly doubled between 1964 and 1968, and given the relatively low level of inflation this meant a 68 percent hike in terms of constant dollars.*

Second, *a pronounced shift in favor of urban and metropolitan areas occurred in federal aid allocations.* Compared to the 50-50 rural-urban division in 1960, the split eight years later was 30-70, reflecting roughly the actual geographic distribution of the population. Part of this change was caused by the "by-passing" of the states and the pick-up in direct federal grants to local, generally urban, governments. By 1968, 12 percent of all federal aid was channeled to local governments compared to 8 percent in 1960.

Third, *more grant programs (210) were enacted during Johnson's five years than in all of the previous years dating back to the first categorical grant enactment (1879).*

Fourth, *the range of purposes encompassed by the 210 new enactments greatly expanded the definition of what is in the national interest.* From a historical perspective, practically all of the leftover domestic items from Truman's Fair Deal, the congressional Democrat's legislative agenda of the fifties, and the Democratic platform of 1960 were enacted. Put differently, the national liberal programmatic pipeline was wholly decongested under Johnson. But Johnson (and in part Kennedy) pushed beyond the past and initiated programs that were not part of the liberal legacy. From antipoverty programs and Model Cities to Medicaid as well as numerous smaller grants, many Johnson proposals were newly conceived, thus adding fresh, frequently controversial, and vastly expanded programmatic dimensions to the national liberal implementation agenda.

Fifth, and as an outgrowth of much of the above, *the partnership principle under Johnson's aegis took on a more panoramic character.* With the increasing tendency to allocate federal aid directly to substate jurisdictions, a growing number of cities, school districts, special districts, and some counties as well as a range of nonprofit organizations joined the states as recipients of grant funds.

Sixth, *with Creative Federalism the beginning of a new regulatory era was launched—an era wherein states and localities became the objects of and/or implementers of federal regulations.* Relying on the Fourteenth Amendment, the commerce power, or the conditional spending power (and increasingly on the last), legislation was enacted that established new approaches to achieving national regulatory goals. With the Civil Rights Acts of 1964 and 1968 (Titles VI and VIII, respectively), the Architectural Barriers Act of 1968, and the National Historic Preservation Act of 1966, four major crosscutting conditions were established (that is, requirements that apply to all or all relevant grant programs). The Highway Beautification Act of 1965 was one of the first examples of a crossover sanction, under which aid provided under one or more specified programs would be terminated or reduced if the requirements of another program were not satisfied. Finally, with the Water Quality Act (1965), the Wholesome Meat Act (1967), and the Wholesome Poultry Act (1968), three early case studies of partial preemption emerge (that is, the federal government establishes the standards but their administration is delegated to the states provided they adopt standards equivalent to the national ones). These approaches represent a major departure—admittedly in areas of crucial national concern, for the most part—from the carrot of grant funds to the stick of coercive grant conditions.

Finally, *a largely unrecognized, but significant managerial thrust was also part of Creative Federalism.* Largely in response to criticisms following the 1966 midterm elections from leading Democratic governors, a cluster of efforts were launched to improve grants management, to establish clearer lines of communication with the states and localities, to rationalize headquarters–field office relations, and to reorganize the federal bureaucracy. Not all of these undertakings occurred during Johnson's last two years, but the overall drive to apply systematically a cluster of fairly conventional public administration principles did occur in that period.

In more specific terms, the following should be noted (for in many instances, they set the scene for follow-up efforts lasting to 1980):

(1) To provide better information and achieve better communication with states (especially) and localities, intergovernmental liaison officers were established in all the domestic departments, Circular A-85 was promulgated to facilitate public interest group participation in the development of grant conditions, and trips were made by the "Flying Feds" to all fifty states.

(2) To help standardize and simplify certain phases of grants management, executive branch attention focused on the "letter of credit" technique of disbursing grant funds in a timely fashion, the problem of separately required grant accounts,[1] overhead costs (that resulted in Circular A-87), and audits (Circular A-74).

(3) Efforts to improve headquarters-field relationships were reflected in the experimental establishment of Federal Regional Councils and in developing plans for full-scale regional reform that came to fruition in June 1969 under President Nixon.

(4) Major drives to rationalize the federal bureaucracy were marked

by the reorganizations that produced the departments of Housing and Urban Development and Transportation.

While most of these undertakings in better management and better communication proved by the late seventies to have their shortcomings, they conformed largely to the administrative reform principles of the day, and they were expanded and embellished by Johnson's three successors during the next decade. Yet even in the Johnson period a note of caution was voiced by budget director Charles Schultz when in 1967 he commented on the irrelevance of "the hierarchic concept of management" in intergovernmental relations and called for the development of new techniques that "would enable many governmental units, all of equal status, to work together on a voluntary basis."

IMMEDIATE IMPACTS

All but the last of these seven Johnson-engendered intergovernmental trends produced negative reactions even as they were getting under way. By 1966 the governors began complaining of the increased "bypassing," poor communications, the mounting number of conditions, the proliferation of institutional strings, and the general "management muddle" at the national level. The mayors, in term, criticized the direct federal-to-community action group links. Local officials complained of the broad discretion (and potential for favoritism) given to federal aid administrators under project grants.[2] Meanwhile, Black Power and liberal white neighborhood activists resented what they saw as the centralizing, technocratic, vertical functional, integrationist, or paternalistic tendencies in Creative Federalism.

The 1968 Nixon campaign focused on the proliferation of categorical (especially project) grants and conditions, centralized decision-making, and the "management mess" that had been created. Both members of the Humphrey-Muskie ticket echoed some of these same concerns in their advocacy of more management reforms, general revenue-sharing, and better intergovernmental cooperation.

THE SEVENTIES: A SCHIZOIDAL DECADE

Despite these criticisms, the seventies witnessed both a major extension of and major additions to the Johnson legacy—all paradoxically during a decade that many have labeled as "conservative." Witness the following five examples:

(1) Despite the advent of GRS (General Revenue Sharing) in 1972

and of five block grants, the total of federal aid for these newer, less restrictive forms of federal aid never surpassed the 25 percent mark reached in 1975.[3] Put differently, categorical grants continued to dominate the aid picture and although over fifty were merged under the block grants, 120 new ones were enacted during the Nixon-Ford years and over sixty in the Carter period, for a total of 532 funded and operational categorical programs by the end of the decade.

(2) Retrenchment was a rhetorical response to the growth in federal grant outlays through much of decade, but it did not become an operative policy until the last two years of the Carter administration. Outlays in constant dollar terms doubled between 1970 and 1980.

(3) Though grant conditions were condemned throughout the period, more intrusive conditions involving all of the newer approaches to regulation were enacted than ever before.

(4) The Johnson precept of a panoramic partnership was carried to its ultimate in the seventies. The substate jurisdictional dimensions of General Revenue Sharing, Community Development Block Grants, and Comprehensive Employment Training Act were not fully appreciated by their sponsors. The tendency of a substate allocational formula to spread federal monies to more jurisdictions, despite efforts to draft rigorous eligibility provisions, was a major cause of this expansion. The three countercyclical programs of the mid-seventies only strengthened this trend. Ironically, these developments occurred chiefly during the administrations of two presidents who honored the primacy of the federal-state connection. So it was that bypassing of state governments doubled during the Nixon years (from 12 percent in 1968 to 24 percent by 1974) and reached 29 percent of total federal aid by 1977.

(5) The proliferation of program thrusts also continued throughout the period. During the second- and third-generation renewals of the Johnson programs, specialized groupings within each of the aided functional areas sought to capture their "piece of the pie," whether it was a project grant or a regulation. The "concert of interests" approach to renewals usually took the form of an omnibus bill that renewed the Great Society program, expanded it with new but narrow program thrusts, and usually added intrusive conditions. By the end of the decade, hardly any agency of a state or local government was unable to find at least one grant in the Federal Catalog of Domestic Assistance that would meet some of its needs. The admittedly expansive Johnsonian view of the national interest had become nearly all encompassing. Moreover, the uncertain but very real line between private and public concerns in the sixties had been obliterated by the late seventies, and what

the national decision-makers of the early sixties understood to be a state or local rather than a federal matter was practically eclipsed. No delimiting concept of the national interest remained. The concept became trivialized as policemen's pensions, potholes, jellyfish, fire protection, rural as well as urban libraries, and noise control became the object of congressional attention.

THE FALLOUT

These extraordinary extensions of the Johnson legacy occurred in large measure because the fiscal caution he exhibited did not reappear until 1978 (with Proposition 13, the revamped effort for a balanced budget amendment, and Carter's last two budgets) and because the role of the Democratic party as a mediating, mollifying, moderating instrumentality collapsed. Reasons for the latter included: Johnson's departure, the representational reforms of Democratic convention rules, the ostensibly liberal changes in the procedures in Congress, and the quintupling of the number of pressure groups that were housed in Washington. Not to be overlooked here is the fact that Johnson's commonsense approach to programs, high-sounding principles, and pressure groups was lost amid efforts to legislate morality at the behest of narrow interest groups, with little to no attention paid to implementation, cost, and the inevitably resulting public cynicism. Witness the enactment of environmental legislation based on technology that did not exist and the passage of regulatory programs (notably for the disabled) that presumably involved no public outlays.

Congress became the dominant architect of the intergovernmental system after 1973 (until 1981). But the legatees of the Johnson heritage remembered only part of his legacy. Liberal Democrats began to dominate all but a handful of the standing committees. At the same time their senior members had their formal powers curbed and the growing junior contingent was composed increasingly of inexperienced, bright, assertive, though increasingly politically exposed members. The minority party and many conservative members of the majority campaigned against the congressional excesses on the stump and on television, but the final votes for renewals indicated their own capacity to be co-opted by the interest-group pressures of the period.

By the end of the decade, discerning conservatives and liberals could and did condemn the inordinate role of interest groups in the system, though few recognized that the decline of the parties and of generalist state and local officials was the main cause of much of the problem. John Gardner could speak of the dangers of the "interest group state" and others could describe and prescribe for an overloaded system. Still others could depict the majority party as a loose aggregation of countless factional groupings, many of which were fundamentally hostile to one another but were held together by their common desire for federal aid and/or the conditions attached to it.

All this, of course, captures some of the extraordinary pressures that were placed on the Carter presidency. Once its history is written with some measure of compassion and political understanding, these developments no doubt will loom large. Even a Johnson would have had a tough time functioning as a broker—masterful or otherwise—in the stifling atmosphere of the powerful, proliferating, and loudly insistent pressure groups of the late seventies.

THE REAGAN REACTION

The most pronounced rejection of the Creative Federalism legacy was, of course, the election of Ronald Reagan. Yet the trends of the seventies were a major conditioner of Reagan's campaign strategy, and these, as has been noted, cannot be wholly or even reasonably attributed to Johnson. While it was never conceded, the Reagan domestic speeches in 1980 were addressed as much against his two Republican predecessors as against Johnson, the Democratic congresses, and Carter. It was during their tenure, after all, that the entitlements were indexed, social welfare spending really soared, the federal regulation of subnational governments got seriously under way, large deficits became the norm, and defense outlays were significantly reduced. But Carter and the Democrats were the main objects of his strictures, even though the Georgian had hiked defense expenditures, curbed grant outlays, initiated an effort to curb regulations, and even sponsored four block grants (though unsuccessfully).

Reagan then continued the trends begun under Carter, but with more flair, more force, and greater success. In its approach to federalism the Reagan administration should be judged in terms of each of its years, since somewhat different intergovernmental strategies characterized each. Yet throughout these years the themes of devolution and reducing the flow of federal aid dominated, while deregulation and deinstitutionalization of federal multistate and substate regional efforts were major subthemes. The one clear call for greater centralization occurred in the 1982 State of the Union address with the president's proposed "big swap," but it unfortunately failed.[4] What then has and has not Reagan federalism accomplished?

In the drive for devolution, the president secured congressional approval of nine block grants in 1981 and the Job Training Partnership Act a year later, as well as the elimination of funding for at least sixty programs in the Budget Reconciliation Act (1981). At the same time, none of the new block grants matched the proposals that left his desk either in programs merged or in format, and his chief efforts to devolve through the "big swap" and his subsequent (1983–84) four "megablock" proposals (and seven minor mergers) went nowhere.

The effort of New Federalism (and Reaganomics) to reduce federal aid succeeded in achieving a static growth in grant outlays from 1981 to 1984, in reducing the number of grants to a little above 400 (from 537 in 1980), and in bringing the proportion of federal aid down to 20 percent of state and local revenues (the 1973 level). He also succeeded in curbing the rate of growth in social spending, notably in Medicaid, food stamps, AFDC, and Section 8 housing—largely by cost controls and tightened eligibility requirements. Yet he failed to achieve a continuing absolute reduction in aid outlays (as was called for in the 1981 reconciliation legislation), and he signed appropriation bills in 1982 and 1983 that totaled more than his initial budget proposals.

In his deregulatory drive the rate and number of issuances were reduced and many regulations were "softened," thanks to his appointed personnel and their generally permissive style of administration. A few (chiefly Davis-Bacon) were fought out successfully in the courts, and certain procedural crosscutting conditions were scrapped (A-95 and A-111, for example). Not to be overlooked was the increase in the devolving of standard-setting authority under certain environmental and health-safety programs to the states that under the relevant laws meet certain federal requirements. At the same time, no basic changes as yet have occurred in the basic legislation establishing these intergovernmental regulatory programs. Furthermore, the stance of the solicitor general's office in federal district court cases involving states' rights (police power) and business concerns indicates no consistent position on the part of the administration on the states' regulatory powers. The "Baby Doe" medical life-support controversy and the administration's support for raising the drinking age are other examples of this selective approach.

The unheralded campaign against regional institution-building achieved the elimination of funds for Title V (federal-multistate economic development commissions) and Title II (counterpart river basin commissions), both Johnson programs. At the substate regional level, of the thirty-nine federal programs funding such efforts in 1980, twelve were terminated, eleven experienced major budget cuts, nine lost their regional features, six were revised, and one was left untouched. Yet some of the multistate bodies have been continued as wholly multistate ventures, and federal support for some of the substate instrumentalities continues through the Department of Transportation's MPO (Metropolitan Planning Organization) requirements, the AAA (Areawide Agency for the Aged) program, and prospectively the Clean Water Act, as amended. Moreover, Executive Order 12372 (the successor to A-95) does not eliminate a federal role in supporting regional councils.

All of the above, along with the Reagan administration's failure to get any real change thus far in the Supreme Court's handling of most federalism issues, its meager success in modifying significantly Congress's approach to intergovernmental questions, its marked inability to make any significant dent in the volume of interest-group activity in Washington, and its barren effort to arrive at a viable definition of the proper federal role(s) suggest a Reagan incrementalist reaction, not a Reagan revolution. The only real revolution occurred as a result of Reagan economics, and that is the gradual realization across the country that answers to many state, local, and even private problems—fiscal or otherwise—may well find no real solution in Washington. This is in marked contrast to thinking during much of the seventies.

How does all this relate to Creative Federalism and its progenitor, Lyndon B. Johnson? Most of his major health, education, environmental (even as amended in the seventies), and regulatory programs are alive and a little uncomfortable perhaps but well. His urban-metropolitan emphasis has not disappeared and even his "bypassing" propensity persists (at least one-fifth of all federal aid still bypasses state governments). While the federal role in manpower training, economic development, social services, and poverty has changed and in some cases has been reduced, it has not been eliminated. To put it differently, many of his programs—even as expanded in the seventies—have become based in consensus with strong bipartisan support in Congress and strong interest-group support outside. Reaganism, in short, has generated a process whereby agreements finally are being hammered out on the worth of the Johnsonian programmatic legacy. And Johnson is faring fairly well.

So we return to the opening characterization of Lyndon Johnson—as the president who had more of an impact on the federal system than any since. The foregoing tracing of the post-Johnson years and especially the real Reagan record on federalism provide ample basis for this judgment. Certainly the intergovernmental system is even bigger, broader, deeper, and more complex than it was in 1968. Yet in my opinion the long-term fate of the Johnson legacy hangs heavily on whether his party recaptures some of the political party strength, fiscal caution, and principled pragmatism that characterized the Johnson era and Johnson the man. These after all still are essential foundations for a viable liberalism, and in an era of "deficit politics" they are indispensable.

The Great Society and the Growth of "Juridical Federalism": Protecting Civil Rights and Welfare

DAVID H. ROSENBLOOM

The Great Society's concept of federalism marked a significant turning point in the relationship of the federal government to other governmental jurisdictions in three respects. Philosophically, "the Great Society programs were a triumph for those who believed that the federal government should establish national goals and standards for social welfare and civil rights," and that "neither state-by-state variations in political belief nor fiscal capacity should prevent any citizen from having a full opportunity to develop his potential and to enjoy the benefits of the nation's prosperity."[1] This philosophical approach necessarily had fiscal and structural implications for American federalism. Fiscally, it involved the explosive expansion of federal grants-in-aid to other governmental units. Structurally, the Great Society changed the traditional character of federalism by dealing directly with local governments and agencies, rather than through state governments as intermediaries. This development was largely a result of the belief that the Great Society's philosophical and political objectives could not be achieved without a direct federal assault on the "urban crisis."[2]

Many of these developments have been extensively researched and reported upon elsewhere. Some have become the object of intense political opposition, as is manifested in the Reagan administration's call for a "New Federalism." One aspect, however, has gone relatively unnoticed until very recent years—that of the growth of "juridical federalism."[3] This is the direct involvement of the federal judiciary in a variety of aspects of state and local governance, including administrative operations and the allocation of funds. Juridical federalism may have arisen in any event as a check on the modern administrative state,[4] but philosophically it comports very well with the ideas of the Great Society toward federalism generally.

FEDERAL PROTECTION OF INDIVIDUAL'S RIGHTS AND WELFARE

A fundamental premise of the Great Society was that the federal government had an obligation to protect the basic civil and political rights of individuals from actions by the states in which they resided. Historically, this same premise was the basis of the Reconstruction era.[5] In the aftermath of the Civil War, it was first thought that military occupation of the South could protect the rights of the freedmen. Subsequently, it was believed that federal civil rights statutes, as well as the Thirteenth, Fourteenth, and Fifteenth constitutional amendments, which were enforceable in federal courts, could accomplish this objective. However, by the 1880s and 1890s it had become clear that this approach was ineffective because the federal courts themselves were reluctant to alter drastically the traditional character of American federalism by becoming actively involved in determining how the states could treat their own citizens.[6]

But if the federal judiciary did not act vigorously to enforce these federal guarantees of individual rights, who would? The obvious answer by the 1960s was that unless additional federal action were taken, many of these rights would in fact go unenforced. In particular, blacks would continue to be deprived of their federally "protected" civil and political rights as a result of discriminatory actions and policies undertaken by the various states. The Great Society was partly an effort by the federal government once again to afford genuine protection of the citizenry's federally guaranteed rights. This was most evident in the Voting Rights Act of 1965, but was also present in some aspects of the Civil Rights Act of 1964 and in other Great Society legislation. The Voting Rights Act authorized federal intervention in state and local elections where racial discrimination existed on a pervasive scale. In particular, the act allowed the Department of Justice to suspend the use of literacy tests and other prerequisites to voting in states or local subdivisions where less than 50 percent of the voting age populations were registered on 1 November 1964 or had voted in the presidential election that month. Such suspensions had a five-year duration, and the states could adopt new voting laws only with federal approval. The act was unsuccessfully challenged as a violation of the Tenth Amendment by South Carolina before the Supreme Court. A majority of the court in *South Carolina* v. *Katzenbach* (1966)[7] found it to be within Congress's power under the Fifteenth Amendment. However, Justice Black dissented in part on the grounds that the act did violence to traditional notions of American federalism:

> Section 5, by providing that some of the States cannot pass state laws or adopt state constitutional amendments without first being compelled to beg federal authorities to approve their policies, so distorts our constitutional structure of government as to render any distinction drawn in the Constitution between state and federal power almost meaningless. . . .[8]

Experience suggested that many of the Great Society's efforts to secure the basic civil and political rights of blacks and other groups would fail if the federal judiciary were largely unsympathetic to them. Indeed, President Johnson was acutely aware of this. He apparently viewed Franklin Roosevelt's early troubles with the Supreme Court as a key factor in limiting presidential power and the success of the New Deal.[9] According to Joseph A. Califano, Jr., "Johnson nominated scores of men and women to federal circuit and district judgeships, in large part because he believed they shared his philosophy about equal rights and racial discrimination."[10] Many of these judicial appointments are still on the bench, and many have been instrumental in the development and growth of the new juridical federalism.

JURIDICAL FEDERALISM

Although it could be defined to include additional elements, contemporary juridical federalism rests largely on two legal developments of great importance. The first is known as 42 U.S. Code, section 1983; this was originally part of the Civil Rights Act of 1871. It provides that:

> Every person who, under color of any statute, ordinance, regulation, custom, or usage, of any State or Territory, subjects, or causes to be subjected, any citizen of the United States or any other person within the jurisdiction thereof to the deprivation of any rights, privileges, or immunities secured by the Constitution and laws, shall be liable to the party injured in an action at law, suit in equity, or other proper proceeding for redress.

Until the 1970s this section of law was almost moribund because the federal judiciary had held that despite the apparent broad sweep of the statute in establishing liability, many public officials had a common law immunity from civil suits for damages. By the end of the 1970s, however, the federal judiciary had reversed the presumption that state and local administrative officials had an absolute immunity from such suits. Instead, it was reasoned that for the most part they had only a "qualified immunity." The current criterion is principally whether the state or local administrator knew or reasonably should have known that his or her actions would violate the federal constitutional or legal rights of the individuals upon whom he or she acted.[11] Governmental entities such as cities or administrative agencies are liable if their policies resulted in violation of such rights, regardless of what they "knew" or should have known.[12] The resuscitation of section 1983 has had a major impact on federalism because it enables federal judges to determine what state administrators should know about the constitutional and federal legal rights of those individuals with whom they interact in an official capacity. Federal courts can also assess personal and even punitive damages against them.[13]

The second major development is public law litigation. This is a fundamentally new model of lawsuit that has been developed primarily by the federal judiciary. It is seen as more of an exercise in "problem-solving" than as an exercise in specific dispute resolution.[14] Public law litigation tends to involve class action suits against governmental agencies or subdivisions. Often whole communities are directly involved, as in school desegregation suits. Consequently, judges must assess the interests of even those who are not direct parties to the case and are unrepresented in the litigation. This is a radical departure from the traditional litigation involving two well-defined parties. If relief is warranted, the judicial decree "seeks to adjust future behavior, not to compensate for past wrong. It is deliberately fashioned rather than logically deduced from the nature of the legal harm suffered. It provides for a complex, ongoing performance rather than a simple, one-shot, one-way transfer . . . [I]t prolongs and deepens, rather than terminates, the court's involvement with the dispute."[15] Common examples of public law litigation affecting federalism involve school desegregation and conditions in prisons and public mental health facilities.

Both these legal developments affected the basic nature of federalism. Both were outgrowths of judicial decision-making and interpretation. A new type of law suit was developed and a rarely enforced statute from the 1870s was revitalized by the federal judiciary itself. No outside political body thrust juridical federalism upon the federal judiciary. Cases had to be brought, to be sure, but juridical federalism is the federal judiciary's own creation. Its impact on federalism has been monumental. As James D. Carroll notes:

> [I]n the last decade several thousand damage suits have been filed by Americans against hundreds of state and local governments and thousands of state and local officials. The face amount of the damages claimed adds up to billions of dollars. In over half the states, one or more institutions—prisons, mental institutions, institutions for the retarded, juvenile homes—have been declared unconstitutional, as structured and administered. Many state and local government officials have found themselves subject to demands that they be held personally liable in money damages to individuals and organizations claiming they have been harmed by actions of these officials.[16]

THE GREAT SOCIETY ON THE BENCH: SOME EXAMPLES

Many of President Johnson's judicial appointees have been key participants in the development and application of the new juridical federalism. The judicial appointees of other presidents have also been participants, and no doubt some of Johnson's appointees have opposed the new approach. Nonetheless, as one goes down the list of federal judges sitting during the 1970s and early 1980s and considers some of the major cases of public law litigation, it is abundantly clear that many of the Great Society judges shared the Great Society's premise that the federal government had a direct responsibility to protect individuals against the actions of state governments, even at the cost of fundamentally altering traditional notions of federalism.

An illustrative review of some of the activities of some of President Johnson's judicial appointees pertaining to juridical federalism is facilitated by *The American Lawyer*'s "Complete Guide to Federal District Judges."[17] This publication reviewed the background, major rulings, philosophy, and courtroom style of all 560 federal district court judges in 1983. Johnson's appointees constituted 12.9 percent of the total. Among their decisions promoting juridical federalism were decrees requiring vast administrative and fiscal reforms of state and local school systems, electoral arrangements, personnel practices, prisons, and mental health facilities. Their decisions have created magnet schools, school busing to achieve desegregation, and racial quotas for integrating the public personnel systems. Federal judges have "ordered" the improvement of state and local administrative management. They have also had an impact on states' fiscal decision-making by holding that when it comes to prisons, facilities for the mentally ill or retarded, and, implicitly, school systems, "lack of funds is not an acceptable excuse for unconstitutional conditions."[18]

THE FUTURE OF JURIDICAL FEDERALISM

Opponents of juridical federalism view it as unduly invasive of state sovereignty under the Constitution. They find it particularly inappropriate that nonelected federal judges, holding office during good behavior, have "arrogated" to themselves functions traditionally performed by state and local elected and politically appointed officials. Opposition to juridical federalism tends to focus on three subissues: state sovereignty, representative appearance, and fiscal impacts.

Critics of juridical federalism often view it as a devastating encroachment by the federal judiciary upon matters of state governance. They argue that the essence of state sovereignty is a state's authority to govern itself as it sees fit within the broad parameters of the constitutional requirement that it have a republican form of government. On the other hand, proponents of juridical federalism note that the Fourteenth Amendment protects individuals from the deprivation of life, liberty, or property without due process of law and guarantees them equal protection of the law.

A clash between state governance and individual civil rights and liberties is often found in the treatment of state civil servants. One of the many opportunities to address the matter was presented by *Elrod* v. *Burns* (1976).[19] The issue, simply stated, was whether a state could choose by legislative design to use a patronage system for the appointment and dismissal of its public employees. The Supreme Court's judgment was that patronage dismissals constituted unconstitutional infringement of public employees' freedom of political belief and association. Justice Brennan stated this position most forcefully in an opinion joined by Justices White and Marshall. In dissent, Justice Powell, joined by Chief Justice Burger and Justice Rehnquist, denounced the federal judiciary's interference with a matter so intimately connected to the state's right:

. . . I would hold that a state or local government may elect to condition employment on the political affiliation of a prospective employee and on the political fortunes of the hiring incumbent. History and long-prevailing practice across the country support the view that patronage hiring practices make a sufficiently substantial contribution to the practical functioning of our democratic system to support their relatively modest intrusion on First Amendment interests. The judgment today unnecessarily constitutionalizes another element of American life. . . .[20]

Opponents of juridical federalism also view it as a serious breach of the principles of representative government. Nonelected federal judges are viewed as substituting their values for those of elected state and local representatives of the citizenry, thereby denying the population a substantial measure of political representation. This issue was addressed by the Supreme Court in *Milliken* v. *Bradley* (1974). The case involved the desegregation of the public schools in the Detroit metropolitan area. After finding the schools to be unconstitutionally racially segregated, the district court proposed to implement a sweeping remedy involving the consolidation of fifty-four independent school districts. The Supreme Court, through Chief Justice Burger, strongly opposed such an exercise of juridical federalism: "it is obvious from the scope of the interdistrict remedy itself that absent a complete restructuring of the laws of Michigan relating to school districts the District Court will become first, a *de facto* 'legislative authority' . . . and then the 'school superintendent' for the entire area. This is a task which few, if any, judges are qualified to perform and one which would deprive the people of control of the schools through their elected representatives."[21] Justices White, Douglas, Brennan, and Marshall dissented. Justice Marshall, in particular, dismissed the majority's argument on this point as "constructed of the flimsiest of threads."[22] In his view, juridical federalism was necessary to protect the constitutional rights of a minority against the tyranny of the representatives of the majority.

A third criticism of juridical federalism involves its pressures on state budgeting decisions. Judicial decisions giving states a choice of either upgrading their prisons and mental health facilities or closing them altogether place substantial pressures on state budgeting. States may virtually be forced to allocate additional funds to these functions. Funds must come from elsewhere, but unlike the typical legislature, the federal court does not formally consider the alternative sources: additional taxes, libraries, housing for the elderly, etc. In other words, the court does not prioritize when it considers the constitutional rights of prisoners or those in public mental health facilities. Sometimes, as when a federal court requires a very pleasant temperature range to be maintained in an institution,[23] critics have found juridical federalism particularly inept. The Supreme Court addressed some of these issues in *Pennhurst State School and Hospital* v. *Halderman* (1981).[24] A federal district court found that conditions at the Pennhurst facility for the retarded violated a federal constitutional right to be provided with minimally adequate habilitation in the least restrictive environment and to be free from harm. On appeal, the court of appeals avoided these constitutional issues and found instead that conditions at Pennhurst violated the federal Developmentally Disabled Assistance and Bill of Rights Act of 1975. The act was a federal-state funding statute. Whether it made federal funds contingent upon fulfillment of the act's "bill of rights" was the issue considered by the Supreme Court. A majority thought not, believing that based on the legislative history Congress was merely "encouraging" the states to meet such conditions. Justice White dissented in part in an opinion joined by Justices Brennan and Marshall. He argued that the state had a legal obligation not to spend public funds on any such facility that did not provide appropriate treatment, services, and habilitation. Moreover, he thought that the case could properly be litigated under 42 U.S. Code, section 1983—an issue upon which the majority expressed some skepticism.

These cases illustrate some of the complexities and problems associated with juridical federalism. They show how deeply it can cut into traditional concepts and exercises of state sovereignty. They also suggest that to a considerable extent the fate of juridical federalism will rest with future Supreme Court decisions—and consequently, future appointments to the court. Clearly, the concept may find less support as the number of Johnson's judicial appointees continues to dwindle. The impetus for juridical federalism also could be blunted by the states themselves through policies and programs that protect the constitutional rights of their more disadvantaged and vulnerable residents.

Regardless of the specific directions taken in the immediate future, however, the advent and growth of juridical federalism has made it a fundamental aspect of contemporary federalism. Although federal judicial intervention in state and local governance may become less frequent in the future, the means for such intervention have been fully established. In keeping with the Great Society's concept of federalism, the federal judiciary has expanded its role in directly protecting individuals' rights and opportunities against encroachments by state and local governments. The constitutional landscape of American federalism has consequently been substantially altered.

Conclusion

Great Society—Past, Present,
and Possible Future

POLICIES, THEMES, AND PROGRAMS

The federal government's efforts to expand the choices of the poor and revitalize downtrodden areas during the sixties and the seventies were unique. Contrary to the massive federal intervention in American domestic life that occurred in the thirties, the primary genesis was not the restoration of the economy but the improved well-being of people and their environment. Different from the comprehensive and pervasive federal involvement in the nation's civic affairs that often occurs during war, the basic objective was not the destruction of a distant enemy but the construction of a better society.

For one relatively brief period, the national government—the president, the bureaucracy, Congress, and the courts—discovered poverty and assumed responsibility for ameliorating its burden and finding a cure. In doing so the federal government affirmed the concept of America as a single national community rather than as thousands of separate communities divided by class or caste. For the first time in the nation's history, cities, the orphans of the American constitution, became visible players in the federal system. Similarly, for the first time in the nation's evolution, electoral politics, both in theory and practice, often took a backseat to "something" we couldn't quite define but called citizen participation or participatory democracy.

The initiatives, begun during the sixties and subsequently expanded during the seventies, reflected a national commitment to changing the rules of behavior that historically governed our relationships to one another, the distribution of private income, the balance between public and private consumption, and the number and range of public services provided to white and minority, affluent and poor citizens.

In the span of twenty short years the nation outlawed most forms of overt public- and private-sector discrimination; it granted minorities preference with respect to certain jobs and educational opportunities; it significantly expanded income-support programs for the needy and sometimes the not-so-needy; it invented and initiated numerous disparate federal programs to support basic local public services for poor people and poor neighborhoods. It tried both to help people help themselves and to provide a basic level of life-saving or life-giving support to those who ostensibly could not help themselves.

Federal efforts or initiatives during the sixties and seventies were not always neat or logical. While rhetoric often focused on achievement of equality of opportunity, activities at times appeared premised on securing equality of outcome or condition. Although the very visible War on Poverty program appeared to be aimed at assisting the poor find a competitive place in the system, the less visible but far larger entitlement programs that evolved seemed premised on a commitment to assist a poverty population that could not, should not, or would not compete.

Consistency regarding long-term or even intermediate-term objectives was not a perceived virtue. Heuristic goals associated with many programs defied strategic "how to" knowledge and the related capacity of federal, state, and local government institutions to deliver. It was a period where moral rather than strategic imperatives often governed. Policy-makers and policy advocates *believed* that government intervention combined with money could make a difference. Faith, more often than not, substituted for the absence of predictable cause-and-effect relationships in the design and development of programs. It was a heady period defined by decent, committed, and competent people.

But did it work?

As several chapters in this book suggest, opinion on this question varies widely. Put two scholars, evaluators, or practitioners in a room and they are likely to offer three conclusions regarding the wisdom of social policies and programs initiated during the last two decades. Two relatively popular and positively reviewed books have recently been published, each claiming to give its readers the final or almost final word on the effect of the Great Society and its successor policies. To John Schwarz, author of *America's Hidden Success*,[1] the domestic initiatives of the last twenty years were unambiguously successful. Strong economic growth proved the validity of Keynesian economics; the reduction of poverty testified to the wisdom of federal efforts to expand job, education, health, and income support programs. He notes:

> The introduction and enlargement after 1960 of the many governmental programs to reduce poverty and environmental pollution were associated with solid progress over a broad spectrum of national concerns. During the past twenty years of the post-Eisenhower era, government programs led to a diminishing of poverty among Americans by more than half. They significantly reduced flagrant malnutrition, lessened inequality in access to medical services, and were associated with dramatic declines in infant mortality rates among the poor and the minorities. They helped relieve overcrowded and substandard housing. They also improved the education of impoverished children and gave employable skills to thousands of otherwise unemployed adults. In the wake of the environmental programs, pollution levels in the nation's air were generally reversed, and pollution of the nation's waters was checked. A single generation of Americans realized these accomplishments, enough perhaps for any generation to leave as its legacy. Notwithstanding the crescendo of criticism that ushered out the decade of the 1970s, the post-Eisenhower era was in fact an age of distinguished public achievement.[2]

Charles Murray, author of *Losing Ground*,[3] saw these domestic policies and programs as almost an unambiguous disaster. If trends observed during the fifties had been allowed to continue, unimpeded by government intervention, America likely would have (in Murray's view) witnessed continued progress in reducing poverty. More to the point, the tremendous growth in the dollar volume and number of federal domestic programs during the seventies coincided with a halt in any statistically significant reduction in the numbers of people living in poverty. Indeed, despite continued economic growth and a quantum leap in the availability of federal assistance to the poor, the absolute and relative percentages of Americans living in poverty seemed impervious to change.

In other words, more federal aid to the poor, according to Murray, has not brought more opportunity and a better life for recipients. Quite the contrary: the poor—generally synonymous in his book with minorities—were actually worse off in 1980 than before the beginning of the Great Society. Irrespective of the indices—jobs, education, crime—the picture of the poor during the seventies was not a bright one. Federal social policy and programs muted the incentive of the poor to participate in the system, to achieve, to compete, to leave the ranks of the poor. Murray notes:

> The unadorned statistic gives pause. In 1968, when Lyndon John-son left office, 13 percent of Americans were poor, using the official definition. Over the next twelve years, our expenditures on social welfare quadrupled. And, in 1980, the percentage of poor Ameri-cans was—13 percent. Can it be that nothing had changed?[4]
>
> Then, after two decades of reasonably steady progress, improve-ment slowed in the late sixties and stopped altogether in the seven-ties. The proportion dipped to its low point, 11 percent, in 1973. A higher proportion of the American population was officially poor in 1980 than at any time since 1967. By then it stood at 13 percent and was heading up. The number of people living in poverty stopped declining just as the public-assistance program budgets and the rate of increase in those budgets were highest. The question is why this should be.[5]
>
> The proposition . . . is that things not only got worse for the poor and disadvantaged beginning (in most cases) in the last half of the 1960s, they got much worse than they "should have gotten" under the economic and social conditions that prevailed in the so-ciety at large. This is of course a hazardous assertion. It is not sus-ceptible to proof, and, ex post facto, we concoct some sort of benign explanation for almost any catastrophe—benign in that it tells us we were helpless to prevent it.[6]
>
> I have for the most part used the data to make a case that the reforms flowing from the new wisdom of the 1960s were a blunder on purely pragmatic grounds.[7]

Will the real Great Society come forward?

Regrettably, in light of the needed debate prompted by President Reagan's desire to reduce domestic spending and by the administration's penchant for defining its commitment to the "safety net" primarily in terms of middle-class entitlements, neither the Schwarz nor the Murray book provides precise or conclusive analytical direction. Indeed both books, like much of the literature concerning the Great Society and its aftermath, end up using partial data to support the seemingly preformed or preanalysis conclusions of their authors.

Clearly, Murray is correct in faulting much of the analysis concerning the Great Society for its failure to acknowledge that there was life be-fore 1964 and that poverty numbers were moving downward during the quiescent Eisenhower years. Just as clearly, however, Murray's contribution as a statistical historian is effectively limited by his unwillingness to link the behavior of the economy and demographic changes in the seventies to the failure to make progress in reducing poverty. Indeed, as Frank Levy has noted, Murray's frequent use of increases in per capita gross national product (GNP) to support the assertion that the economy should be held blameless for static poverty levels during the seventies hides more relevant negative economic data.[8] With the maturing of the baby-boom generation and changes in life-style, household formation rates were at unprecedently high levels. While GNP per capita increased, real GNP per worker did not. In addition, the economy suffered stronger cyclical cycles than in the recent past. Succinctly speaking, if as most economists agree robust and sustained economic growth is essential to a significant reduction in poverty, then the uneven performance of the economy from 1970 to 1980 at least helps explain the sluggishness of aggregate poverty data. The economy had all it could do to accommodate the more than 30 million new labor force participants who entered the scene between 1965 and 1980.[9]

Arguments over the relevance or irrelevance of trends and their relationship to federal social welfare policies are interesting. But they blur still underanalyzed relationships between specific programs and the behavior of specific individuals and groups. Any policy debate worth its analytical weight should, at a minimum, note what several authors in this book indicate:

(1) Poverty rates without federal transfer programs would have been significantly higher in the seventies and the eighties. Far more people who could not or should not have worked—the old, the infirm, the discriminated against—would have been hungry, without adequate shelter, and without decent health care.

(2) Many millions of previously poor minority households appeared to escape from poverty and dependence during the sixties and early seventies. Even Murray admits that "employed blacks" made important gains in the struggle against wage discrimination, and he notes that the ratio of black to white income improved for full-time workers.[10]

Cause and effect relationships concerning income and mobility remain difficult to discern in a precise manner. But economic growth alone cannot explain black progress. Overall the economy likely accounted for only about 2 percent of the reduction in poverty levels. Expanded education and training options combined with affirmative action efforts clearly helped expand minority employment options.

(3) While, as Murray suggests, negative job, education, and crime trends affecting minorities—particularly the young—during the seventies

should raise issues concerning the relevance of related domestic policies and programs, positive data (not mentioned by Murray) concerning housing, health, and educational improvements suggest that the problem, if one exists, may well be in program design and execution rather than in basic commitments.

Direct and in-kind income transfer programs constitute at present the most significant and controversial federal commitment to the poor. Many argue that the beneficence of programs such as AFDC, Medicaid, and unemployment insurance has decreased the willingness or desire of recipients to work hard at finding a job or securing a good education. Why should they if household opportunity costing equations favor remaining on welfare? Or so the story line goes! It is reminiscent of Harold and Phyllis—a mythical couple Murray uses to illustrate the positive economics and related benefits of welfare.[11]

But the data regarding the behavior of welfare recipients are neither as pejorative as the rhetoric or as clear-cut as classroom theories and models suggest. Despite numerous experiments and millions of dollars worth of evaluation, the precise link between diverse welfare benefits and household decisions to work or not to work has not been defined conclusively.

Perhaps equally relevant, the characteristics associated with welfare recipients suggest that considerable misunderstanding exists concerning their behavior patterns. Contrary to what many critics say, most recipients are not permanent receivers of welfare. Many are labor force participants, and many who do not work are unable to find or hold a job. In March 1979 more than one-fourth (28.5 percent of the families receiving AFDC had been on the rolls continuously for less than thirteen months and nearly 57 percent had been receiving assistance for three years or less. Almost 75 percent had been receiving assistance for five years or less, and only about one in fourteen families (7.1 percent) had been on the rolls for more than ten consecutive years.[12] Preliminary estimates show that the net effect of eligibility restrictions imposed by the Reagan administration to limit welfare to the nonworking poor did not cause former recipients to withdraw from work to gain welfare. According to the Urban Institute, the recidivism rate of 10 to 20 percent was no higher than before the administration's changes.[13]

Where do we go from here?

Historians and makers of history have popularized the cyclical nature of social welfare policy development. Accordingly, the president, Congress, and indeed the American public will be willing to accept or initiate major new domestic programs relatively infrequently. Short periods of executive and/or legislative activity will be followed by long periods of relative quiet. Major breaks in or departures from public policy will ordinarily not occur or will occur only in periods of visible crisis or need.

Unanticipated events often disrupt predictions based on the recorded past. In this context, although analysts may dispute the impact of the Reagan administration's domestic policies, they do seem to constitute more than a blip or idiosyncrasy. Whether or not they should generate a modification of the cyclical model of public policy making or the in-crementalist's assumption regarding policy development is still open to question. Clearly the president's

> rejection of moderate to liberal consensus that had come to domi-nate both Republican and democratic administrations over the pre-vious forty years, his vision of a better America based on less gov-ernment and more individual enterprise, and his efforts to translate this division into a new agenda for the nation have been both dis-tinctive and controversial. Not since 1932 has there been such a re-direction of public purposes. . . .[14]

The president would have eradicated most of the hallmarks of the Great Society and would have shrunk social insurance programs to a scope approximating their New Deal origins. As things have turned out, Congress and the courts have moderated the president's intentions. Congress acted to protect many of the more effective programs and to hold together the bottom tier of the safety net. Congress and the courts have moderated the president's intentions. Congress and the courts rejected several of the administration's more ambitious efforts to narrow or reinterpret civil rights laws. Nevertheless, President Reagan has successfully shifted the nation's social policy agenda from problem solving to budget cutting, and as long as the federal deficit remains a problem, there is little room for the agenda to shift back.[15]

THE FUTURE

Regrettably, for those who cherish simple ideologies or easy answers, absolute wisdom and clairvoyance are not characteristics associated with most public policy-makers. Often, as the Dutch proverb has it, the best "cause is best, not because its anticipated results provide conclusive evi-dence regarding benefits and costs, but because it has the best pleader." In this context, increasing numbers of poor Americans have failed of late to secure their share of academic, business, and government pleaders. Indeed, concern for poverty and deteriorated neighborhoods occupied by poor people no longer appears fashionable or politically viable. Yet problems remain and a strong case can be made that the policies of the last four years have exacerbated them.

Increased social ills have occurred simultaneously with, and many would indicate partly because of, severe administration-generated budget cuts in social programs and because of administration-supported restrictive monetary policies. The administration held that both policies were essential to remedy economic ills and that tight monetary policies and domestic spending reductions would lead to greater economic growth, more jobs, and lower unemployment. The administration hoped that the rising tide would float all ships and their crews—including their minority and low-income crews. But it has not worked out that way.

As indicated earlier in this book, since 1980 for the first time in almost twenty years the numbers—absolute and relative—of poor people have increased significantly. Job and labor market statistics among low-income individuals—particularly young minority individuals—are not good. Further, data indicate that low- and moderate-income households face growing difficulties in maintaining their historical share of total income.

Current economic and fiscal constraints, however, are real. Combined with visible political antipathy in Congress and the nation regarding any increases in the federal social welfare role, these constraints likely will defeat any major effort to secure a significant increase in federal resources for the poor or for distressed neighborhoods.

But consensus—between liberals and conservatives, between Republicans and Democrats, among Americans of all political persuasion—may be able to be reached on the following set of principles, policies, and programs.

(1) *The poor have suffered enough:* The aggregate impact of recent budget and tax policies have left the poor in a net deficit position. Their share of income has declined and they have lost on average over $500 in real income. Similarly, means-tested programs have been reduced from nearly 4 percent to approximately 3 percent of the gross national product, while nonmeans-tested programs have hardly been touched.[16]

Congress, in its necessary and continuous efforts to shave the budget deficit, should exclude from this process programs aiding the poor. Ending tax expenditures or closing tax loopholes, reductions in nonmeans-tested programs, strategic tax increases, and reductions in the rate of growth of the defense budget would be more equitable options to choose from to reduce the federal budget deficit.

(2) *Equity and efficiency concerns should mandate more targeting of scarce existing resources to the needy:* Recent legislative and regulatory changes have led to diversion of federal block-grant and categorical program funds away from needy people and communities. While a conscious strategy aimed at helping deteriorating as opposed to already deteriorated neighborhoods and the "new" or working poor as opposed to the chronically poor could well be appropriate in light of resource constraints, the sustained leakage of funds, once focused on poverty, raises serious issues related to equity. Congress should consider specific legislative amendments to retarget key "still on the books" social policy initiatives of the sixties and seventies.

(3) *Across-the-board cuts or reductions in the rate of growth of nonmeans-tested programs (such as Social Security) is neither strategic nor fair:* Repetitive proposals to slow down the rate of growth in Social Security and other nonmeans-tested programs affecting the elderly by postponing or changing COLAS, by amending computations regarding benefits, or by increasing taxes are often regressive. When *all* recipients are treated alike, lower-income elderly households end up bearing a relatively larger share of the burden.

Perhaps it is time to reconceptualize programs like Social Security. To reduce their collective drain on resources, to open up options regarding other expenditures, and to protect needy beneficiaries, consideration should be given to applying a means test for the receipt of benefits and further extending the progressive characteristics associated with wage-based taxes. Social Security, in particular, ought to be restructured as an insurance not as a pension program. Benefits should flow primarily to low-income needy elderly.

(4) *The "safety net" has become full of gaps. Many innocent people have been hurt. While further budget-cutting will be essential, selective budget increases are warranted in instances where basic life-giving or life-protecting support has been withdrawn precipitately from the chronically poor and/or the new cyclically poor:* During the eighties, benefits cuts (real value) exacerbated the effect on the poor of unfavorable economic conditions. Further, "while the average value of public assistance received by a poor family rose 5 percent after inflation between 1974

and 1977, that value declined 17 percent between 1979 and 1982. Since the distribution of income other than transfers appears to be unequal, even a period of substantial growth may not lead to reductions in poverty . . . unless recent declines in the real value of means tested transfers are reversed." Maintaining key transfer programs at current real values, combined with increasing coverage of Medicaid to include all families with children and incomes below the poverty level (including families not eligible for welfare), should be a congressional priority.

(5) *Welfare has become subject to several myths—myths that mute the need for a legitimate debate concerning often inconsistent welfare objectives and programs:* Contrary to conventional wisdom—wisdom now fed by revisionist scholars—most people receiving welfare are not shiftless and are not on welfare on a permanent basis. Clearly the relationships between benefit levels, marginal tax rates, and work incentives need to be continually reviewed; just as clearly the assumption that abolition of all welfare programs would generate an increased quality of life for recipients is facile. Neither the nonprofit nor the private sector is capable of picking up the tab, nor does the job market look particularly good for often undertrained, undereducated, underskilled recipients.

It is conceivable that we as a nation have relied too much on or overemphasized welfare as a response to poverty. While the nation's current mood does not grant legitimacy to the idea that economic status alone should determine eligibility, neither does it lend credence to the idea that only the disabled, aged, and others in similar categories should receive welfare. While welfare in some states may provide a disincentive to work for some people, conclusive data do not exist regarding the extent. Clearly, we have yet to define a response to the increasing feminization of poverty. Do we want female heads of poor households to work, or to maintain often already fragile households?

Our limited knowledge argues the need for analysis and reform, not for across-the-board reduction and elimination. Strategies to develop a national threshold eliminating state-by-state inequities and to develop a clearer link between welfare benefits and training as well as work options are appropriate to examine. Revoking welfare benefits is not!

(6) *Elimination of discrimination and racism remains an unfinished agenda. To argue that increased participation by the poor in the economic life of the nation is important without strongly affirming the need to reduce artificial barriers denying minorities decent housing, jobs, and educational choices suggests logical malfeasance or worse:* The

Reagan administration's symbolic and substantive record on civil rights is at best uneven. It has not rigorously enforced fair housing laws; it has canceled the executive orders of the previous administration linking availability of grants to overt actions extending equal opportunity; it has cut back on aid aimed at fostering urban school desegregation efforts; it has wavered on affirmative action programs related to jobs.

While debate concerning strategy flourishes, consensus seems to exist among most Americans that discrimination and racism are wrong. Congressional efforts to strengthen federal equal opportunity initiatives appear to be in order. Increasing the penalty for housing discrimination and providing for administrative adjudication of housing discriminatory cases would be a good first step.

(7) *Improved education and better job opportunities remain crucial to efforts to help the poor become self-supporting. While recent test data suggest improvement, elementary and secondary education programs now available or accessible to the poor are often inferior. Similarly, unemployment and nonlabor force participation rates among the poor, particularly young minority poor, remain appalling:* In light of the less than overwhelming results of many federally supported programs of the sixties, seventies, and early eighties, certainty is lacking about how best to extend job and educational opportunities to the underemployed or undereducated. However, a number of promising options deserve consideration.

One such option is federal reaffirmation and encouragement of court or school desegreation efforts. Despite waning political support, school integration, when successful, has expanded the educational opportunities of involved minorities. Assistance should also be increased to financially strapped school districts to help them secure and/or train top-notch principals—principals capable of providing educational leadership to their schools. The need to find principals who can lead and are given the opportunity to lead is the key reform agreed on by most recent analysts of America's educational problems. Aid—perhaps in the form of wage and training subsidies—should be considered in order to develop close linkages between the availability of jobs and successful completion of high school educational programs. New incentives to encourage the private sector to guarantee summer, after-school, and postgraduate jobs to high school students would be desirable. Assured access to employment will increase student desire and willingness to perform well in school and to remain in school through graduation.

Ultimately a nation committed to reducing dependency, if guided by standards of both equity and efficiency, will equate strategies to reduce welfare assistance to the poor who can and should work with strategies to increase and if necessary guarantee jobs. If "workfare" is to diminish the need or substitute for welfare, then consideration by Congress of possible "last resort" job strategies may well be essential, in light of the gap between the skills of many unemployed people and the job market.

POSSIBILITIES AND PROBABILITIES

Despite the rhetoric of the administration, it has not eliminated the need for a national government. Expenditures continue to grow for programs to assist people who are not poor and for efforts to increase the nation's defense readiness. Like many of the initiatives aimed at helping the needy, the nonmeans-tested programs and programs to build up the military are often premised more on partial data, possibilities, and ultimately faith than on proof. But unlike many of the antipoverty initiatives, these programs have received the support of the American president, Congress, and the people. This bit of moral ambivalence is related to the new facts of American life. Declining growth rates have created a smaller economic pie to distribute or redistribute. Competition for resources has placed the poor and minorities at a political disadvantage. In this context our ability to expand the opportunities of the needy will be sorely tested. Our failure to do so will convert the American dream into an American nightmare.

Notes

INTRODUCTION

1 Speaker John McCormack and an unnamed reporter as quoted in James L. Sundquist, *Politics and Policy: The Eisenhower, Kennedy and Johnson Years* (Washington, D.C.: Brookings Institution, 1968), p. 1.
2 The term "private affluence and public squalor" was initially used by Adlai Stevenson. It is a recurring theme, however, in the liberal thought of the period. See, for example, John Kenneth Galbraith, *The Affluent Society* (Boston: Houghton Mifflin, 1960).
3 Lyndon Johnson, speech delivered at the University of Michigan, 22 May 1964.

THE GREAT SOCIETY 1984: RELIC OR REALITY

1 Sar A. Levitan and Robert Taggart, *The Promise of Greatness: The Social Programs of the Last Decade and Their Major Achievements* (Cambridge, Mass.: Harvard University Press, 1976).
2 John E. Schwarz, *America's Hidden Success: A Reassessment of Twenty Years of Public Policy* (New York: Norton, 1983).
3 Doris Kearns, *Lyndon Johnson and the American Dream* (New York: Harper and Row, 1976).
4 Robert A. Caro, *The Years of Lyndon Johnson* (New York: Knopf, 1982).
5 James MacGregor Burns, *Leadership* (New York: Harper and Row, 1978).
6 Merle Miller, *Lyndon: An Oral Biography* (New York: Putnam, 1980), p. xix.
7 The authors cited are among the academic pioneers in the field of policy implementation. All of their major works can be found in the bibliography included in Robert T. Nakamura and Frank Smallwood, *The Politics of Policy Implementation* (New York: St. Martin's, 1980).
8 Peter Rossi, "Issues in the Evaluation of Human Services Delivery," *Evaluation Quarterly* 2, 4 (November 1978): 574.

IS NEW FEDERALISM THE WAVE OF THE FUTURE?

1 Brochures describing Great Society Conference, spring 1984, University of Colorado, co-hosted by the president of the university and the Graduate School of Public Affairs.
2 New Leftists Marvin Gettleman and David Mermelstein suggested that the

Great Society's "strategy of social change initiated 'from the top down'" was intended to "bring about such reforms in America that a socialist program will be rendered obsolete." They conceded that this was not quite "Bismarckian authoritarianism," but it "is certainly a kind of bureaucratic elitism that can be contrasted with the tradition of American pluralism and voluntarism" (Marvin Gettleman and David Mermelstein, Great Society Reader [New York: Vintage Books, 1967], p. 455).

3 "Selections from the Port Huron Statement," in How Democratic Is America?, edited by Robert A. Goldwin (Chicago: Rand-McNally, 1969), p. 7.

4 Stokely Carmichael and Charles V. Hamilton, Black Power: The Politics of Liberation in America (New York: Vintage Books, 1967), pp. 53, 37, 39.

5 Michael Novak, The Rise of the Unmeltable Ethnics (New York: Macmillan, 1973), p. 321.

6 "Liberalism and the National Idea," in Left, Right and Center, edited by Robert A. Goldwin (Chicago: Rand-McNally, 1967), p. 143. Samuel Beer is perhaps the most thoughtful analyst of the community-building emphasis of contemporary American liberalism, which found its sharpest expression in Herbert Croly's The Promise of American Life, published in 1909. See also Beer's "The Idea of the Nation," The New Republic 19 and 26 (April 1982): 23–29.

7 According to Michael Harrington, the isolation of the underprivileged from the larger society—the fact that they did not "belong" in any sense to the greater, national community—was at the core of the problem of poverty. This led to his "vision" for America: the "political, economic, and social integration of the poor with the rest of the society. The second nation in our midst, the other America, must be brought into the Union" (Michael Harrington, The Other America [Baltimore: Penguin Books, 1967], p. 164).

8 Lyndon B. Johnson, My Hope for America (New York: Random House, 1964), pp. 44–45. Alvin Schorr, as deputy assistant secretary at HEW under Johnson, captured perfectly the connection between the goal of building a national community and the Great Society's social welfare initiatives in several essays written in the late 1960s and published as Explorations in Social Policy (New York: Basic Books, 1968). As he noted in one, Johnson's "attack on poverty . . . sets out to commit the nation to oneness." The goal of "an integrated society," he argued, would inspire the sacrifices necessary to eradicate poverty: "we should be relieved and delighted to substitute for a new refrigerator or a second television set a sense of commitment and community" (p. 268). In another essay tellingly entitled "National Community and Housing Policy," Schorr maintains that "if we are to be one nation, those who have money and power must devote the resources required to produce housing for poor people" (p. 274).

9 Johnson, My Hope, p. 51. The idea of national community also lay behind Johnson's emphasis on "consensus" throughout his administration. His "basic theme" in meetings with national leaders immediately after Kennedy's assassination was that "people must put aside their selfish aims in the larger cause of the nation's interest. They must start trusting each other; they must start communicating with each other; and they must start working together." These meetings persuaded Johnson that "there was a consensus—a broad, deep and pervasive consensus among most groups within our diverse society" (Lyndon Johnson, The Vantage Point [New York: Popular Library, 1971], pp. 30, 41). This led Johnson to believe that "someday we will see an America that knows

no North or South, no East or West—an America undivided by creed or color, untorn by suspicion or strife." Johnson, *My Hope*, p. 17.

10 Johnson, *Vantage Point*, p. 74.

11 See especially Herbert J. Storing, *What the Anti-Federalists Were For* (Chicago: University of Chicago Press, 1981), pp. 15–23.

12 In one sense, of course, the Great Society acknowledged—and may even have helped stimulate—the "small republican" renaissance through its community action programs. As Johnson noted, The Community Action Program (CAP) was based on "one of the oldest ideas of our democracy, as old as the New England town meeting—self determination at the local level" (Johnson, *Vantage Point*, p. 74). Nonetheless, if we may take Daniel P. Moynihan's word for it, Johnson was never entirely comfortable with the CAP idea, precisely because it focused on building local communities rather than the national community. CAP, Moynihan suggests, was a product of heterogeneous New York, while the broader war on poverty was a product of homogeneous Washington; the former was "fascinated by racial, ethnic and religious diversity," while the latter was "fiercely loyal to the Republic and still trying to fashion a nation out of continent" (Daniel P. Moynihan, *Maximum Feasible Misunderstanding* [New York: Free Press, 1970], p. 147).

13 In a symposium on the Great Society organized by *Commentary* in 1973, Bayard Rustin noted the curious but nonetheless real connection between Nixon's "New Federalism" proposals and the New Left and Black Power critiques of the Great Society. He suggested that "the Left bears substantial responsibility for [Nixon's federalism program]. Decentralization has become attractive at least partially because of those who have decried the powers of Washington while insisting, from a leftward vision, that the fundamental task is bringing government 'closer to the people.' Among whites, this attitude permeated the New Left. . . . For blacks, it was reflected in the emphasis on 'nation-building' at the expense of broad strategies for social change" (Bayard Rustin, *Commentary* [May 1973], p. 14, cited in Henry J. Schmandt et al., "CDBG: Continuity or Change?" *Publius* [Summer 1983]: 7).

14 Jimmy Carter, *The Presidential Campaign, 1976*, 2 vols. (Washington, D.C.: Government Printing Office, 1978), 1:705–9.

15 Jimmy Carter, "Let the People Rule," remarks to the Executive Club of Chicago, September 1975 (unpublished manuscript).

16 S. Kenneth Howard, "DeFacto New Federalism," *Intergovernmental Perspective* (Winter 1984), pp. 4ff.

17 Walter F. Mondale, statement for the National Council on Aging's magazine, *Perspective on Aging*, 20 February 1984, press release, Mondale for President Campaign.

18 Walter F. Mondale, "That Old-Time Mondale Religion that the Californians Loved," *Washington Post*, 23 January 1983.

19 Senator Gary Hart, "Address to the Yale Divinity School Convocation," 18 September 1982, press release. Hart's rejection of centralized federal programs and embrace of decentralization typifies what has come to be called neoliberalism. Robert Reich, for instance, argues that social welfare programs in the future will be provided not through central government bureaucracies, but through democratically reorganized local businesses: "Public funds now spent directly on . . . services"—these include "health care, social security, day care, disabil-

ity benefits, unemployment benefits, relocation assistance"—will be "made available to businesses, according to the number of chronically unemployed they agree to hire" (Robert Reich, *The Next American Frontier* [New York: Times Books, 1983], p. 248).

The emphasis on decentralization and localism becomes even more pronounced as we move toward the far left of today's political spectrum, as a quick perusal of *The Nation, Dissent, In These Times,* and (until recently) *democracy* would demonstrate. John Schaar, for instance, is pleased that "thousands of people and small groups have seen through the destructiveness and logic of bigness, centralization, and technology run amok" and are looking for "new ways to act and work, ways that stress place, community and commitment, decentralization and local control. . . ." (John Schaar, *In These Times*, 8–14 February 1984, p. 18). William Appleman Williams calls upon American radicals to "confront centralized nationalism" and to begin to "create a human-scale participatory democracy to establish priorities and procedures at each [level] of everyday life" (William Appleman Williams, *democracy*, October 1981, p. 95). Bruce Stokes argues that "participatory community groups can reestablish a central role in solving problems at the local level, leading to political decentralization and cultural pluralism that is impossible in a welfare state dominated by the federal government" (Bruce Stokes, "Self-Help in the Welfare State," in *Rethinking Liberalism*, edited by Walter T. Anderson [New York: Avon Books, 1983], p. 98).

20   Jesse Jackson, "A Call to Black America," *Chicago Tribune*, 18 April 1976.

TAX REFORM FROM 1964 TO 1984—A BRIEF RETROSPECT

1   Since the Great Society Conference, the president has recommended major changes in the tax system.

POVERTY IN THE UNITED STATES

1   U.S. House of Representatives, Subcommittee on Oversight and Subcommittee on Public Assistance of the Committee on Ways and Means, *Background Material on Poverty* (Washington, D.C.: Government Printing Office, 17 October 1983).

2   Sheldon Danziger, Peter Gottschalk, Robert J. Rubin, and Timothy M. Smeeding, "Recent Increases in Poverty: Testimony before the House Ways and Means Committee," IRP Discussion Paper no. 740-83. Cited in "Poverty in the United States: Where Do We Stand Now?" IRP *Focus* (Madison: University of Wisconsin, Institute for Research on Poverty, Winter 1984), p. 2.

3   Robert Pear, "Rate of Poverty Found to Persist in Face of Gains," *New York Times*, 3 August 1984. Pp. A1, B8.

4   Robert Pear, "Study Finds Poverty Among Children is Increasing," *New York Times*, 22 May 1985. Pp. A1, D26.

5   "Poverty in the United States," pp. 2–5.

6   Ibid., p. 7.

7   Ibid., p. 8.

8   Ibid., pp. 2–4.
9   "Facts and Figures," *Boston Globe*, 27 July 1985.
10 "A Further Look at the Budget Debate," *Monitor* (Washington, D.C.: Center for Community Change, April 1984), p. 3.
11 U.S. Bureau of the Census, *Money Income and Poverty Status of Families and Persons in the United States*, P-60, no. 149 (Washington, D.C.: Government Printing Office, 1985).

WAR ON POVERTY: ASSUMPTIONS, HISTORY,
AND RESULTS

1   Carl M. Brauer, *John F. Kennedy and the Second Reconstruction* (New York: Columbia University Press, 1977), p. 103.
2   Michael Harrington, *The Other America* (New York: Macmillan, 1962), p. 179.
3   Ibid., p. 12.
4   Ibid., p. 15.
5   James T. Patterson, *America's Struggle Against Poverty, 1900–1980* (Cambridge, Mass.: Harvard University Press, 1981), p. 176.
6   Dwight MacDonald, "Our Invisible Poor," *New Yorker*, 19 January 1963, pp. 82–132.
7   Godfrey Hodgson, *America in Our Time* (New York: Vintage Books, 1978), pp. 172–73.
8   Brauer, *John F. Kennedy*, p. 106.
9   Ibid., p. 112. See also James L. Sundquist, ed., *On Fighting Poverty* (New York: Basic Books, 1969), p. 29.
10 Charles Silberman, "The Misguided War on Poverty," *Fortune* 72 (August 1965): 224, 226.
11 John A. Garraty, *Unemployment in History: Economic Thought and Public Policy* (New York: Harper and Row, 1978), p. 242.
12 Brauer, *John F. Kennedy*, p. 115.
13 Hannah H. Meissner, *Poverty in the Affluent Society*, rev. ed. (New York: Harper and Row, 1973), pp. 202–9.
14 Sundquist, ed., *On Fighting Poverty*, p. 29; Meissner, *Poverty*, pp. 210–15.
15 Frances Fox Piven and Richard A. Cloward, *Regulating the Poor: The Functions of Public Welfare* (New York: Random House, 1971), pp. 248–82.
16 Patterson, *America's Struggle*, p. 172.
17 Ibid., p. 171.
18 Lester Thurow, *The Zero Sum Society* (New York: Penguin Books, 1981), p. 160.
19 Daniel P. Moynihan, ed., *On Understanding Poverty* (New York: Basic Books, 1969), p. 5.
20 Ibid., pp. 30, 47.
21 Lee Rainwater and William L. Yancey, *The Moynihan Report and the Politics of Controversy* (Cambridge, Mass.: MIT Press, 1967).
22 Christopher Lasch, *Haven in a Heartless World* (New York: Basic Books, 1977), p. 160.
23 Rainwater and Yancey, *The Moynihan Report*, p. 200.

24 Lasch, *Haven in a Heartless World*, p. 164.

25 Ibid., p. 165.

26 William Julius Wilson, *The Declining Significance of Race*, 2nd ed. (Chicago: University of Chicago Press, 1980), p. 160.

27 Silberman, "The Misguided War," p. 158.

28 Ibid.

29 Michael Harrington, "The Will to Abolish Poverty," *Saturday Review* 173 (27 July 1968): 12, 40.

30 Edward C. Banfield, *The Unheavenly City Revisited* (Boston: Little, Brown, 1974), p. 236.

31 Ibid., p. 237.

32 Ibid., pp. 238, 266.

33 Martin Anderson, *Welfare: The Political Economy of Welfare Reform in the United States* (Stanford: Hoover Institution Press, 1978).

34 Ben J. Wattenberg and Richard M. Scammon, "Black Progress and Liberal Rhetoric," *Commentary* 56 (April 1973): 35–44.

35 Clayborne Carson, "Black Power after Ten Years," in *A History of Our Time*, edited by William H. Chafe and Harvard Sitkoff (New York: Oxford University Press, 1983).

36 Wilson, *The Declining Significance of Race*, p. 160; Carl Gershman and Kenneth B. Clark, "Race or Class?" *New York Times Magazine*, 6 October 1980, pp. 22ff.

37 Henry S. Reuss, *To Save Our Cities: What Needs To Be Done* (Washington, D.C.: Public Affairs Press, 1977), p. iii.

38 Piven and Cloward, *Regulating the Poor*, p. 348.

39 Michael Petrowsky, "Race, Poverty, and Unemployment," *Philadelphia: Past, Present, and Future* (Philadelphia Social History Project, Interim Report: Fall 1984), pp. 9, 11.

DID THE GREAT SOCIETY AND SUBSEQUENT INITIATIVES WORK?

1 Kristin A. Moore et al., *Teenage Motherhood: Social and Economic Consequences* (Washington, D.C.: Urban Institute, 1979); Kristin A. Moore, Margaret Simms, and Charles Betsy, *Information Services and Aspirations: Race Differences in Adolescent Fertility* (Washington, D.C.: Urban Institute, 1984).

2 Julius B. Richmond, testimony before the U.S. House Subcommittee on Elementary, Secondary, and Vocational Education, 21 September 1982.

3 Children's Defense Fund, "A Children's Defense Budget: An Analysis of the President's FY 1984 Budget and Children" (Washington, D.C.: Children's Defense Fund, February 1983), p. 39.

4 Ibid., p. 141.

5 Irving Lazar and Richard Darlington, "Lasting Effects of Early Education: A Report from the Consortium for Longitudinal Studies," *Monographs of the Society for Research in Child Development* (Ithaca, N.Y.: Cornell University, 1982).

6 Raymond Collins, "Headstart: Foundation for Excellence," distributed by the Administration for Children, Youth and Families (U.S. Department of Health and Human Services, 1983), pp. 11–13.

7   *Changed Lives: The Effects of the Perry Preschool Program on Youths Through Age 19* (Ypsilanti, Mich.: High/Scope Press, 1984).

8   Henry Zagorski et al., "Overview of Report 12: Does Compensatory Education Narrow the Achievement Gap?" *Study of the Sustaining Effects of Compensatory Education on Basic Skills* (Santa Monica: System Development Corporation, December 1981); Judith Anderson and Robert Stonehill, *A Report to Congress: An Evaluation of the Elementary and Secondary Education Act Title I—Program Operations and Educational Effects* (Washington, D.C.: U.S. Department of Education, March 1982).

9   Children's Defense Fund, "A Children's Defense Budget," p. 39.

10 Sar Levitan and Benjamin H. Johnston, *The Job Corps: A Social Experiment That Works* (Baltimore: Johns Hopkins University Press, 1975); *Job Corps in Brief, Fiscal 1980* (Washington, D.C.: U.S. Employment and Training Administration, 1981); Charles Mallar et al., *The Lasting Impacts of Job Corps Participation* (Washington, D.C.: Government Printing Office, 1980).

11 Robert Taggart, *A Fisherman's Guide: An Assessment of Training and Remediation Strategies* (Kalamazoo, Mich.: W.E. Upjohn Institute for Employment Research, 1981), pp. 282–86.

12 Mathematica, *Evaluation of the Economic Impact of the Job Corps Programs* (Princeton, N.J.: Mathematica, 1978).

13 Taggart, *A Fisherman's Guide*, p. 287.

14 Paul L. Franklin, "A Study of Talent Search and Educational Opportunity Centers" (Washington, D.C.: College Board, 4 October 1983).

15 W. A. Blakey et al., "Briefing for Members of U.S. Congress, House Committee on Education and Labor and New Members of Congress" (Washington, D.C.: Government Printing Office, January 1983).

16 National Commission on Student Financial Assistance, "Changes in College Participation Rates and Student Financial Assistance: 1969, 1974, 1981" (Washington, D.C.: Applied Systems Institute, 28 January 1983).

17 Taggart, *A Fisherman's Guide*, p. 283.

18 Peter Kemper, David Long, and Craig Thornton, *The Supported Work Evaluation: Final Benefit-Cost Analysis* (New York: Manpower Development Research Corporation, 1980).

19 U.S. Department of Commerce, Bureau of the Census, *Money Income and Poverty Status of Families and Persons in the United States: 1983*, series P-60, no. 145, July 1984, p. 6; *Consumer Income*, no. 101, January 1976, p. 27.

20 U.S. Department of Commerce, Bureau of the Census, *Statistical Abstract of the United States: 1984*, p. 434.

21 U.S. Department of Commerce, Bureau of the Census, *Changing Family Composition and Income Differentials*, Special Demographic Analyses CDS-80-7, 1982, p. 12.

22 U.S. Department of Commerce, Bureau of the Census, *Statistical Abstract of the United States: 1982–83*, pp. 388–90.

CREATING JOBS FOR AMERICANS:
FROM MDTA TO INDUSTRIAL POLICY

1   Regional distress is nothing new. The "modern" period began with Paul Douglas and the Depressed Areas Act of 1961, 75 Stat. 47; Appalachia was the focus of

a program of its own in the 1960s, Appalachian Regional Development Act of 1965, 79 Stat. 5. The magnitude of the displaced worker problem now is unprecedented.

2   Full Employment Action Council, "A First Friday Report: Whose Recovery Is It Anyway?," 7 September 1984, p. 1 (reporting government statistics).

3   U.S. Department of Labor, Bureau of Labor Statistics, "The Employment Situation, September, 1984," 5 October 1984, table A-7.

4   Roosevelt Centennial Youth Project, "The Youth Employment Situation August, 1984." The statistics reported by the Roosevelt Project each month are government figures.

5   Children's Defense Fund, American Children in Poverty (Washington, D.C.: Children's Defense Fund, 1984), p. 23.

6   Some 70.7 percent of children in female-headed black families are poor, while 71.8 percent in female-headed Hispanic families are poor. Children's Defense Fund, American Children, p. 23.

7   Center for the Study of Social Policy, The Flip Side of Black Families Headed by Women (Washington, D.C.: Center for the Study of Social Policy, April 1984). This study takes into consideration the number of adult black males who were not counted by the 1980 Census.

8   I am indebted to Arnold E. Packer, assistant secretary of labor for policy and evaluation in the Carter administration, for this material.

9   See, for example, Robert Taggart, A Fisherman's Guide: An Assessment of Training and Remediation Strategies (Kalamazoo, Mich.: W. E. Upjohn Institute for Employment Research, 1981).

10   Manpower Development and Training Act of 1962, 76 Stat. 23 (1962), codified at 42 U.S.C. ([2571 et seq. (1970).

11   Former Supreme Court Justice Arthur J. Goldberg, as secretary of labor, had tried to convince President Kennedy that a billion-dollar program, to include a significant job creation component, would be appropriate, but he did not succeed. The prevailing assumption was that if people were appropriately trained they would find jobs, just as it was assumed that if young people could be persuaded to stay in school, a high school diploma would gain them entry into the labor market. Thus legislative interest in the early and middle sixties focused on education and training rather than on jobs.

12   The Economic Opportunity Act of 1964 had included some modest job-creation provisions, and the summer jobs program became a fairly major strategy toward the limited objective of keeping urban streets a bit cooler between June and September. But year-round public service employment was an idea whose time for large-scale implementation had not yet come. Robert Kennedy cosponsored a billion-dollar authorization of the Economic Opportunity Act of 1967, but the Johnson administration opposed him and the proposal lost by five votes.

13   87 STAT. 839 (1973), codified in 29 U.S.C. ([801 et seq. (1976).

14   See, for example, Martin Neil Baily, "The Problem of Unemployment in the United States," in Jobs for the Future: Strategies in a New Framework (Washington, D.C.: Center for National Policy, 1984), pp. 15–27.

15   Ibid., pp. 15–16.

16   Welfare is often not available to two-parent households even in states that make AFDC available to intact families. AFDC-UP (Unemployed Parent) is offered

by about half the states (the number fluctuates from year to year), including nearly all the urban industrial states. But the person seeking benefits must have fairly extensive recent work experience in order to be regarded as unemployed. The people we are discussing have for the most part never had a regular job, so AFDC-UP is of no value to them. Many states have state-financed general assistance or home relief programs for people who do not qualify for AFDC. These programs, however, are very limited in the benefits they offer, and state budget cuts have made them even more inadequate in recent years. Food stamps are available to virtually all needy people, but they are by definition inadequate to support costs of living other than food. AFDC, therefore, remains the only viable source of income to a young woman with a child and no job, and she will be effectively excluded from that if she marries or lives with the father of her child.

17 Gilbert Y. Steiner, *The Futility of Family Policy* (Washington, D.C.: Brookings Institution, 1981), p. 97; Arthur J. Altmayer, *The Formative Years of Social Security* (Madison: University of Wisconsin Press, 1968), pp. 28, 33.

18 For a confirmation of this trend, see U.S. Department of Labor, Bureau of Labor Statistics, *Employment and Earnings* (Washington, D.C.: Government Printing Office, June 1984), pp. 116, 121.

19 *A Summary Report of the Vice President's Task Force on Youth Employment* (Washington, D.C.: GPO, 1980), pp. 17–18, 20–29. See also Kathleen Teltsch, "Survey Finds Young People Lack Work Skills," *New York Times*, 16 January 1983, p. 21.

20 Children's Defense Fund, *A Children's Defense Budget: An Analysis of the President's FY 1985 Budget and Children* (Washington, D.C.: Children's Defense Fund, 1984), p. 42.

21 *A Summary Report of the Vice President's Task Force*, p. 21.

22 Judith M. Gueron, *Lessons from a Job Guarantee: The Youth Incentive Entitlement Pilot Projects* (New York: Manpower Demonstration Research Corporation, 1984).

23 Ibid., p. 16.

24 Ibid., p. 7.

25 The unemployment rate of 1983 black high school graduates as of the summer of 1984 was 37.5 percent. That of white high school dropouts of the same year was 23.5 percent. Roosevelt Centennial Youth Project, "Youth Employment."

26 The National Child Labor Committee, an organization based in New York City, has been working on a foundation-financed project to encourage greater utilization of cooperative education. Its staff has gathered the literature reporting on the efficacy of this approach. While this is not, strictly speaking, an employment policy, I think it is also timely.

27 The Roosevelt Centennial Youth Project has developed a specific proposal for a federally funded community service initiative for young people that it has circulated widely in draft form to interested people. The proposal is detailed in Frank J. Slobig and Calvin George, *A Policy Blueprint for Community Service and Youth Employment* (Washington, D.C.: Roosevelt Centennial Youth Project, 1984). The Ford Foundation has financed a major study of options for domestic community service that is being carried out by the consulting firm of

Hamilton, Rabinowitz, and Szanton. Publication of this study is expected in early 1986.

28   See, for example, Andrew Hahn and Robert Lerman, *What Works in Youth Employment Policy?* (Waltham, Mass.: Brandeis University, 1984), pp. 15–16, 21–22.

29   Children's Defense Fund, *American Children in Poverty*, pp. 22–23.

30   Manpower Demonstration Research Corporation, *Summary and Findings of the National Supported Work Demonstration* (Cambridge, Mass.: Ballinger, 1980), pp. 2, 5–7, 51–75.

31   Taggart, *A Fisherman's Guide*, pp. 135–36. David Mundel makes a similar statement about the literature in a draft paper, written for the Southern Education Foundation, which will be published in early 1986. The main point of the paper is that governors have the authority under the Job Training Partnership Act to require a more disadvantaged population to be served, and Mundel's argument is that this would *increase* the cost-benefit efficacy of the program.

32   Computed by author, based on Bureau of Labor Statistics, *Employment and Earnings*, p. 105.

33   Center on Budget and Policy Priorities, *Taxing the Poor* (Washington, D.C., 1984), pp. 4–5.

34   See Omnibus Budget Reconciliation Act of 1981, 95 Stat. 357, ¶ 2301 (1981), codified at 42 U.S.C. ¶ 602 (1983).

35   See Senate Democratic Caucus, *Jobs for the Future* (Washington, D.C., 1983), p. 23.

36   Gary Burtless, "Why Is Insured Employment so Low?" in *Brookings Papers on Economic Activity*, 1 (1983): p. 226.

37   See Senate Democratic Caucus, *Jobs for the Future*, pp. 23–24.

SIX WELFARE QUESTIONS STILL
SEARCHING FOR ANSWERS

1   I recall a debate in the mid-1960s during which Milton Friedman and James Tobin were allied in defending the negative income tax against two critics, one from the right and one from the left. At one point Friedman noted the irony that he and Tobin were paired and commented that "disciplinary blood is thicker than ideological water."

2   Real AFDC benefits have declined steadily since 1974 because payments have not been adjusted to fully offset the effects of inflation. Richard A. Kasten and John E. Todd, "Transfer Recipients and the Poor During the 1970s," unpublished paper, 1980.

3   Robert A. Levine wrote: "Most proponents of the negative income tax believed, in the early days, that the greatest political problem that would arise in attempting to legislate an actual program would be the belief, among the public and in Congress, that any form of income maintenance for adult males would bring about a large increase in idleness among those who otherwise would have worked. The whole thrust of the negative income tax, of course, was precisely to avoid this outcome—to provide such men with financial incentives to work. But the advocates felt that, without evidence to the contrary, the conventional perception would prevail" (Robert A. Levine, "How and Why the Experiment Came About," in *Work Incentives and Income Guarantees: The New Jersey*

Negative Income Tax Experiment, edited by Joseph A. Pechman and P. Michael Timpane [Washington, D.C.: Brookings Institution, 1975], pp. 16–17).

4 For a survey of the results of all four of the income maintenance experiments, see *Final Report of the Seattle-Denver Income Maintenance Experiment, Volume 1, Design and Results* (Stanford: SRI International, May 1983). For a review of the results regarding labor supply, see part 3, "Labor Supply Response," pp. 91–198. The estimates of the proportion of extra costs required to replace lost earnings were based on benefits payable under President Carter's Program for Better Jobs and Income and are reported in Henry J. Aaron and John Todd, "The Use of Income Maintenance Experiment Findings in Public Policy, 1977–78," *Industrial Relations Research Association Proceedings* (1979), pp. 46–56.

5 "[I]f work does not pay, a work requirement in most places and times would be ineffectual and inoperative, a costly and largely futile effort to compel the poor to behave in ways contrary to their own self-interest. It is unimaginable that a large bureaucracy would be capable of sifting millions of individual cases, each fraught with special problems, needs, and ambiguity, all requiring judgment if not wisdom. To inspire hard work is a laudable goal, but one not likely to be achieved through a work requirement without more authoritarian administration than most Americans are likely to accept" (Henry J. Aaron, *Why Is Welfare So Hard to Reform?* [Washington, D.C.: Brookings Institution, 1972], pp. 49–50).

6 The first was the finding, noted above, that a sizable proportion of the increased cost of noncategorical aid provided without an effective work requirement would go to replace reduced earnings.

7 *Final Report,* p. 291.

8 These statistics are taken from an unpublished memorandum by Glen Cain (2 September 1981), who chaired a panel appointed by the Department of Health and Human Services to review the *Final Report.* Cain and the panel emphatically urged that the importance of the interaction between cash assistance and counseling be mentioned prominently in the *Final Report.* He maintained that this anomaly, as well as a number of others, made unjustifiable any firm statements about the effects of cash assistance taken alone on family stability. Among these anomalies were gross discrepancies in response across ethnic groups and the fact that increases in cash assistance seemed to reduce family dissolution.

The *Final Report* ignored the conclusions of the Cain panel on the importance of mentioning the effects of counseling and education subsidies. The Office of Planning and Evaluation, which sponsored the experiments, on which more than $70 million was spent, refused to support any further research to resolve this question.

9 The income maintenance experiments devoted a small effort to examining the effects of cash assistance on health and housing and found some modest effects.

10 In fact, strong analytical explanations can be advanced for why assistance in kind, rather than in cash, may be socially optimal, even it is not viewed as optimal by recipients. These arguments have nothing to do with what may be the dominant practical argument for in-kind programs—logrolling—but require only that taxpayers care about how welfare recipients spend the assistance they are given.

RANDOM REFLECTIONS ON THE GREAT SOCIETY'S
POLITICS AND HEALTH CARE PROGRAMS
AFTER TWENTY YEARS

1   Henry Aaron and William B. Schwartz, *The Painful Prescription* (Washington, D.C.: Brookings Institution, 1984).

REVITALIZING THE CITIES:
FROM GREAT EXPECTATIONS TO A NEW REALISM

1   Marshall Kaplan was in charge of coordinating development of the Carter urban policy.
2   Jane Jacobs, *Cities and the Wealth of Nations: Principles of Economic Life* (New York: Random House, 1984), pp. 3–44.
3   Martin Grodzins first used the term "marble cake federalism" to describe the absence of clear-cut boundaries between federal, state, and local governments. Among Grodzins's several articles are "The American Federal System," in *A Nation of States*, edited by Robert A. Goldwin (Chicago: Rand-McNally, 1964); and *The American System*, edited by Daniel J. Elazor (Chicago: Rand-McNally, 1969).
4   Edward D. Banfield, *The Unheavenly City Revisited* (Boston: Little, Brown, 1974). Banfield's initial version was widely read during the early days of the first Nixon administration.
5   President Reagan proposed a massive change in federal domestic responsibilities in 1982. His administration sought to turn over AFDC and food stamps to the states in return for complete federal responsibility for Medicaid. In addition, the federal government would end or vastly reduce its role in many other domestic programs. The critical response to the president's recommendations stemmed primarily from their diminution of the federal role regarding income support.
6   National Urban Advisory Committee, *Urban America, 1984, A Report Card* (Subcommittee on Investment, Jobs and Prices, Joint Economic Committee of the Congress), pp. 17–22.
7   From a working paper by Donald Mason (Washington, D.C.: Urban Institute, 1983).
8   The Urban Development Action Grant Program (UDAG) provides grants to cities that leverage public- and private-sector funds for economic development purposes.

DOWNTOWN SHOPPING MALLS AND
THE NEW PUBLIC-PRIVATE STRATEGY

1   Raymond E. Wolfinger, *The Politics of Progress* (Englewood Cliffs, N.J.: Prentice-Hall, 1974), p. 143.
2   U.S. National Commission on Urban Problems, *Report: Building the American City* (Washington, D.C.: Government Printing Office, 1968), pp. 158, 160.
3   Heywood T. Sanders, "Urban Renewal and the Revitalized City: A Reconsid-

eration of Recent History," in *Urban Revitalization*, edited by Donald B. Rosenthal (Beverly Hills: Sage Publications, 1980), pp. 103–26.

4   See Bernard J. Frieden, "Housing Allowances: An Experiment That Worked," *The Public Interest* 59 (Spring 1980): 15–35.

5   Martha Derthick, *New Towns In-Town* (Washington, D.C.: Urban Institute, 1972).

6   Urban Land Institute, *Revitalizing Downtown Retailing: Trends and Opportunities* (Washington, D.C.: U.S. Department of Housing and Urban Development, Office of Community Planning and Development, April 1983), pp. B-1 to B-3; "Downtown Shopping Areas Again Drawing Customers," *Wall Street Journal*, 2 May 1983.

7   U.S. Department of Housing and Urban Development, *The President's Urban Policy Report: 1980* (Washington, D.C.: Government Printing Office, 1980), chaps. 1 and 3; Vincent P. Barabba, "The Demographic Future of the Cities of America," in *Cities and Firms*, edited by Herrington J. Brice (Lexington, Mass.: Lexington Books, 1980), pp. 3–45; Urban Land Institute, *Revitalizing Downtown Retailing*, pp. C-2 to C-5.

8   Six projects were studied in detail through interviews and reviews of city and developer files. They are Faneuil Hall Marketplace, Boston; Plaza Pasadena, Pasadena; Town Square, St. Paul; Horton Plaza, San Diego; University Town Centre, San Diego; and Pike Place Market, Seattle. Our research assistants who prepared the case studies were Christie Baxter (Town Square and University Town Center), Nancy Fox (Seattle), and Jacques Gordon (Faneuil Hall Marketplace and Horton Plaza).

9   U.S. Department of Housing and Urban Development, *The President's Urban Policy Report: 1980*, section 6, pp. 8–9, 17.

10   T. D. Allman, "The Urban Crisis Leaves Town," *Harper's* 257 (December 1978): 41–56; Blake Fleetwood, "The New Elite and an Urban Renaissance," *New York Times Magazine*, 14 January 1979, pp. 16–33.

11   U.S. Advisory Commission on Intergovernmental Relations, *Significant Features of Fiscal Federalism: 1981–82 Edition* (Washington, D.C.: Government Printing Office, 1983), pp. 66–67.

12   Bernard J. Frieden and Marshall Kaplan, *The Politics of Neglect: Urban Aid from Model Cities to Revenue Sharing* (Cambridge, Mass.: MIT Press, 1975), chap. 11.

13   On the origin of the UDAG program, see U.S. Department of Housing and Urban Development, *The President's National Urban Policy Report: 1980*, p. 11-9; on uses of the program, see U.S. Department of Housing and Urban Development, *Urban Development Action Grant Program: Second Annual Report* (Washington, D.C.: Department of Housing and Urban Development, 1980).

14   As of 1970, accelerated depreciation was available to firms and individuals that invested in new commercial and industrial buildings but not to those that bought or rehabilitated existing buildings.

15   See George E. Peterson, "Federal Tax Policy and the Shaping of Urban Development," in *The Prospective City*, edited by Arthur P. Solomon, pp. 399–425; and Cynthia F. Gensheimer, "Rehabilitation Tax Credits: A Real Estate Tax Shelter of the 1980s," *Journal of Real Estate and Taxation* 9 (Summer 1982): 299–318.

16   Phillip Clay, *Neighborhood Renewal* (Lexington, Mass.: Lexington Books, 1979);

and Franklin J. James, "The Revitalization of Older Urban Housing and Neighborhoods," in Solomon, ed., *The Prospective City*, pp. 130–60, at p. 148.

17   George Sternlieb and James W. Hughes, *Shopping Centers U.S.A.* (New Brunswick, N.J.: Rutgers Center for Urban Policy Research, 1981), p. 3.

18   See Bernard J. Frieden, *The Environmental Protection Hustle* (Cambridge, Mass.: MIT Press, 1979), chap. 11.

19   See Bernard J. Frieden, "Allocating the Public Service Costs of New Housing," *Urban Land* 39 (January 1980): 12–16.

20   Barry Bluestone, Patricia Hanna, Sarah Kuhn, and Laura Moore, *The Retail Revolution* (Boston: Auburn House, 1981), pp. 32–34.

21   Virginia L. Horler, *Guide to Public Debt Financing in California* (San Francisco: Rauscher Pierce Refsnes, 1982), p. 31.

22   "Milwaukee's Grand Avenue," *The Guarantor* (November/December 1982), pp. 2–5.

23   Deirdre Carmody, "Vast Rebuilding of Bryant Park Planned," *New York Times*, 1 December 1983, p. A-1.

24   Manuel Padron, "Build Here: Transit's Rallying Cry," *Planning* 50 (June 1984): 6–10.

OBSERVATIONS ON THE ROLE OF THE MEDIA
IN COVERING THE WAR ON POVERTY

1   Bernard J. Frieden and Marshall Kaplan, *The Politics of Neglect: Urban Aid from Model Cities to Revenue Sharing* (Cambridge, Mass.: MIT Press, 1975).

THE ROLE OF THE MEDIA IN
SHAPING PUBLIC POLICY

1   The original Mencken article and Mencken's later comments upon it are quoted from H. L. Mencken, *The Bathtub Hoax*, edited by Robert McHugh (New York: Knopf, 1958), pp. 4–9.

2   Ibid.

3   John Schwarz, *New Republic*, 18 June 1984.

4   Harry G. Summers, *On Strategy: A Critical Analysis of the Vietnam War* (New York: Dell, 1982).

SOCIAL SCIENCE AND THE GREAT SOCIETY

1   Ronald Reagan, radio address to the nation, 3 December 1983, p. 1.

2   The evaluation studies include James S. Coleman et al., *Equality of Educational Opportunity* (Washington, D.C.: Government Printing Office, 1966); Harvey A. Averch et al., *How Effective Is Schooling?: A Critical Review and Synthesis of Research Findings* (Santa Monica: Rand Corporation, 1972); and Christopher Jencks et al., *Inequality: A Reassessment of the Effect of Family and Schooling in America* (New York: Harper Colophon Books, 1972). See Henry J. Aaron, *Politics and the Professors: The Great Society in Perspective* (Washington, D.C.: Brookings Institution, 1978), foreword.

3   Ibid., p. 159.

4   Ibid.
5   Many public finance studies, for example, of taxes and their economic effects and incidence, fit into this category. For an example of an urban policy study done at the Woodrow Wilson School of Princeton University that fits this category, see Michael H. Schill and Richard P. Nathan, *Revitalizing America's Cities: Neighborhood Reinvestment and Displacement* (New York: State University of New York Press, 1983).
6   For an excellent and important discussion of what is called the literary character of discussion in economics, see Donald N. McCloskey, "The Rhetoric of Economics," *Journal of Economic Literature* 21 (June 1983): 481–517.
7   Ibid., 482.
8   The term is highly pejorative in professional use.
9   As quoted in *Science News* 115 (31 March 1979): 213.
10 Richard R. Nelson, *The Moon and The Ghetto: An Essay on Public Policy Analysis* (New York: Norton, 1977).
11 Examples of both approaches are treated below in this essay.
12 John R. Commons, *Institutional Economics*, vol. 1. (Madison: University of Wisconsin Press, 1959), chap. 1. I am indebted to V. Lane Rawlins for suggesting these passages from Commons's work, *Institutional Economics* was first published by Macmillan in 1934.
13 Ibid., pp. 70–71.
14 Aaron, *Politics and the Professors*, pp. 65–97.
15 See Alice Rivlin, *Systematic Thinking for Social Action* (Washington, D.C.: Brookings Institution, 1971), p. 45.
16 Wassily Leontief, Letters, *Science* 217 (9 July 1982): 104.
17 Comments by Steven B. Steib, University of Tulsa, responding to an early draft of this essay.
18 For a discussion of this history (from our point of view), see Richard P. Nathan, Robert F. Cook, and V. Lane Rawlins, *Public Service Employment: A Field Evaluation* (Washington, D.C.: Brookings Institution, 1981), chap. 2; and Richard P. Nathan, "The Associates: The Methodology for Field Network Evaluation Studies," in Walter Williams et al., *Studying Implementation: Methodological and Administrative Issues* (Chatham, N.J.: Chatham House, 1982), pp. 83–88.
19 For a summary, see Board of Directors of the Manpower Demonstration Research Corporation, *Summary and Findings of the National Supported Work Demonstration* (Cambridge, Mass.: Ballinger, 1980).
20 The author serves as a member of the MDRC board.
21 Leonard Goodwin, *Do the Poor Want to Work?* (Washington, D.C.: Brookings Institution, 1972).
22 Rivlin, *Systematic Thinking for Social Action*, p. 120. Writing in the same period, Carol H. Weiss, in her influential book on evaluation research, reached the same conclusion. See Carol H. Weiss, *Evaluation Research: Methods of Assessing Program Effectiveness* (Englewood Cliffs, N.J.: Prentice-Hall, 1972). Weiss in this book concluded that "more fundamental social experimentation" is needed.
23 This quotation and the ones that follow are from Jonathan Swift, *Gulliver's Travels* (New York: Dell, 1961), pt. 3, chaps. 4 and 5.

THE NATURE AND SYSTEMIC IMPACT
OF "CREATIVE FEDERALISM"

1 Both of these also were treated in Title II of the ICA.
2 All direct federal-local aid was in the form of project grants in the sixties.
3 Moreover, four of the five exhibited strong tendencies to become recategorized or at least more conditioned over time; note CETA and Safe Streets by 1980.
4 The "swap" initially involved a federalization of Medicaid with AFDC and food stamps being devolved to the states along with the "turn-back" of what turned out to be some thirty-five program groupings over a four-year period, with funding sources ultimately accompanying the state assumptions. Had it been successful, a needed decongestion of the system would have occurred and full federal responsibility for the largest of all the welfare programs, ostensibly a liberal goal, would have been achieved.

THE GREAT SOCIETY AND THE GROWTH
OF "JURIDICAL FEDERALISM"

1 Arnold M. Howitt, *Managing Federalism* (Washington, D.C.: Congressional Quarterly, 1984), p. 7.
2 Ibid.
3 James D. Carroll, "The New Juridical Federalism and the Alienation of Public Policy and Administration," *American Review of Public Administration* 16 (Spring 1982): 89–105.
4 David H. Rosenbloom, *Public Administration and the Law* (New York: Marcel Dekker, 1983).
5 See "Developments in the Law: Section 1983 and Federalism," *Harvard Law Review* 90 (1977): 1133–1361.
6 Ibid., pp. 1141–67.
7 383 U.S. 301 (1966).
8 Ibid., at 358–60.
9 Rowland Evans and Robert Novak, *Lyndon B. Johnson: The Exercise of Power* (New York: Signet Books, 1968), pp. 513–14.
10 Joseph A. Califano, Jr., *A Presidential Nation* (New York: Norton, 1975), p. 252.
11 *Wood v. Strickland*, 420 U.S. 308 (1975); *Harlow v. Fitzgerald*, 457 U.S. 800 (1982).
12 *Owen v. City of Independence*, 445 U.S. 622 (1980).
13 *Smith v. Wade*, 461 U.S. 30 (1983).
14 Roger Cramton, "Judicial Lawmaking and Administration in the Leviathan State," *Public Administration Review* 36 (September/October, 1976): 551–55.
15 Abram Chayes, "The Role of the Judge in Public Law Litigation," *Harvard Law Review* 89 (1976): 1298.
16 Carroll, "The New Juridical Federalism," p. 90.
17 Steven Brill, ed., "Complete Guide to Federal District Judges," *The American Lawyer* (July-August 1983), special supplement.
18 *Finney v. Arkansas*, 505 F2d 194, 201 (1974); Judge Lay, a Johnson appointee.
19 427 U.S. 347 (1976).
20 Ibid., pp. 388–89.

21   418 U.S. 717, 743–44 (1974).
22   Ibid., p. 809.
23   *Wyatt* v. *Stickney*, 325 F. Supp. 781; 334 F. Supp. 1341 (1971).
24   451 U.S. 1 (1981).

CONCLUSION—GREAT SOCIETY,
PAST, PRESENT, AND POSSIBLE FUTURE

1   John E. Schwarz, *America's Hidden Success: A Reassessment of Twenty Years of Public Policy* (New York: Norton, 1983).
2   Ibid., p. 76.
3   Charles Murray, *Losing Ground: American Social Policy 1950–1980* (New York: Basic Books, 1984).
4   Ibid., p. 8.
5   Ibid., p. 58.
6   Ibid., p. 135.
7   Ibid., p. 219.
8   Phone conversation with Frank Levy, winter 1985.
9   The number of labor force entrants between 1965 and 1980 was two and one-half times the number of entrants between 1950 and 1965.
10   Murray, *Losing Ground*, p. 88.
11   Murray used a mythical or showcase couple, Harold and Phyllis, who chose to remain on welfare, ostensibly because welfare provided more cash and in-kind benefits than available jobs would have done. Murray's example appears out of touch with reality, except perhaps in a very few "high welfare benefit states." His example also doesn't portray options of two working individuals, and it neglects to describe in-kind benefits that would remain even if Harold and/or Phyllis secured jobs.
12   These data correspond with numerous studies concerning the mobility of the poor. Actual data were provided by the Colorado Department of Social Services, spring 1985.
13   John L. Palmer and Isabel V. Sawhill, eds., *The Reagan Record* (Cambridge, Mass.: Ballinger, 1984), p. 199n.
14   Ibid., p. 1.
15   Ibid., pp. 15, 16.
16   The administration's actions (1980–84) have resulted in a 4.1 percent loss in the level of disposable income for families in the bottom quintile of the income distribution. Average annual real growth of low-income assistance to individuals grew by only 0.1 percent. Other grants (compensatory, vocation, and adult education; education for the handicapped; rehabilitation service; health and social services; employment and training programs; and refugee and entrance services) declined by over 7 percent annually (Palmer and Sawhill, eds., *The Reagan Record*, pp. 322, 329–50).

Index

Contributors

EDITORS

Marshall Kaplan is Dean of the University of Colorado's Graduate School of Public Affairs. Prior to his tenure as dean, he was Deputy Assistant Secretary for Urban Policy at the U.S. Department of Housing and Urban Development. From 1965 through the early 1970s, he was a principal in the national policy consulting firm of Marshall Kaplan, Gans & Kahn in San Francisco.

Peggy Cuciti is currently Senior Research Associate in the Graduate School of Public Affairs' Center for Public/Private Sector Cooperation at the University of Colorado at Denver. Formerly she was a senior resident at the U.S. Advisory Commission on Intergovernmental Relations and a policy analyst at the Congressional Budget Office.

CONTRIBUTORS

Henry Aaron of the Brookings Institution is former Assistant Secretary of the Department of Health and Human Services.

Barry Bosworth of the Brookings Institution is a former economic advisor to President Carter.

Wilbur J. Cohen, Professor of Public Policy, Lyndon B. Johnson School of Public Affairs, University of Texas, was Secretary of the Department of Health, Education and Welfare during the Johnson administration.

Peter Edelman, Professor of Law, Georgetown University, was an executive assistant to Senator Robert F. Kennedy.

Bernard Frieden is Professor, Department of Urban Studies and Planning, Massachusetts Institute of Technology.

Bernard Gifford, Dean of Education, University of California at Berkeley, is a former senior executive of the Russell Sage Foundation.

Charles Green is Editor of the *Denver Post*.

Clifford M. Johnson is Coordinator of Youth Employment and Income Support for the Children's Defense Fund, Washington, D.C.

Sar Levitan is Professor of Economics, George Washington University.

Ian Menzies is a columnist for the *Boston Globe*.

Richard Nathan, Professor of Public Policy, Woodrow Wilson School of Public and International Affairs, Princeton University, is a former senior official at the Office of Management and Budget and the Department of Health, Education and Welfare during the Nixon administration.

Joseph Pechman of the Brookings Institution and the Hoover Institute, Stanford University, was an economic advisor to several presidential administrations.

Robert Reischauer, Senior Vice President, the Urban Institute, is former Deputy Director, Congressional Budget Office.

David Rosenbloom is Professor of Public Administration, Maxwell School, Syracuse University.

Lynne Sagalyn is Assistant Professor, Department of Urban Studies and Planning, Massachusetts Institute of Technology.

William Schambra is a Resident Fellow at the American Enterprise Institute for Public Policy Research.

David Walker, Professor of Political Science, University of Connecticut, is the former Assistant Director, Advisory Commission on Intergovernmental Relations.

Robert Wood, Professor of Political Science, Wesleyan University, was Secretary of the Department of Housing and Urban Development during the Johnson administration.

Paul Ylvisaker, Professor of Education and former Dean of Education, Harvard University, is a former senior executive with the Ford Foundation.

Library of Congress Cataloging-in-Publication Data
The Great society and its legacy.
  Includes index.
  1. United States—Social policy.   2. United States—
Social conditions—1960–1980.   3. United States—
Economic policy.   I. Kaplan, Marshall.   II. Cuciti,
Peggy L.
HN65.G74   1986   361.6'1'0973   86-4472
ISBN 0–8223–0589–5
ISBN 0–8223–0738–3 (pbk.)